MASTER CLASS

Essential DOUBLE BASS DRUMMING TECHNIQUES

by JEFF BOWDERS

ALSO AVAILABLE BY JEFF BOWDERS:

Essential Rock Drumming Concepts
Book/Audio
HL00696622

Essential Drumset Fills
Book/Audio
HL00695986

To access audio and video, visit:
www.halleonard.com/mylibrary

Enter Code
7339-9376-2053-3510

Photography by Alex Solca

Audio recorded at Jocean Studios
Mixed and mastered by David Das at Dasbunk Studios

ISBN 978-1-4950-8886-5

7777 W. Bluemound Rd. P.O. Box 13819 Milwaukee, WI 53213

In Australia Contact:
Hal Leonard Australia Pty. Ltd.
4 Lentara Court
Cheltenham, Victoria, 3192 Australia
Email: **ausadmin@halleonard.com.au**

Visit Hal Leonard Online at
www.halleonard.com

About the Author

Jeff Bowders began his drumming journey in 1987. Since then, he has been blessed with opportunities to perform and/or teach in over 50 countries. Whether it's playing with platinum-selling and GRAMMY® award-winning bands or performing as a solo artist at drum festivals and camps, Jeff's passion for drums and drumming education is undeniable. An in-demand and award-winning instructor at Musician's Institute, Jeff's critically-acclaimed MI Press Hal Leonard publications include *Essential Drumset Fills—The Component Fill System* book/audio and *Essential Rock Drumming Concepts—An Encyclopedia of Progressive Rhythmic Techniques* book/audio. Many of the concepts from those publications and this book can be heard on Jeff's two solo albums: *The Pilgrimage of Thingamuhjig* and *Mission*.

For additional info, news and drumming motivation go to:

www.jeffbowders.com
www.drumdisciplinebootcamp.com
www.facebook.com/jeffbowders
www.youtube.com/jeffbowders

Jeff Bowders is beyond humbled to be endorsed by these incredible companies:

Tama drums, pedals and hardware
Sabian cymbals
Vater drumsticks
Evans drumheads
Humes & Berg drum cases

Special Thanks

Mom and dad for the endless support and sacrifice. Jim Tilton, Lou Chavez, Graham Lear, Larry London, Mike Mangini, Rob Carson and PIT '97 for sharing their hard earned wisdom. Jeff Schroedl and everyone at Hal Leonard for trusting and allowing me to share my contributions. David Das for setting the standard in patience and grace. Alex Solca for always being committed to excellence. Jesus Christ for everything.

A reverent thank you for your support:

Aaron Vishria at Tama
Chris Stankee at Sabian
Chad Brandolini at Vater
Steve "Lob" Lobmeier at Evans
Mike Berg at Humes & Berg

CONTENTS

Introduction 

Double bass drumming is not a style, it is a technique. This technique can be applied to any style of music. Just as brush playing may be associated with jazz drumming, brush technique can be used in virtually any musical environment. Even though double bass drumming was birthed in big band drumming, eventually it became associated and/or relegated to only rock and metal music. Today, double bass drumming is ubiquitous within the music world. Jazz, Latin, funk and, of course, rock and metal drummers are all incorporating double bass techniques to help express themselves within their art. *Essential Double Bass Drumming Techniques* is written for the drummer seeking to further expand their rhythmic horizons, regardless of what style they may choose.

Essential Double Bass Drumming Techniques is an updated and greatly expanded version of my previous book, *Double Bass Drumming—The Mirrored Groove System*. Even though that book offered new and effective insights in approaching double bass grooves, I always felt it to be incomplete. Ultimately, I wanted to have a comprehensive resource that would cover virtually every aspect of practical double bass technique. I wanted a book that would cover perspectives on balance, seat positioning, and foot technique—exercises that would help develop the right and left foot equally within grooves and fills—and a guide that will help lay a foundation for applying advanced phrasing techniques. *Essential Double Bass Drumming Techniques* is that book.

There is a lot of material in the following pages. My goal was to be exhaustive, not intimidating. My hope for this book is that it becomes a resource that you use whenever you need new rhythmic inspiration. Working through this book from beginning to end will be greatly beneficial, but exploring certain sections periodically will also render effective gains. Whichever way you choose, practice with intention. Remember that the difference between right and nearly right is greater than the difference between right and wrong. Work with the expectation to grow. Focus completely on the task at hand. Don't compromise your practice time with distractions. Ultimately, develop the discipline to be the drummer you desire to be.

Now, go! Unleash the double bass giant within!

"It had long since come to my attention that people of accomplishment rarely sat back and let things happen to them. They went out and happened to things."

—Leonardo da Vinci

Notation Guide

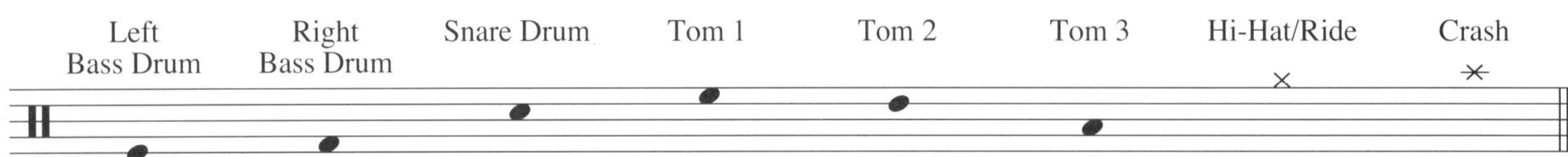

The "Essential" Double Bass Factor: Balance 

No other instrument requires the use of all four limbs to the extent of the modern drumset. Developing the ability to control our feet to the level we've developed our hands is one of the biggest challenges we drummers face. Developing a solid double bass technique completely hinges on the responsibility of what we should and shouldn't assign to our feet.

Naturally, we depend on our feet for balance. Walking, standing, jumping—for just about any physical activity, we rely on our feet to prevent any unnecessary tumbling. However, we play an instrument that requires the equal use of all four limbs. By depending on only our feet for balance, we will greatly hinder our ability to develop our double bass technique to the highest level possible.

Ultimately, we need our feet to be as free as our hands. This is easily achieved by redistributing our body weight off of our feet and onto our seat. Sitting on the front side of the drum throne may seem beneficial (Ex. 1.0), however, sitting in this position distributes all of our body weight down to our feet, which forces them to take on the unnecessary responsibility of maintaining our balance. By sitting on the backside of the drum throne and receiving the support under our thighs (Ex. 1.1), we will be able to "center" our body weight directly on the throne and allow our feet to be free. So now, our freedom mantra becomes "balance off the feet and onto the seat."

Not only will sitting on the backside of the throne free up our feet, it will also allow our lower back, hips, and upper thighs to relax and not be subjected to fatigue and injury.

Ex. 1.0

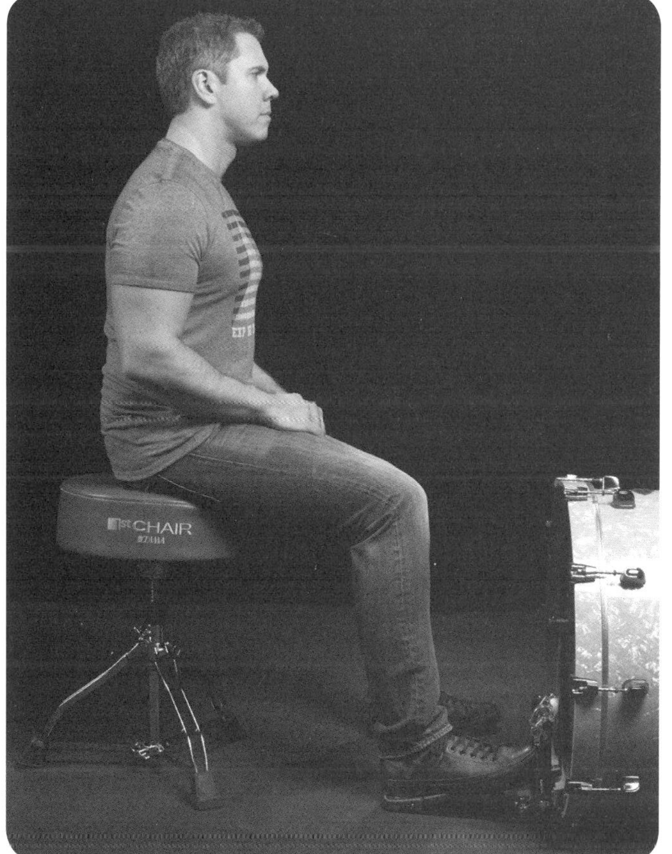

Ex. 1.1

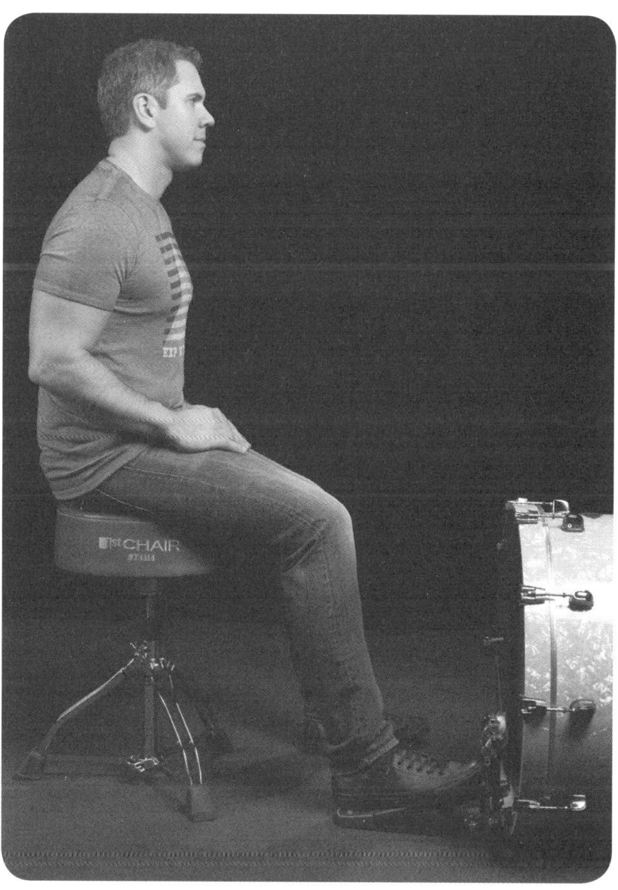

One final note on balance: we want the most support underneath us as possible. This means the more surface area our thrones provide, the better. Small or "bicycle" designed thrones essentially rob us of the maximum support we need. Big, round or square thrones are best.

Seat Height and Positioning

Seat height and positioning is relative to the length of your legs. Drummers come in all shapes and sizes, so to prescribe an absolute measurement for everyone would be irresponsible. However, the following guidelines will provide a strong starting point for you to discover your specific needs.

The best measurement to determine your seat height is the relationship from your hips to your knees. Your hips should be slightly higher than your knees. If you sit so low that your knees come above your hips, your center of gravity will shift and put undesirable pressure on your lower back and hips. If you sit too high, your center of gravity will shift down to your feet, forcing them to maintain your balance. Also, this will limit the use of any ankle motion, which will force a dependency on upper leg technique. This is not the goal (see Foot Technique on page 8).

Seat positioning is the distance between you and your pedals. This is slightly easier to determine. You want your feet to be slightly ahead of where they would rest in a natural sitting position (Ex. 2.0). This will allow you to maintain your balance and also utilize a lower and upper leg technique. Sitting too far away will make you feel imbalanced and put extra stress on your hips and upper thighs (Ex. 2.1). Conversely, you are too close when your ankles are positioned behind your knees (Ex. 2.2). This will add undesirable pressure on the knees and greatly limit the use of any ankle motion.

Ex. 2.0

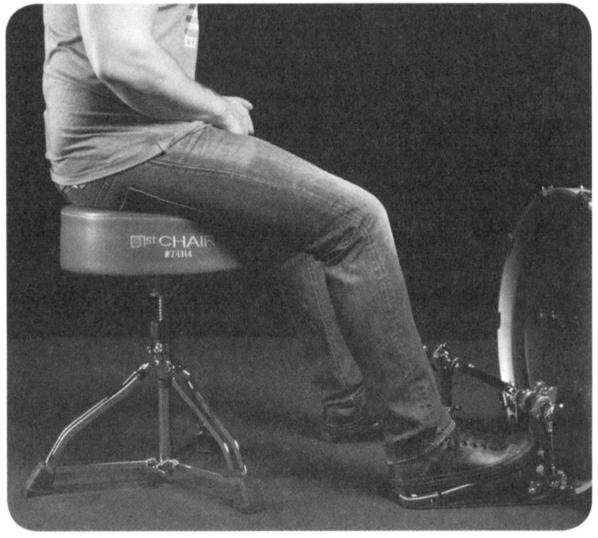

Ex. 2.1

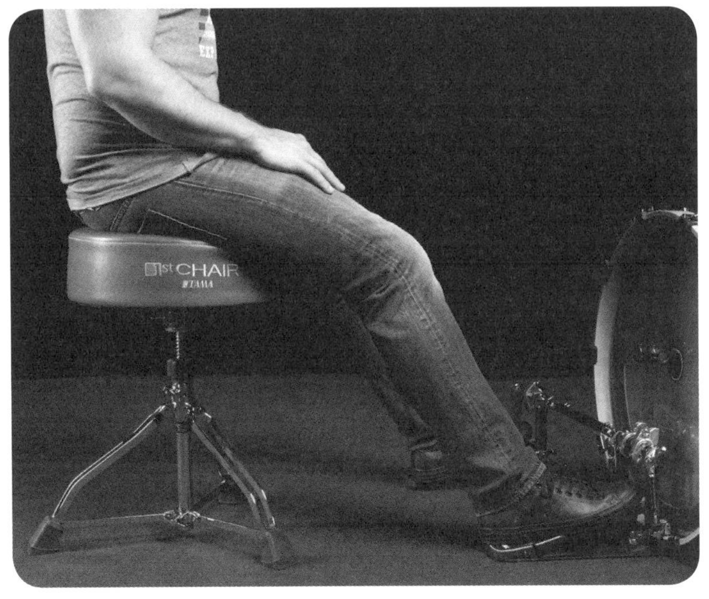

Ex. 2.2

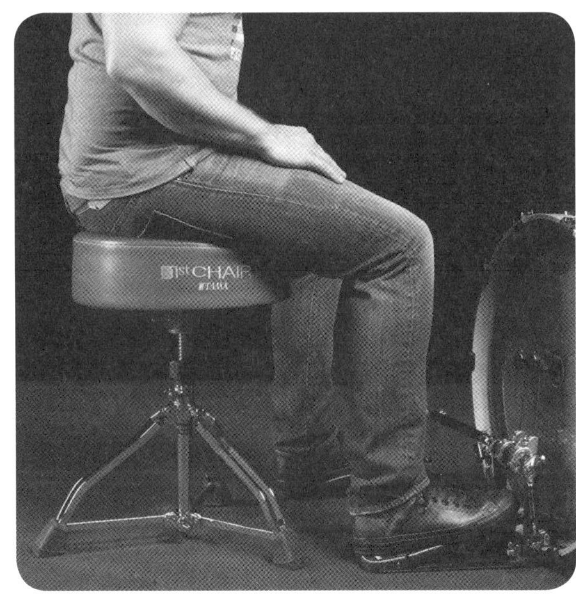

Pedal Position and Placement

Both bass drum pedals should be of equal distance from you. Many of my students position their left pedal closer so that it lines up with their hi-hat pedal. However, this makes it more difficult to achieve an even balance of sound and technique between the two bass drum pedals, not to mention the negative effect on their own physical balance. The hi-hat requires more of an upper leg technique that is not diminished by a closer positioning, but the technique desired for the bass drum will be compromised.

Maintaining contact with your pedals is ideal. Avoid over-exaggerating any motion so that you do not lose contact with the footboard. The main contact point of your foot to the pedalboard should be the "ball," where your toes connect to the rest of your foot. This is the area of the foot that should feel the most contact with the pedal. Due to the flexible nature of toes, you cannot depend on them to maintain consistent feel and sound. The ball of your foot is stronger and not pliable like your toes, thus making it the ideal portion of your foot for pedal contact.

For maximum dynamic leverage, position your feet about 2/3 the way up the pedal. This means the ball of your foot should be near the top third of the pedal surface, and the toes should be positioned toward the top edge of the pedal. Although it's sometimes easier to control, playing too low on the pedal will limit your power and dynamic range. Conversely, playing too high will choke the natural response from the pedal, preventing the full range of motion the beater wants to produce. The correct foot position will offer you a much wider dynamic range.

Both feet should be positioned evenly on the pedals (Ex. 3.0). Having uneven position (Ex. 3.1) will compromise sound, feel, and overall quality of your performance. Often, I find myself looking down while I'm playing to double-check that my feet are in the same position as each other on the pedals. My left foot has a tendency to slide down, and when it does, I make the adjustment as needed.

Ex. 3.0

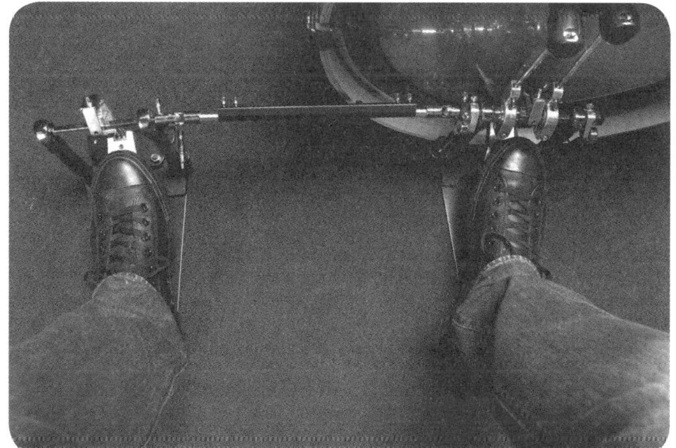

Ex. 3.1

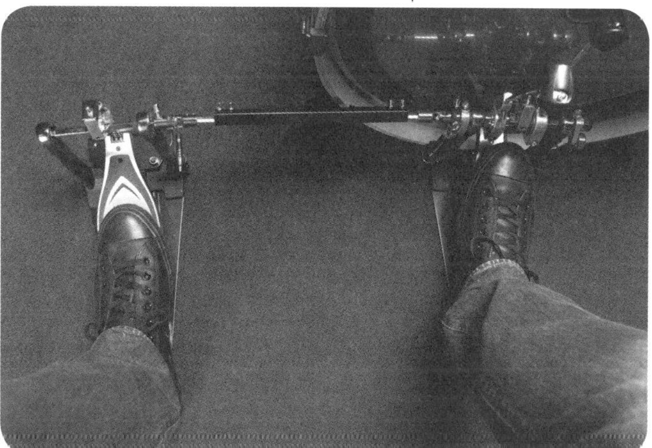

Foot Technique

This section will be addressing foot technique as applied to the bass drum pedal(s)—not the hi-hat or any auxiliary sound source pedal. Different sound sources require different techniques.

Bigger motions and muscle groups are easier to control, which is why we naturally gravitate away from using smaller motions/muscle groups to achieve a specific task. However, taking the time to develop these smaller motions and muscles will render results that are very difficult to achieve otherwise. Developing a strong and reliable foot technique will greatly benefit from focusing on these smaller motions and muscle groups.

Foot technique can be grouped into two categories: "heel-up" and "heel-down." Each technique is exactly what its name implies.

Heel-Down (Ex. 4.0): Place the heel on the heel plate and allow your foot to rest on the remaining surface of the pedalboard. This technique enables you to play softer and can aid in your balance (but we're depending on our seat for balance, not our feet, right?). This position solely relies on the ankle to be the pivot point in transferring the energy from the foot to the pedal. Over time, this can cause some discomfort because it isolates the shin muscle (*tibialis anterior*). Whenever you press down on the pedal, this muscle is doing all the work, and it can quickly become fatigued, especially if you're playing fast and/or loud passages of music.

Ex. 4.0

Heel-Up (Ex. 4.1): This is somewhat similar to heel-down, but the heel is slightly raised off of the pedalboard (about one to two inches.) Heel-up offers more options in terms of dynamics and speed. The heel-up technique is less fatiguing on the shin muscles. Since we have raised our heel, the shin is no longer isolated and now other muscles in our leg are able to take on some of the responsibility. This position also allows us to use some of our upper leg for energy and power. However, we are not relying on our upper leg to provide the energy for the bass drum stroke. The focus is still on pivoting the ankle to provide the stroke, just as we did in the heel-down position.

Ex. 4.1

Think of the heel-up technique as a "heel-down motion in a heel-up position." The pivoting of the ankle should be identical in both techniques (heel-up and heel-down). An effective way to gauge if you're using too much upper leg is to watch your knee as you play. If your knee is bouncing up and down like a piston, you're using too much upper leg. This will change slightly when you have to play accents or louder sections of songs, but generally the knee should only be moving sympathetically within the stroke.

Some misconstrue heels-up to mean the position shown in Ex. 4.2. This will greatly reduce the involvement of the ankle and transfer the responsibility of the stoke mostly to the upper leg. Our quest is to minimize the dependency on our upper leg and focus primarily on developing the ankle motion to control the stroke. Raising the heel too high will also risk the possibility of losing contact with the pedal plate. Just relax, lower your heels, and let your ankles do (most of) the work.

Ex. 4.2

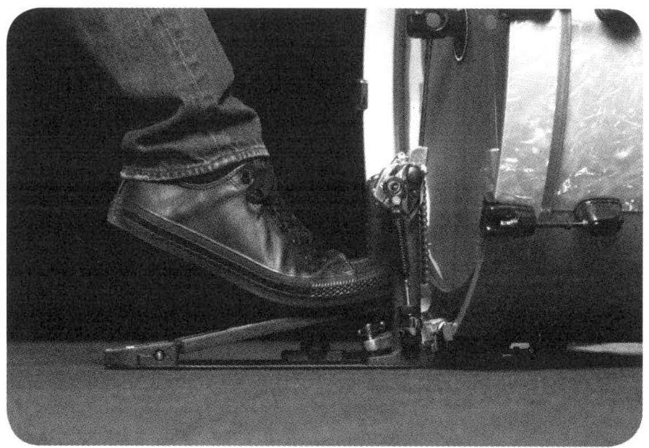

To Bury or Not to Bury... That Is the Question

As within almost every aspect of art therein lies opinions. Within drumming, strong opinions have emerged on whether or not to bury the beater. I feel this debate can easily be resolved by simply investigating what the desired bass drum goal may be.

"Burying the beater" means leaving the beater pressed against the bass drum head after it has been struck. If the bass drum has a certain amount of muffling this will in no way affect the resonance of the drum. However, if there is minimal or no muffling this will choke the drum, just like leaving the stick on the head of any drum after it has been struck. The challenge with this technique is making sure the beater doesn't dribble on the head while you are burying it. This will be almost impossible if you're playing a bass drum with a resonant head that doesn't have a venting hole. This technique does offer more power than not burying the beater. Resting on the head will offer more area and time for the stroke to build up inertia which will produce a bigger and stronger stroke; much like a windup does for a baseball pitcher.

Not burying the beater is allowing the beater to play off of the bass drum head. If there is minimal or no muffling in the bass drum, playing off the head will allow the drum to resonate freely. This will be the preferred stroke if the bass drum has a solid resonant head with no hole. The challenge with this technique is making sure the beater does not touch the head when you prepare for the next stoke. Sometimes the foot or leg will create a small "prep stroke" (similar to the baseball windup) that will position the beater dangerously close to the head. Make sure the only time the beater touches the head is when it is intended. The bottom line is if you want the bass drum to resonate, use minimal to no muffling and don't bury the beater. If you desire a bass drum sound with more attack and power, use more muffling and bury the beater.

The Forgotten Piece of Equipment: Shoes

For the same reason we don't wear mittens on our hands when we play, we don't want our feet to be unnecessarily restrained. In our quest to develop our feet to be as free as our hands, it is in our best interest to eliminate any obstacle that may stand in the way between our feet and the pedals.

Boots, high-tops, or any other footwear that interferes with the ankle's motion will not be your ally. Wearing them will only slow the process in developing a technique which depends on the ankle to move freely and unhindered. Conversely, low-cut shoes or water socks will not obstruct your ankle. They will greatly reduce the weight and resistance on your foot and ankle's range of motion, helping you achieve a strong ankle-based bass drum technique.

Playing barefoot may be the most logical solution if we're making the comparison with our hands, however, I have found that it's just not practical. In some music venues this could work, but I have played on some stages that made me wish I was wearing a full body HazMat suit! Protect your feet...it's worth it.

1 8th and 16th-Note Warm-Ups

Using basic exercises to help focus on fundamental concepts is the purpose of this chapter. Various layered and linear approaches will help establish the development of the right and the left foot in conjunction with the hands.

Don't let the simplicity of some of the exercises distract you from their importance. The goal is quality, not difficulty, even though some may pose some unexpected challenges. Approach these exercises in the same way a pianist will use scales to help prepare them for the work ahead. Focus on each foot producing the same sound and feel. Usually, the left (hi-hat) foot will be weaker—pushing two cymbals together feels much different than pushing a beater against a big drum. Be aware of this new motion and feeling and give it time to develop.

Practice Tips:

- Play to a click track or metronome set at eighth or sixteenth notes and count out loud to ensure a consistent feel of even subdivisions.
- Strive for the right and left foot to sound identical in tone and dynamic.
- Periodically check to see if your technique in your right and left foot look the same.
- Repeat. Rest. Recall.

"Outstanding people have one thing in common: an absolute sense of mission."

—Zig Ziglar

16th-Note Progressive Builder

Focus on evenly subdividing the up-beat 16th notes ("e's" and "a's") within the 8th-note ostinato. Practice to a 16th-note click at 50–100 BPM.

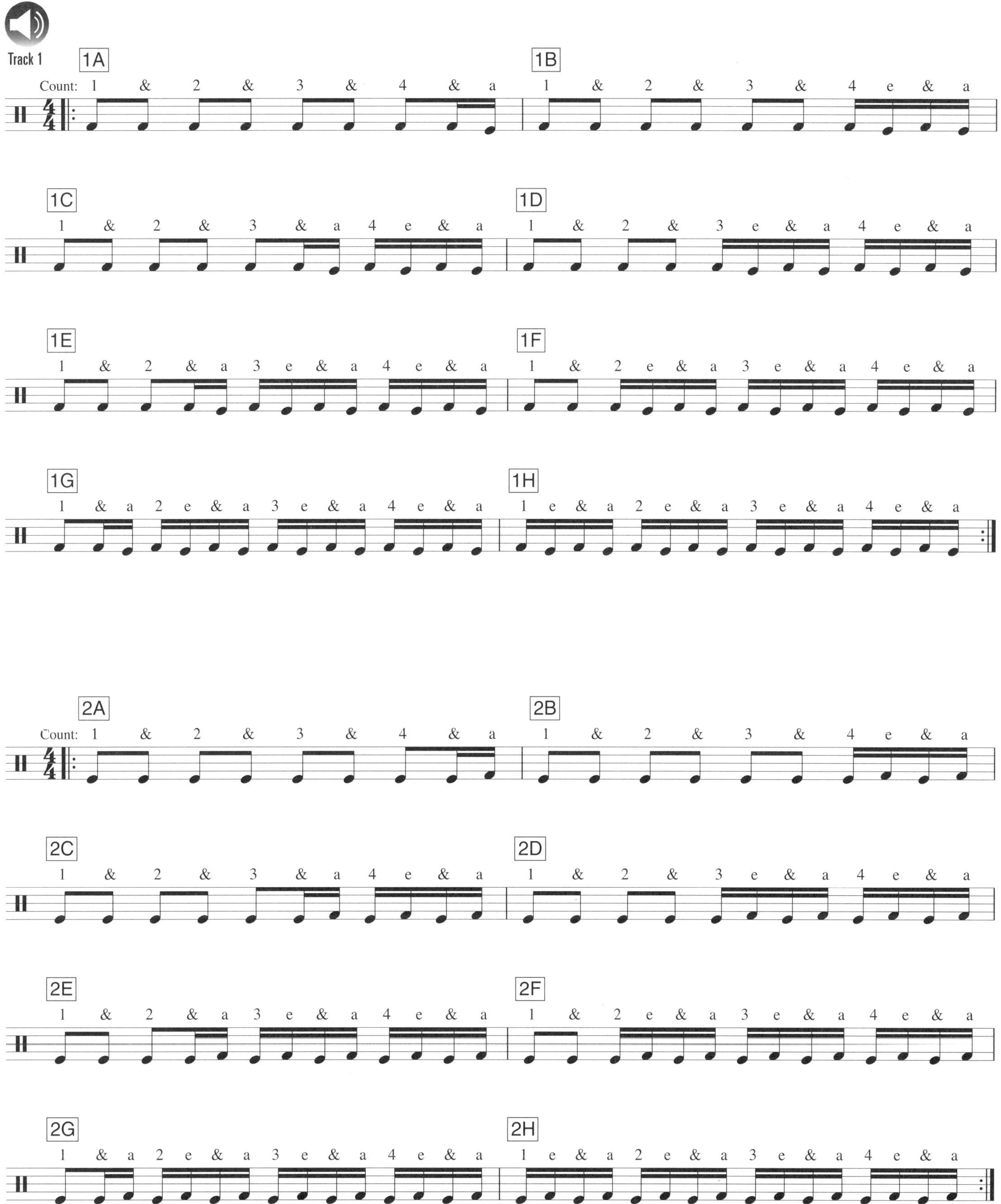

Dynamic Control Builder

To develop speed you first have to develop control. Control is the ability to play at any tempo within any dynamic range. Exploring and pushing yourself outside of your natural dynamics comfort zone will produce the control you need to be able to play faster. True speed is a byproduct of control.

As you play through these "dynamic" exercises, try to create the biggest dynamic separation between the loud and soft notes.

Accent Control Builder

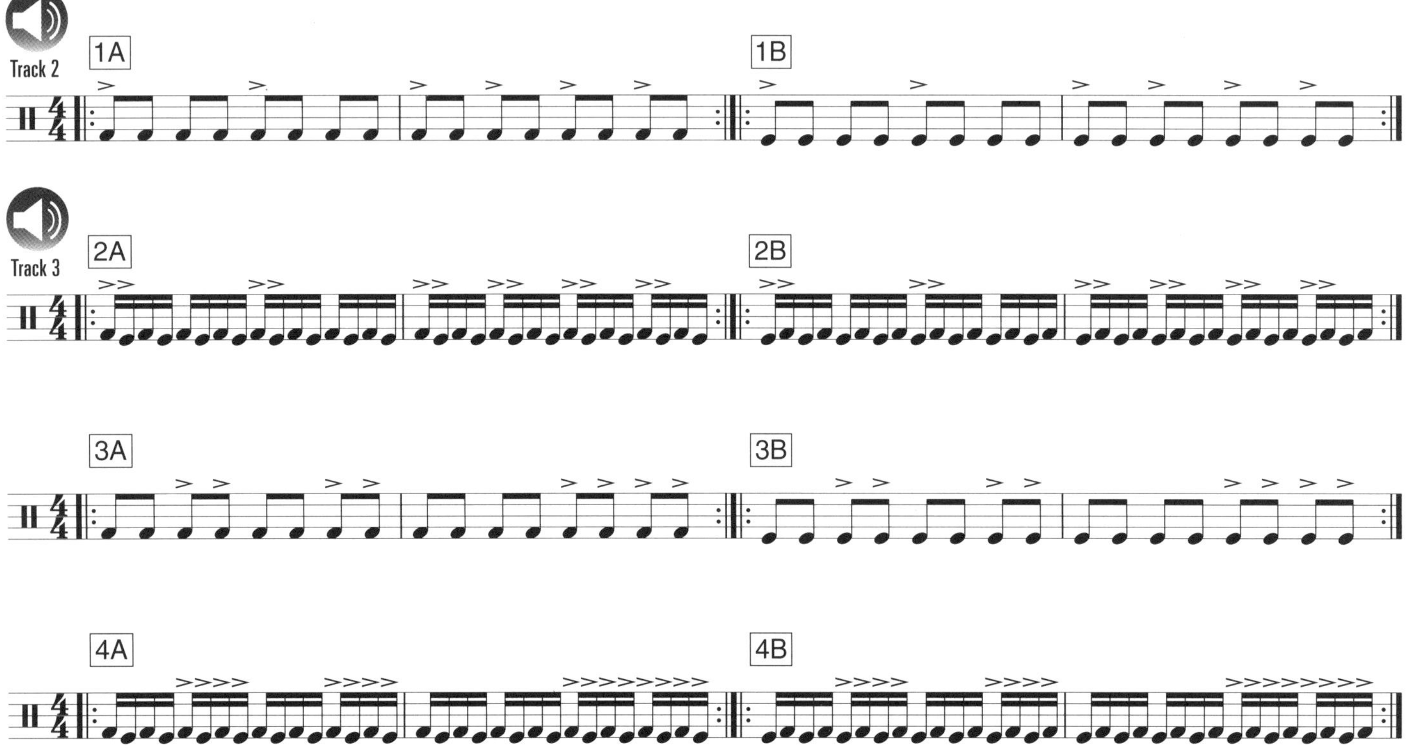

Layered 16th-Note Progressive Builder

One of the most important aspects of drumset coordination is being able to play with two or more limbs at the same time without flamming. The following "layered" exercises are designed to help you develop a heightened awareness of each limb's relationship to one another.

The goal is multiple voices creating one unison sound, not a cacophonous flam!

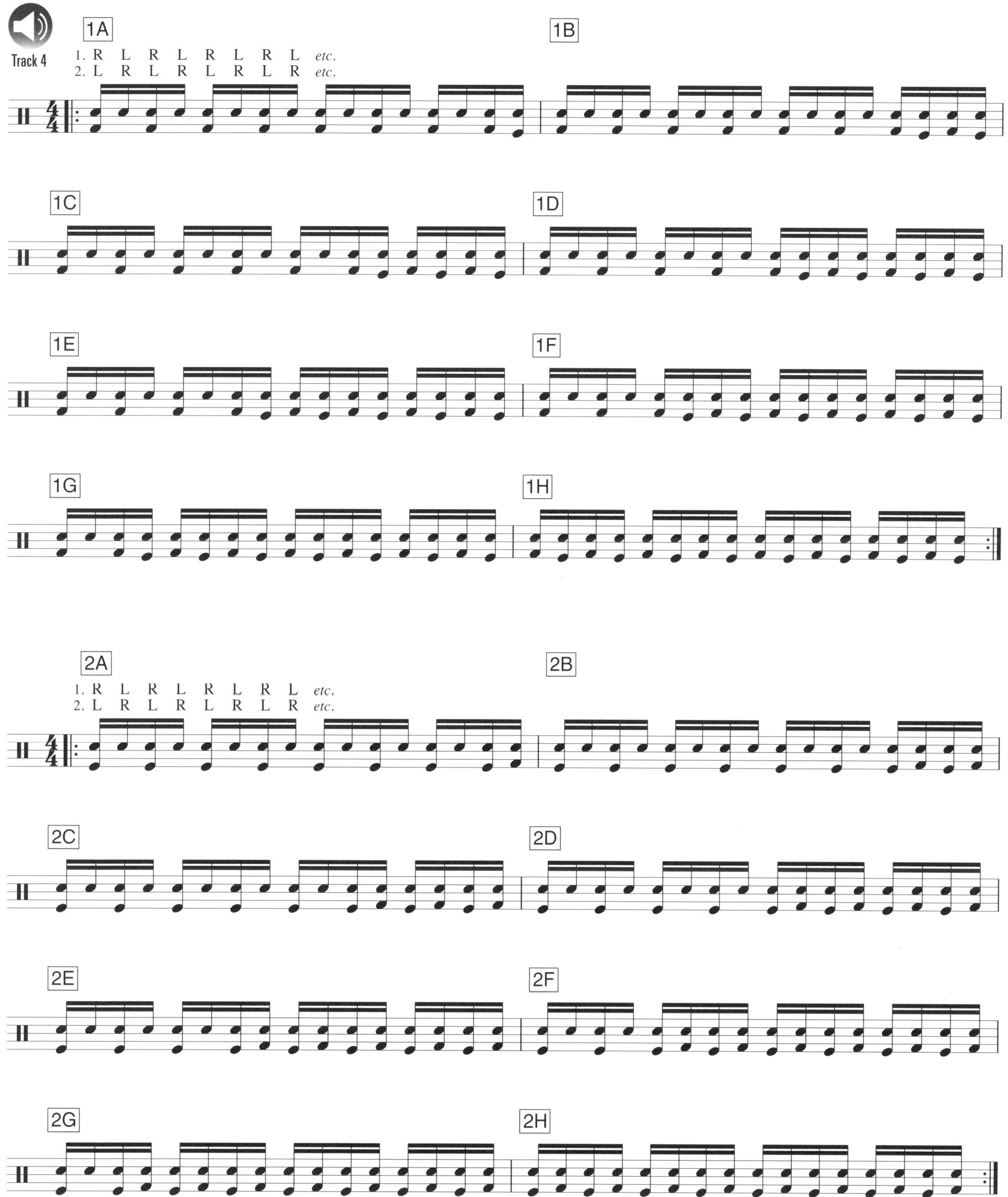

Layered Accent Control Builder

1

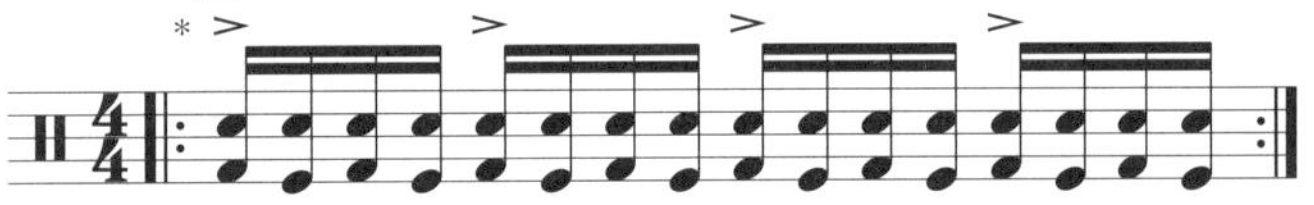

*Accents apply only to the snare drum.

2

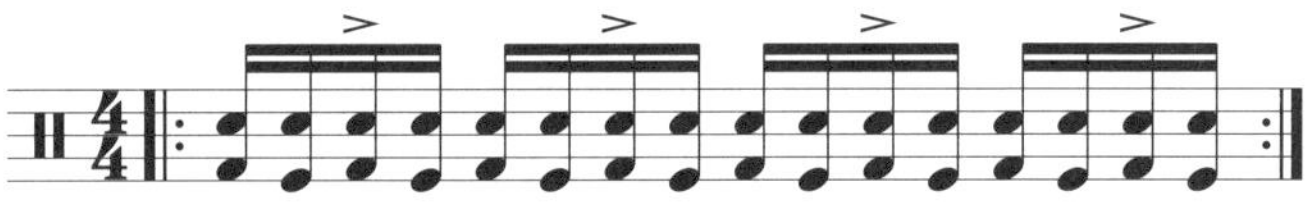

3

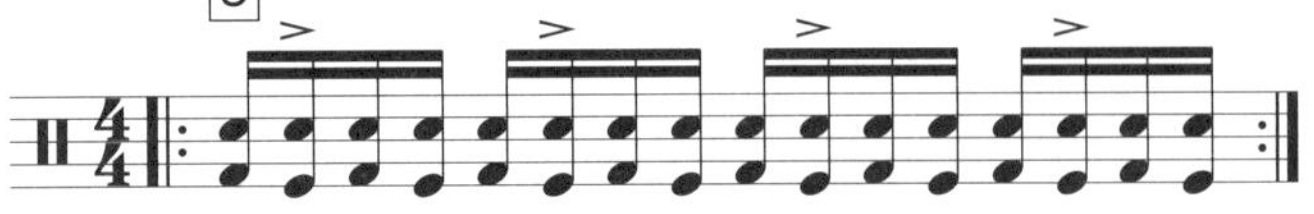

4

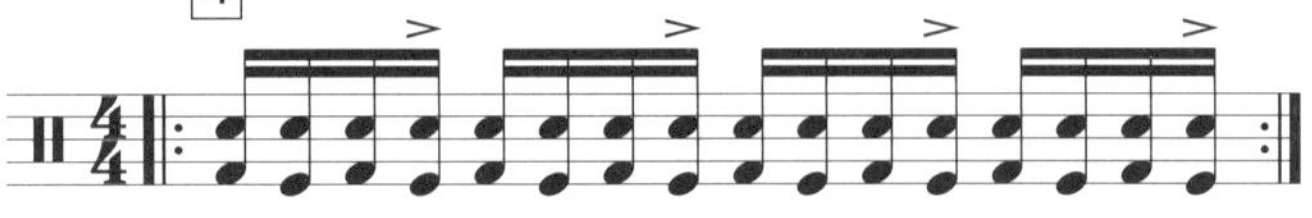

5

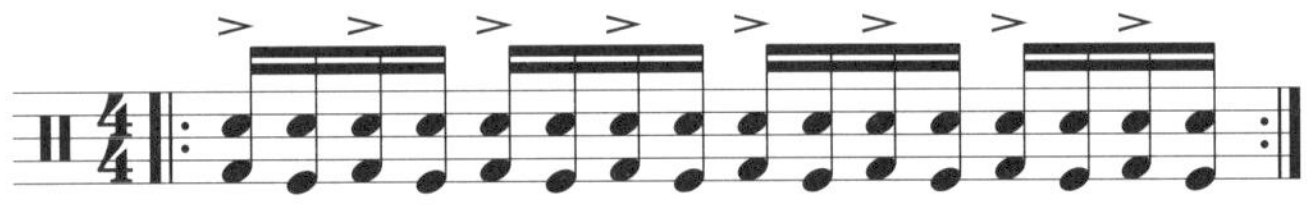

6

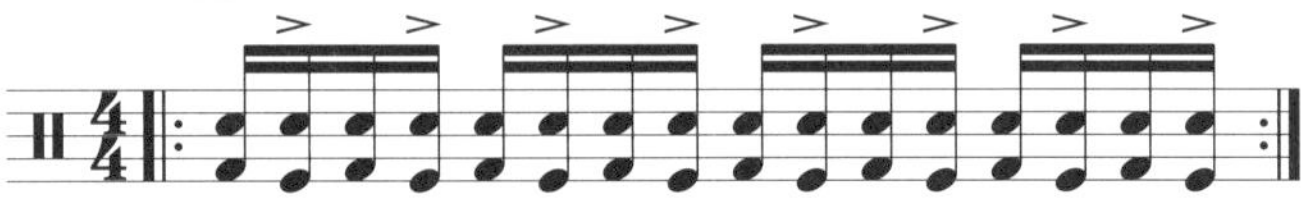

7

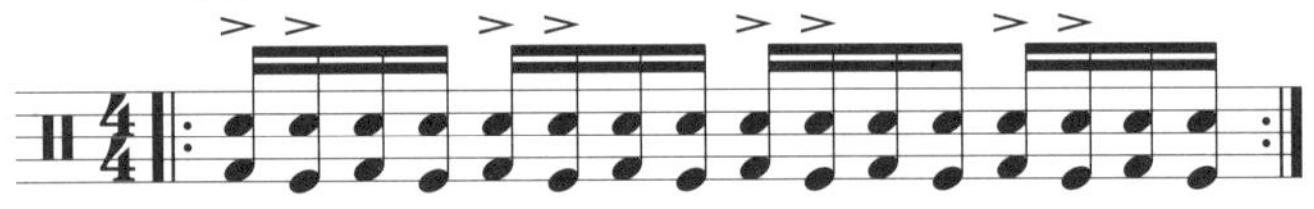

8

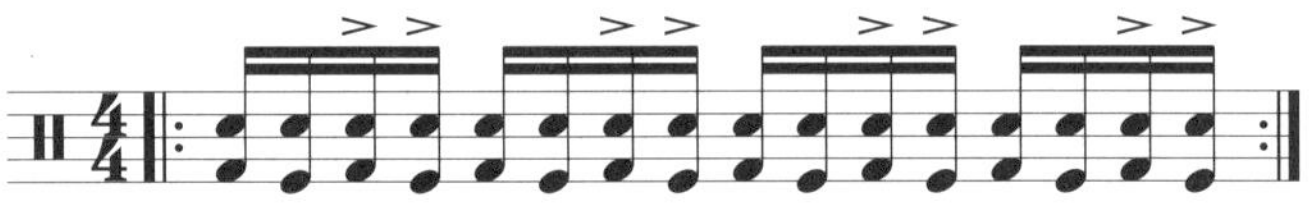

9

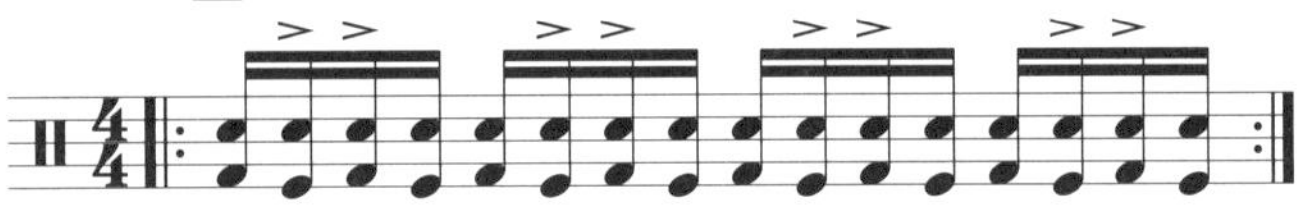

10

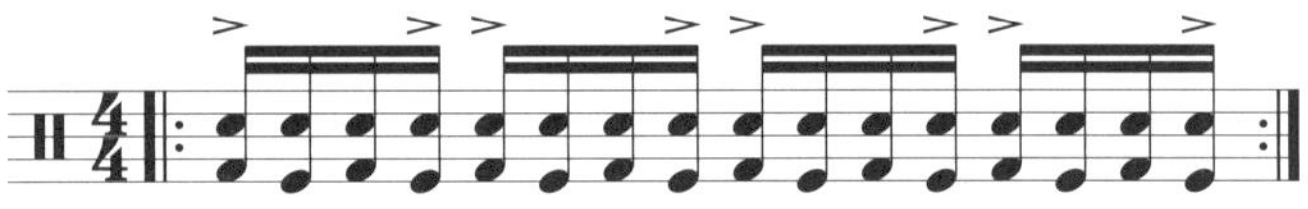

Layered Accent Variations

1

2

3

4

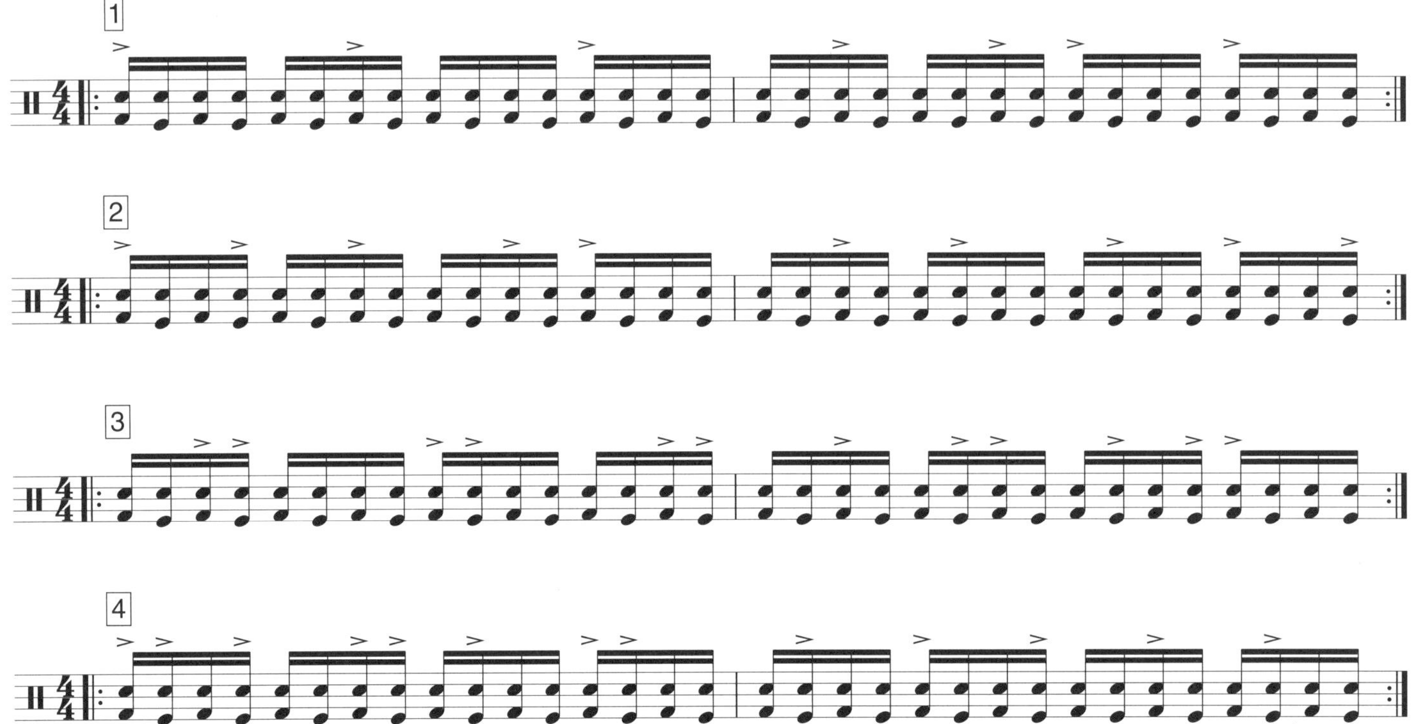

Divided Dynamics

The following dynamic exercises are designed to separate the dynamic approach between your hands and your feet. Generally, it's easier for all of the limbs to play at the same volume, but sometimes music will require one to be able to control their dynamic approach within the limbs interdependently. These exercises will help facilitate this demand.

In the following exercise, try to make each crescendo and decrescendo evenly match their counter-dynamic direction.

Linear Builders (Singles)

In drumming, "linear" means no two voices (or limbs) play at the same time. The opposite of this approach is "layered," which the previous pages had just explored. Linear poses a new challenge in that one can no longer depend on a specific limb to help focus the time or coordination. Now, each limb is soley responsible for evenly subdividing the time. This is extremely valuable when developing a double bass technique in which both feet are prepared to play any given rhythm.

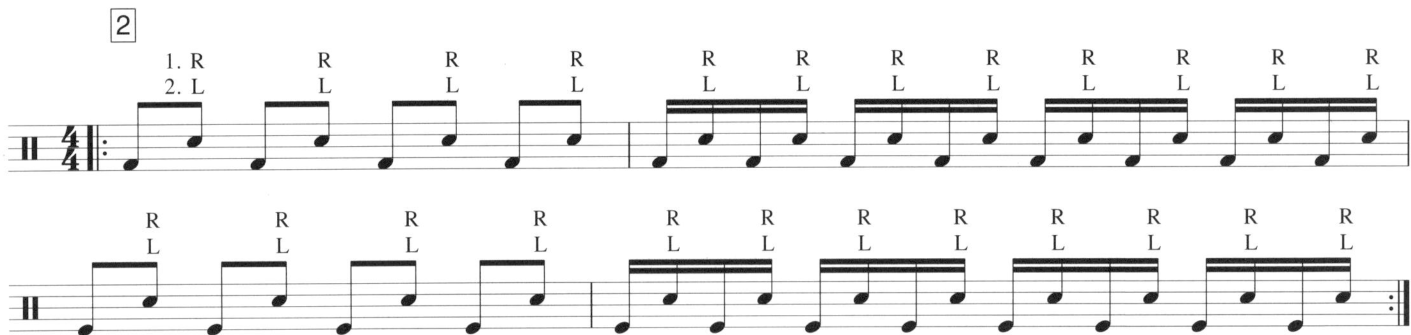

Linear Builders (Doubles)

1

1. R
2. L

2

1. R
2. L

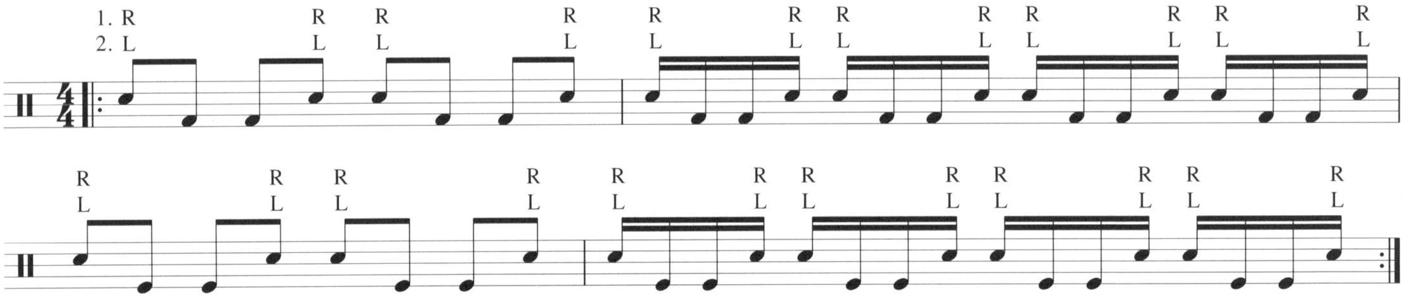

3

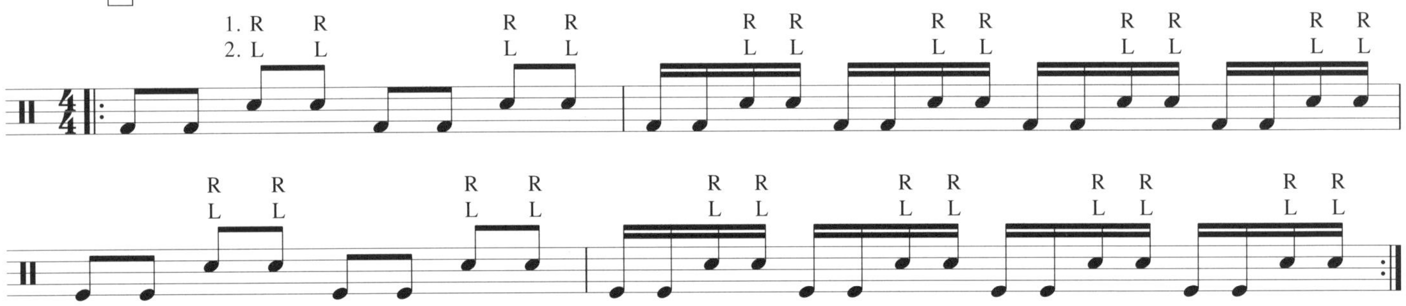

1. R
2. L

4

1. R
2. L

Linear Builders (Paradiddles)

Drumistic Discoveries

Use this page to log your original ideas based on the concepts from this chapter.

1

2

3

4

5

6

7

8

2 8th and 16th-Note Mirrored Grooves

As drummers, one of our main responsibilities is to provide a solid groove. For the most part, the first double bass grooves where consecutive 16th-note or 8th-note-triplet ostinatos, while the hands where responsible for changing the feel and/or motion within the time.

Soon, double bass developed into more than just a powerful ostinato to play with your feet, but rather an integral part of the groove. By using two feet to create various rhythmic patterns, double bass quickly became an effective way to establish powerful and exciting grooves.

Initially, assigning the right and left foot to specific parts of the beat was the approach. The right foot would play all of the eighth-notes (1-&-2-&-3-&-4-&) and the left foot was assigned all the up-beat 16th-notes ("e's" and "a's"). This approach is effective, but has its limitations. Not all rhythms will lend themselves to this system, which is why a new approach to practicing and playing double bass was needed.

Ultimately, the goal is to be able to lead with either foot, regardless of where it is within the beat. We don't want to be limited by depending on a certain foot to play a particular rhythm. We don't (or shouldn't) do this with our hands, so why would we do this with our feet?

The *mirrored groove system* is a double bass practice technique that I developed in 2000. A "mirrored groove" is a two-bar phrase that is rhythmically identical, however, the footings are reversed in each bar, hence "mirrored." By creating two-bar grooves that are rhythmically identical, while always alternating the feet, allowed myself and my students to work each foot equally, while developing a creative double bass groove vocabulary. Since both measures are rhythmically the same, it provided an effective practice tool to equally compare how each foot sounds and feels within the phrase.

The grooves in this chapter are based off the *mirrored groove system*. Take your time with each groove. Memorize the phrase as quickly as possible so you can really focus on making both feet sound equal in tone, dynamic, and feel.

Practice Tips:

- Play the double bass rhythms with your hands before playing them with your feet.
- Count out loud until you can memorize the phrase, then continue to count to yourself.
- Only try the ride variations at the end after you've mastered the eighth-note feel.
- Repeat. Rest. Recall.

"We cannot become what we need by remaining what we are."

—John Maxwell

16-Note Groove Builders

Use the following grooves to focus on the tone, feel, and technique of each foot. Play to a 16th-note click at 50–100 BPM and count out loud as you play.

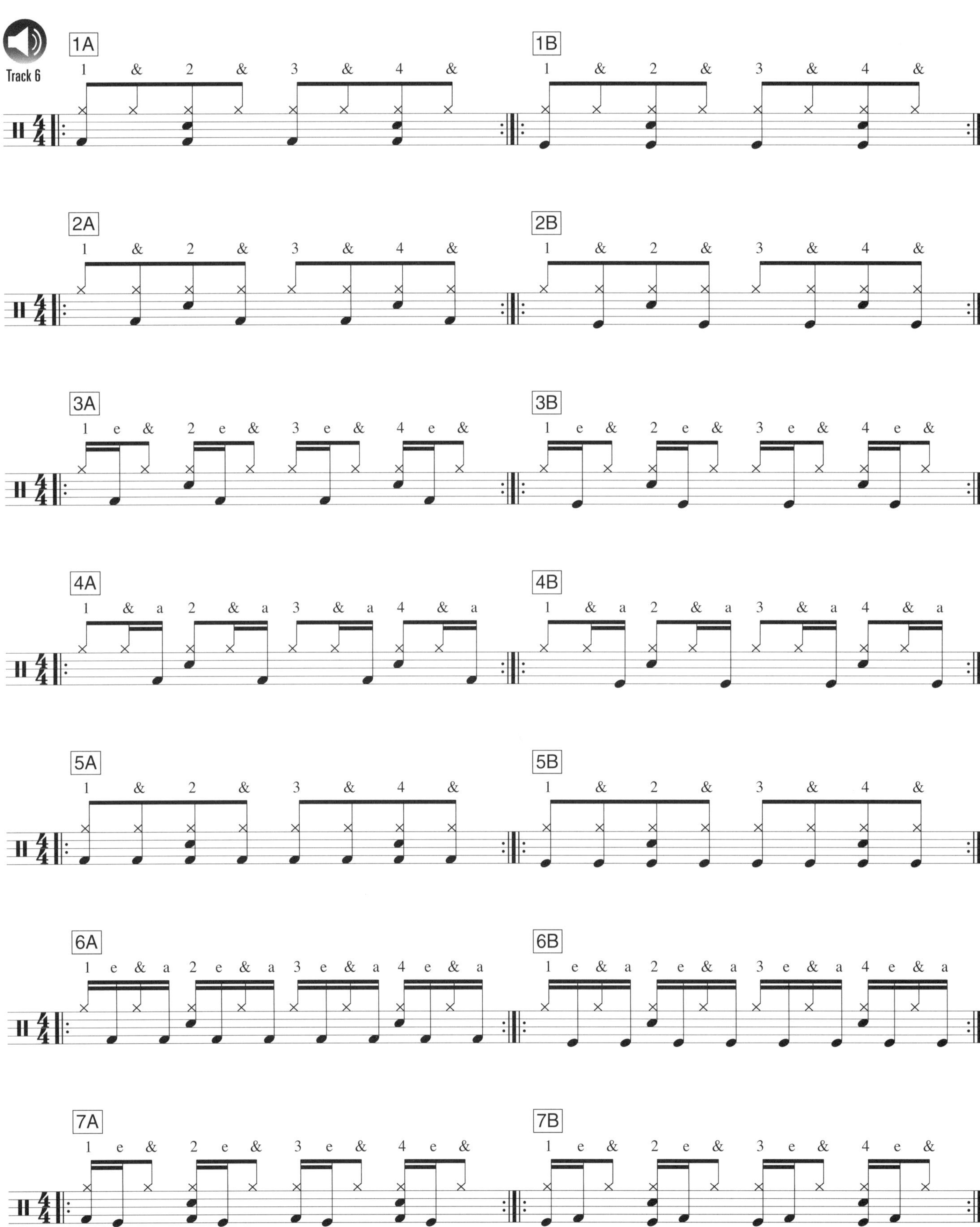

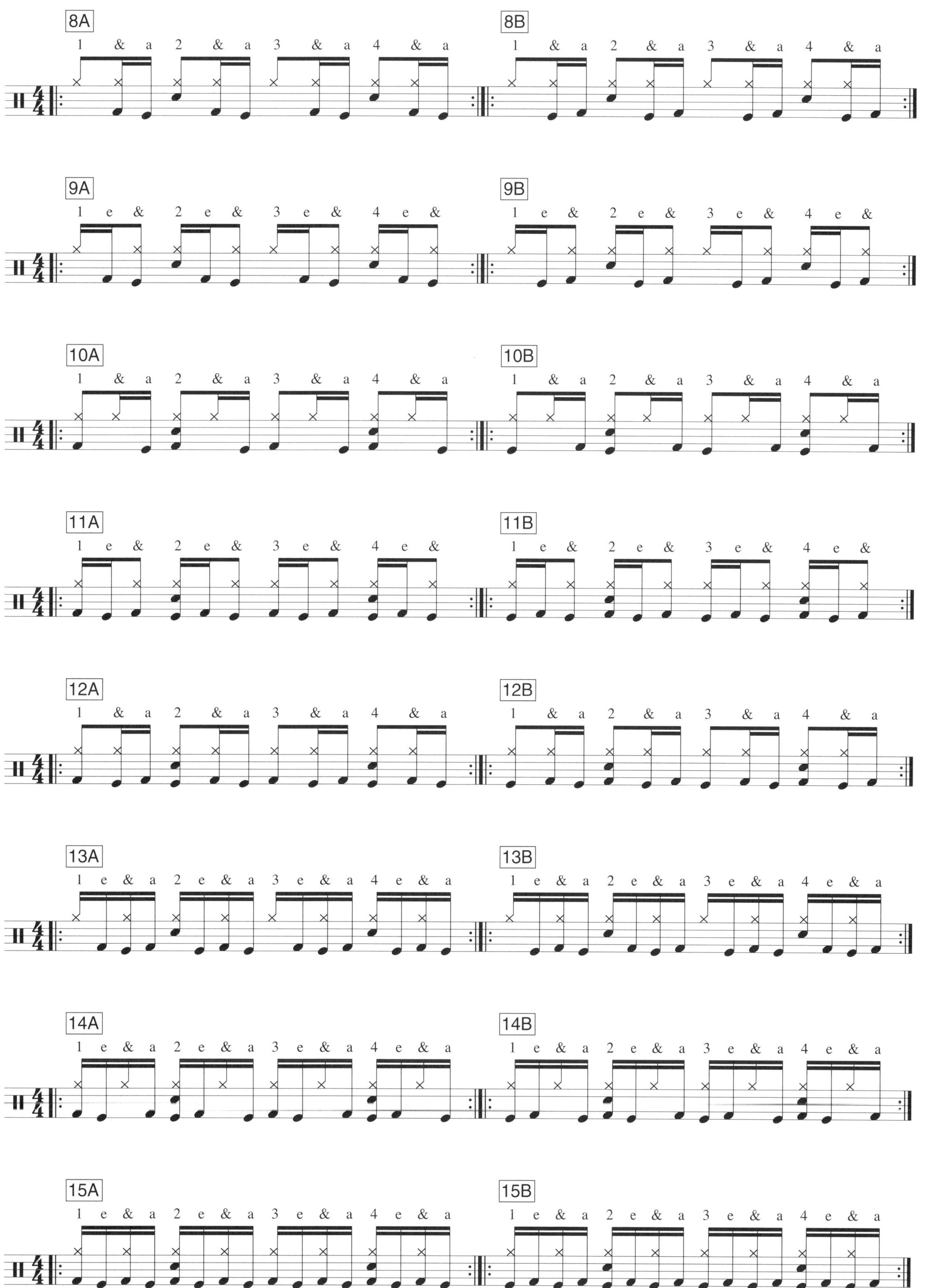
8A
1 & a 2 & a 3 & a 4 & a
8B
1 & a 2 & a 3 & a 4 & a
9A
1 e & 2 e & 3 e & 4 e &
9B
1 e & 2 e & 3 e & 4 e &
10A
1 & a 2 & a 3 & a 4 & a
10B
1 & a 2 & a 3 & a 4 & a
11A
1 e & 2 e & 3 e & 4 e &
11B
1 e & 2 e & 3 e & 4 e &
12A
1 & a 2 & a 3 & a 4 & a
12B
1 & a 2 & a 3 & a 4 & a
13A
1 e & a 2 e & a 3 e & a 4 e & a
13B
1 e & a 2 e & a 3 e & a 4 e & a
14A
1 e & a 2 e & a 3 e & a 4 e & a
14B
1 e & a 2 e & a 3 e & a 4 e & a
15A
1 e & a 2 e & a 3 e & a 4 e & a
15B
1 e & a 2 e & a 3 e & a 4 e & a

Preliminary 8th/16th-Note Mirrored Grooves

8
9
10
11
Track 8
12
13
14
15
16

16th-Note Mirrored Grooves: Snare on 2 and 4

16th-Note Mirrored Grooves: Snare on 3

16th-Note Mirrored Grooves: Snare on "&" of 2 and on 4

16th-Note Mirrored Grooves: Snare on 2 and the "&" of 4

16th-Note Mirrored Grooves: Snare on the "a" of 1 and on 4

16th-Note Mirrored Grooves: Snare on 2 and the "a" of 3

16th-Note Mirrored Grooves: Snare on "e" of 2 and on 4

16th-Notes Mirrored Grooves: Snare on 2 and the "e" of 4

16th-Note Mirrored Grooves: Snare on 1, 2, 3, and 4

16th-Note Mirrored Grooves: Snare on the "&s" of 1, 2, 3, and 4

16th-Note Mirrored Grooves: Snare Combinations

Ride Variations

Apply all of the following ride variations to the previous mirrored grooves. By doing this, you will discover how various ride patterns can alter the entire character of the groove. They may pose some new coordination challenges; in that case, take it slow and count out loud... but you already know this!

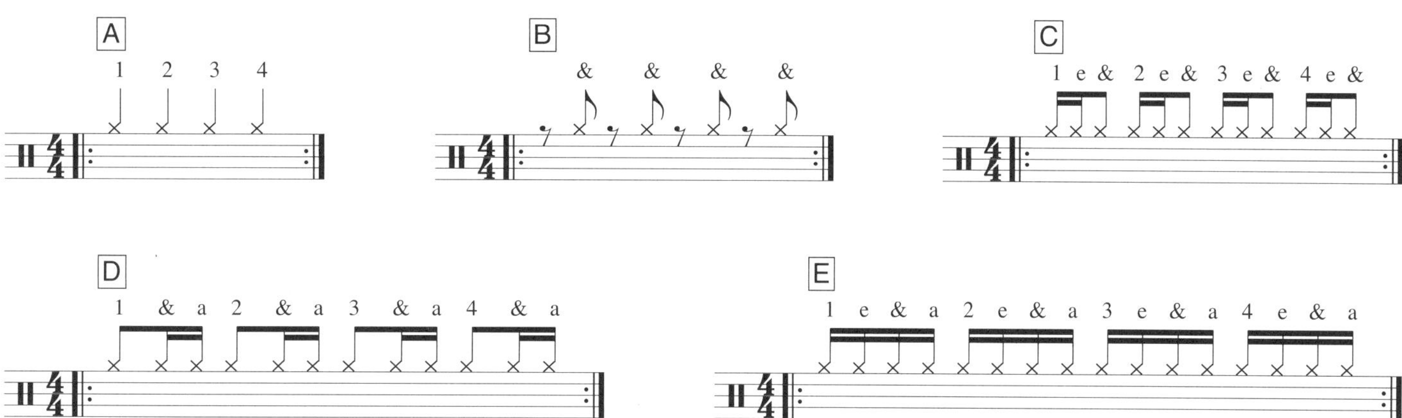

Groove Applications

The following is what the notaion looks like when applying all of the ride variations to one mirrored groove from this chapter.

Track 17a

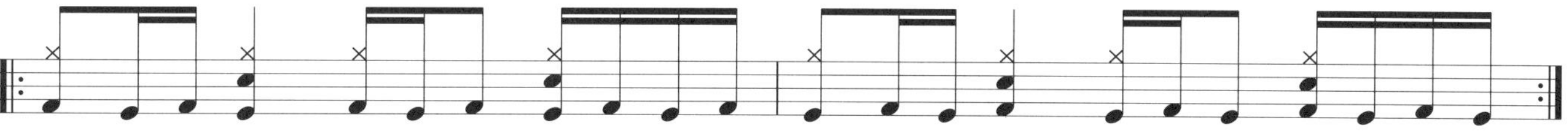

A

Track 17b

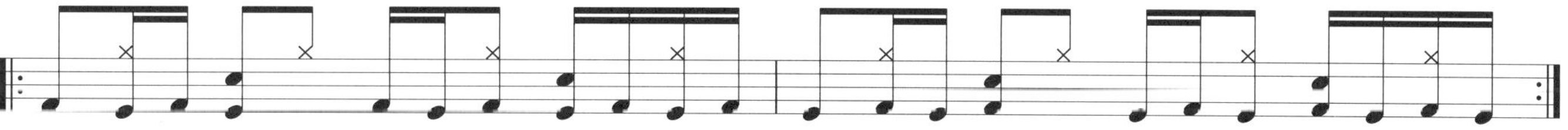

B

Track 17c

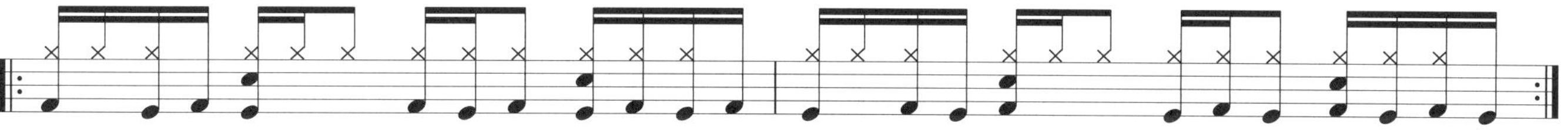

C

Track 17d

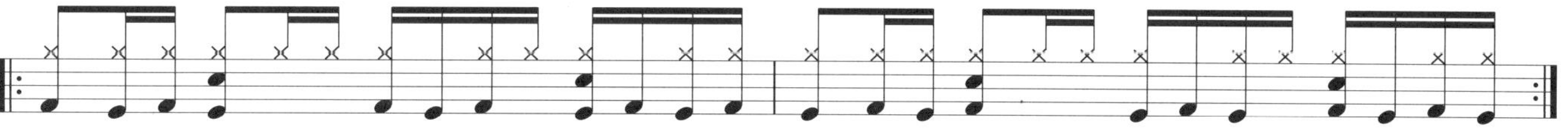

D

Track 17e

E

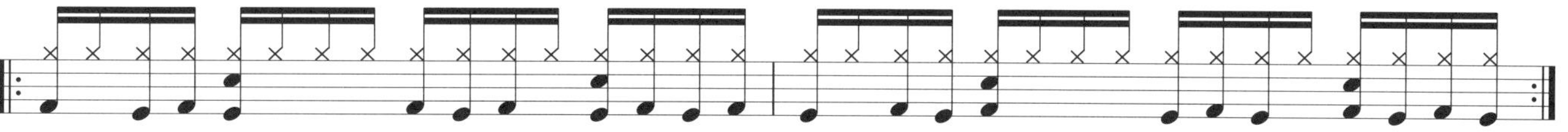

Drumistic Discoveries

Use this page to log your original ideas based on the concepts from this chapter.

1

2

3

4

5

6

7

8

3 16th/32nd-Note Mirrored Grooves

As mentioned previously, the ability to lead with either foot has become the new standard in double bass technique. Focusing on each foot equally is the most efficient way to develop this skill. By now, you should be able to notice more strength and control with your "weaker" foot. However, the fun is just beginning.

This chapter will reinforce why we've been spending equal time on each foot. In the following pages you will encounter rhythms based off various 32nd-note patterns that automatically reverse the footing. This will provide a great opportunity for you to further refine your double bass technique and prepare you for any rhythmic challenge!

Practice Tips:

- 16th and 32nd notes have the same relationship that 8th and 16th notes have—the values are doubled, meaning, you play (subdivide) them twice as fast.
- Count 16th notes even if you're playing 32nd notes.
- Approach these grooves at a slower tempo than you did with the grooves in Chapter 2.
- Repeat. Rest. Recall.

"Some people want it to happen, some wish it would happen, others make it happen."

—Michael Jordan

Ride/Snare Patterns

Since some of these grooves may initially be rhythmically challenging, these 32nd-note groove builders will provide a thorough primer in preparing you for the ensuing double bass adventure.

First, play each bass drum pattern with your hands to help internalize the rhythm, then try to play it with your feet. Next, add the 8th ride pattern. Finally, add these following snare drum patterns.

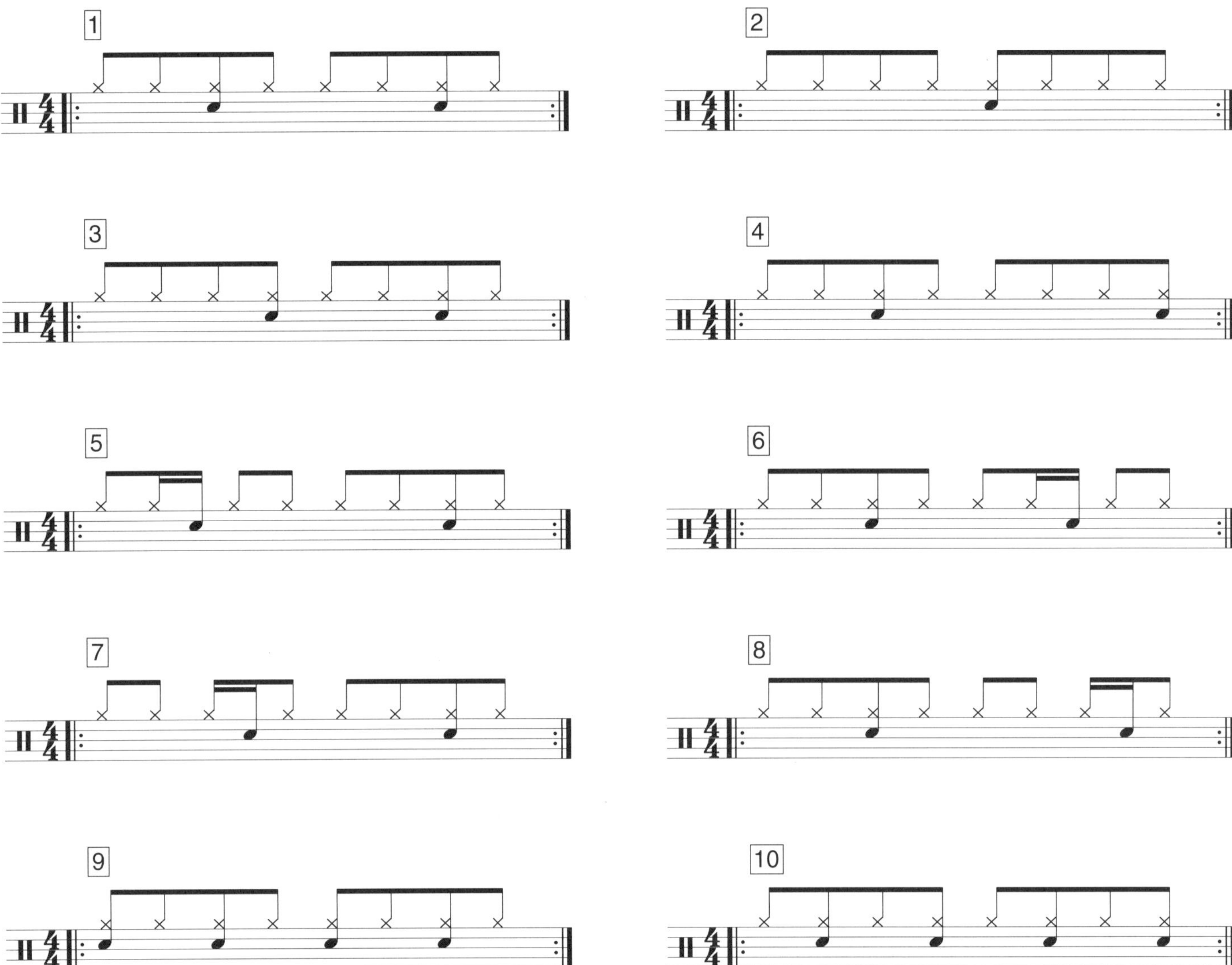

32nd-Note Groove Builders: 2-Note

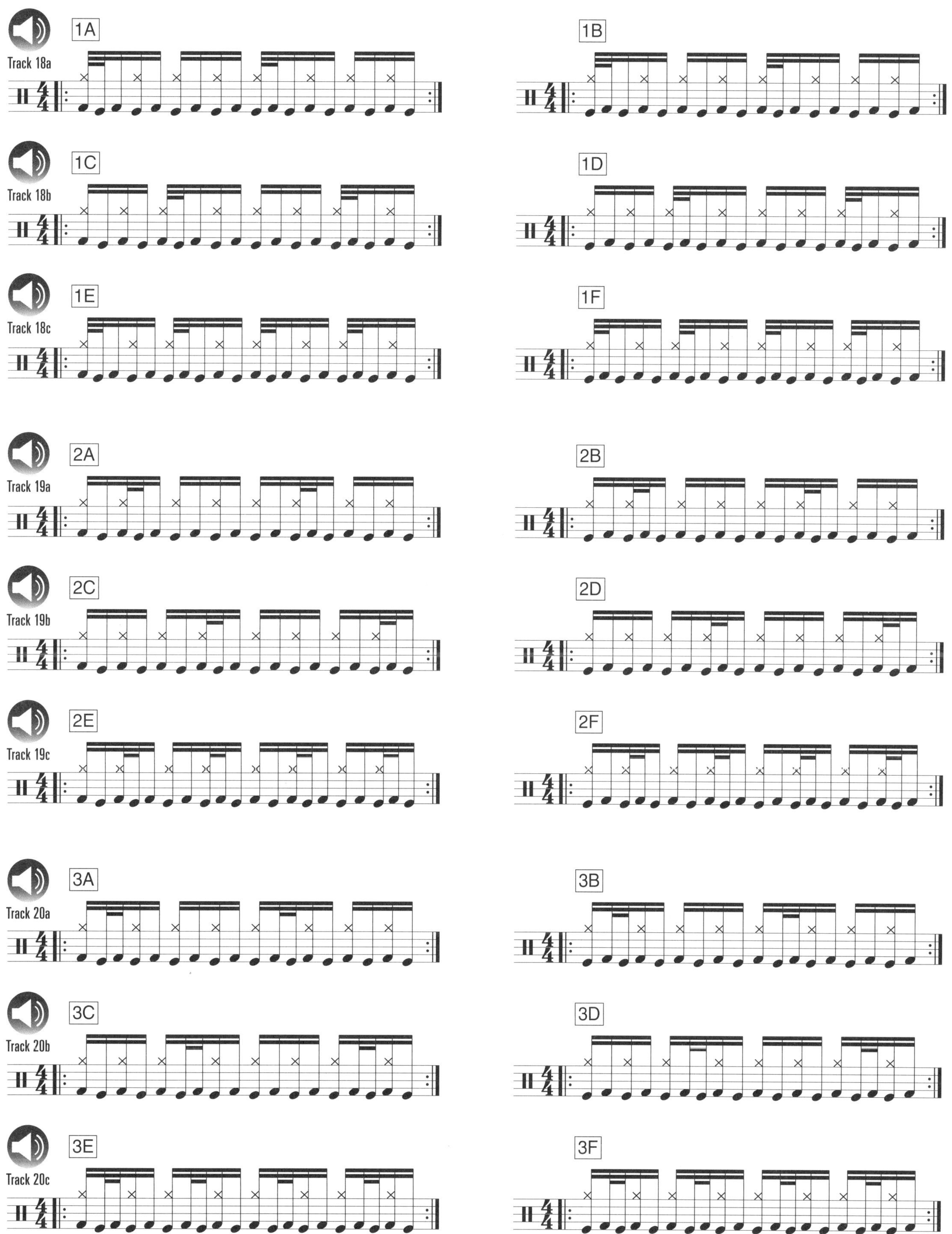

4A
Track 21a
4B
4C
Track 21b
4D
4E
Track 21c
4F
5A
Track 22a
5B
5C
Track 22b
5D
5E
Track 22c
5F
6A
Track 23a
6B
6C
Track 23b
6D
6E
Track 23c
6F

32nd-Note Groove Builders: 4-Note

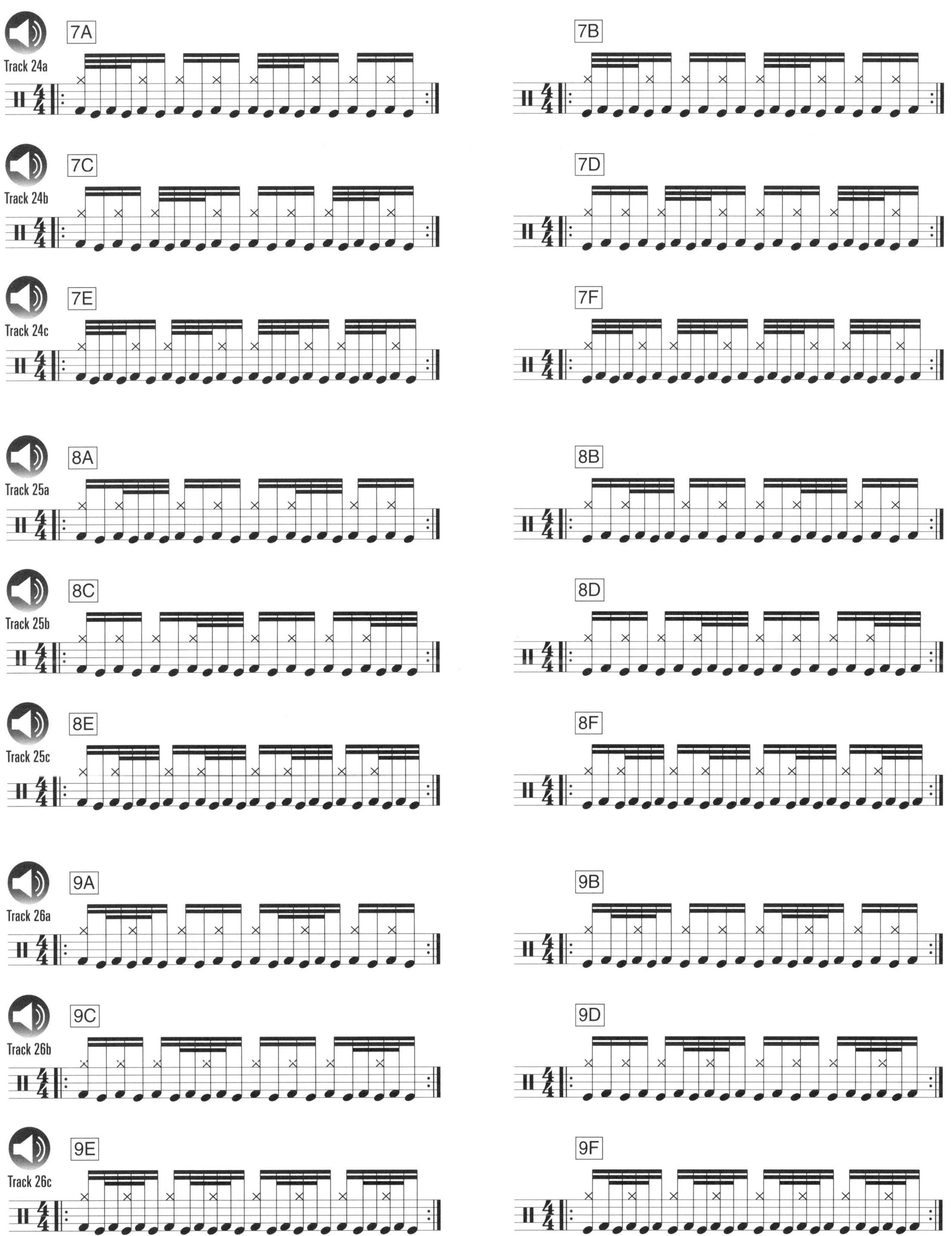

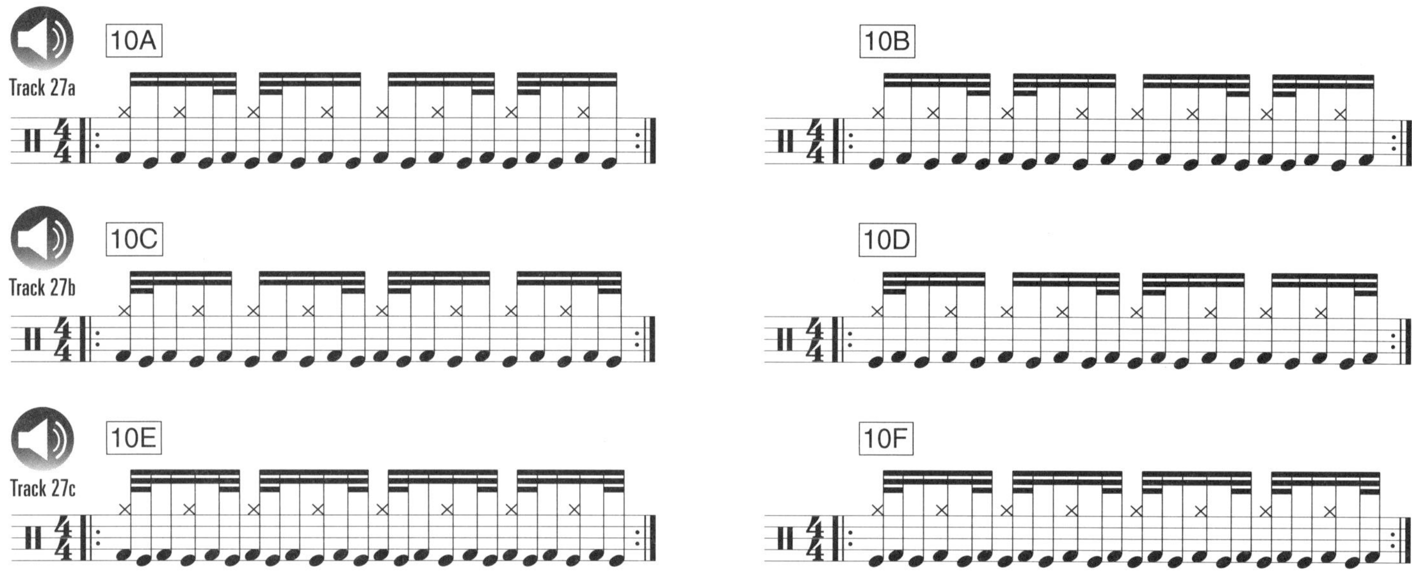

Progressive Groove Builder: 16th-Note and 32nd-Note

The main objective for this exercise is to play measure 1A to measure 16 without stopping. However, as with most exercises, feel free to repeat any measure as long as it takes before moving on; this is practicing proficiently.

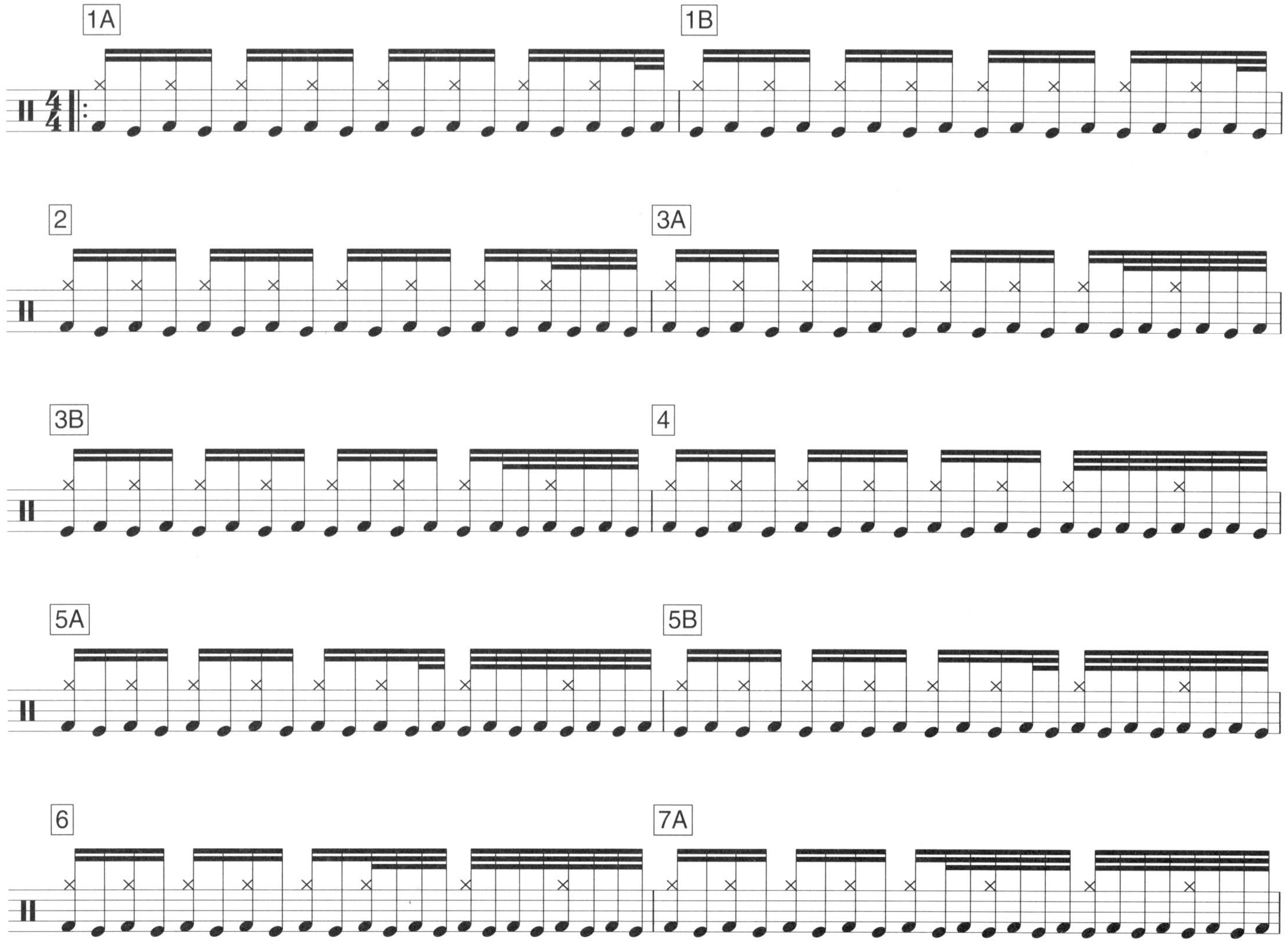

1A 1B

2 3A

3B 4

5A 5B

6 7A

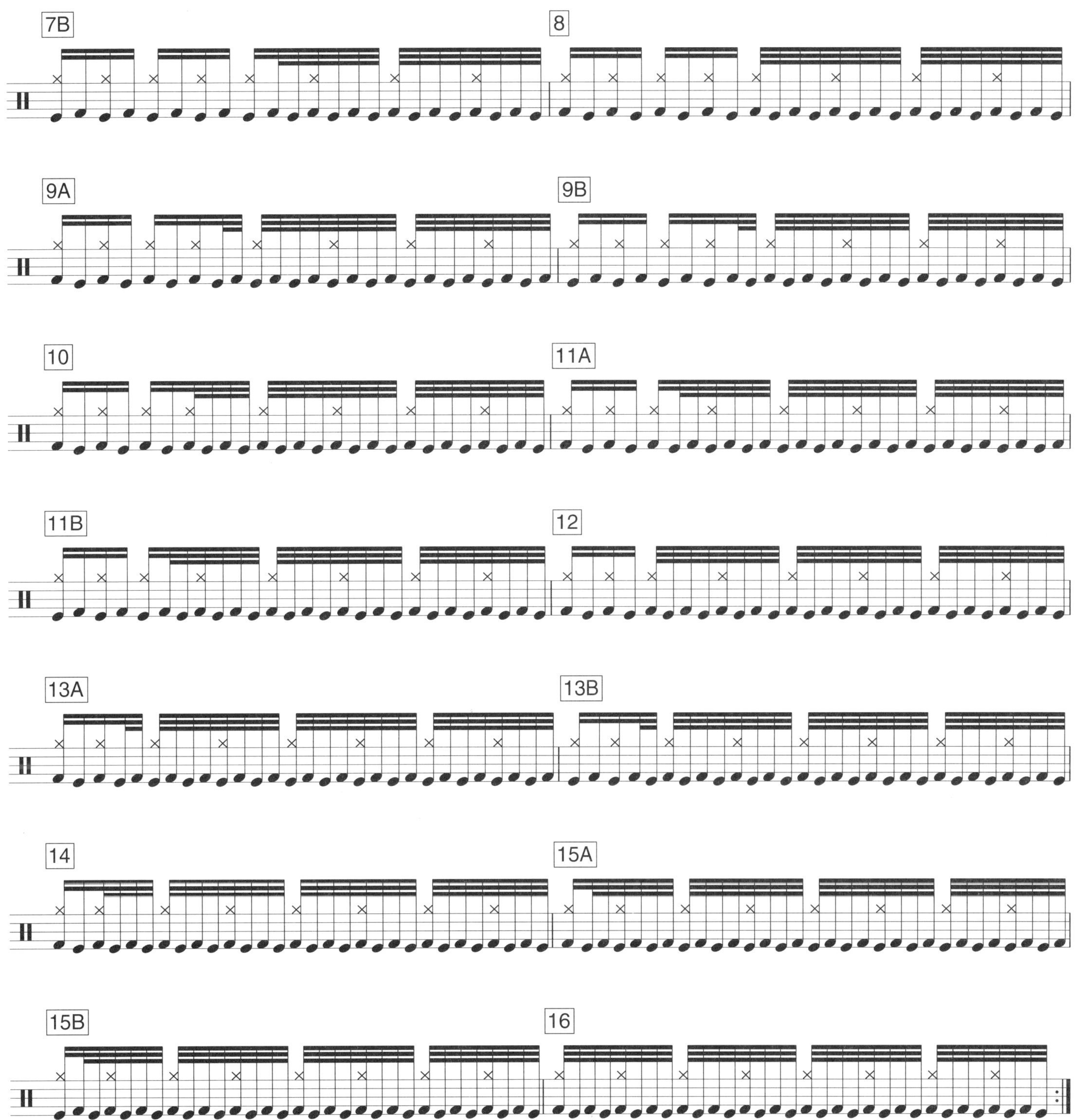
7B
8
9A
9B
10
11A
11B
12
13A
13B
14
15A
15B
16

16th/32nd-Note Mirrored Grooves: Snare on 2 and 4

16th/32nd-Note Mirrored Grooves: Snare on 3

16th/32nd-Note Mirrored Grooves: Snare on "&" of 2 and on 4

16th/32nd-Note Mirrored Grooves: Snare on 2 and the "&" of 4

16th/32nd-Note Mirrored Grooves: Snare on the "a" of 1 and on 4

16th/32nd-Note Mirrored Grooves: Snare on 2 and the "a" of 3

16th/32nd-Note Mirrored Grooves: Snare on "e" of 2 and on 4

16th/32nd-Note Mirrored Grooves: Snare on 2 and "e" of 4

16th/32nd-Note Mirrored Grooves: Snare on 1, 2, 3, and 4

16th/32nd-Note Mirrored Grooves: Snare on the "&s" of 1, 2, 3, and 4

16th/32nd-Note Mirrored Grooves: Snare Combinations

Ride Variations

Apply all of the following ride variations to the previous mirrored grooves. By doing this, you will discover how various ride patterns can alter the entire character of the groove. They may pose some new coordination challenges—in that case, take it slow and count out loud... but again, you already know this!

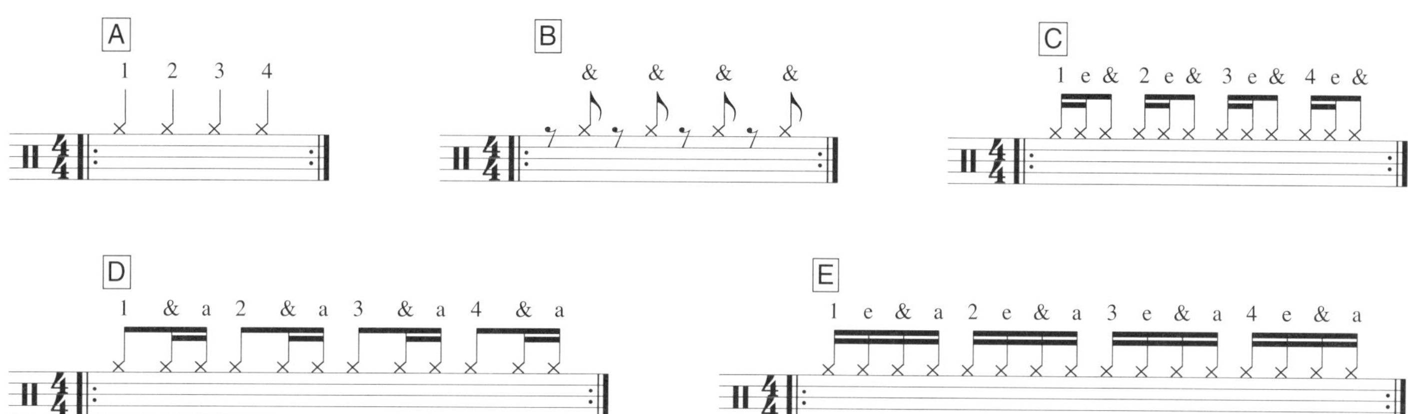

Groove Variations

This is what the notaion looks like when applying all of the ride variations to one mirrored groove from this chapter.

A
Track 34a

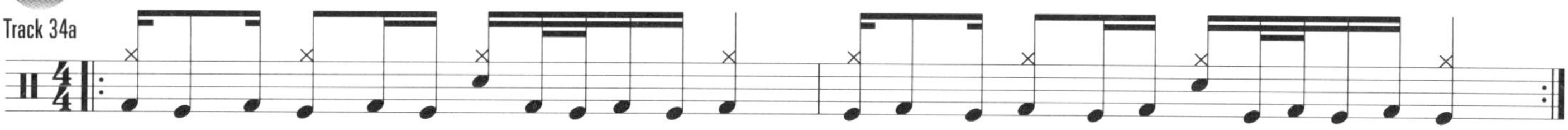

B
Track 34b

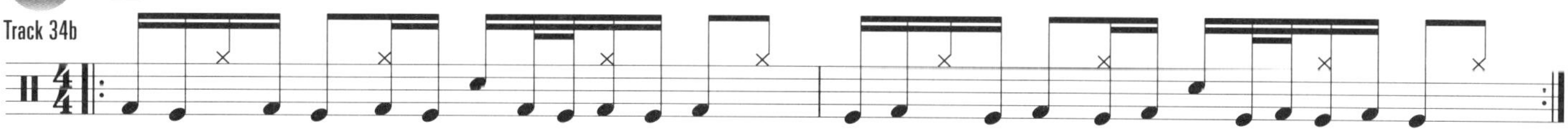

C
Track 34c

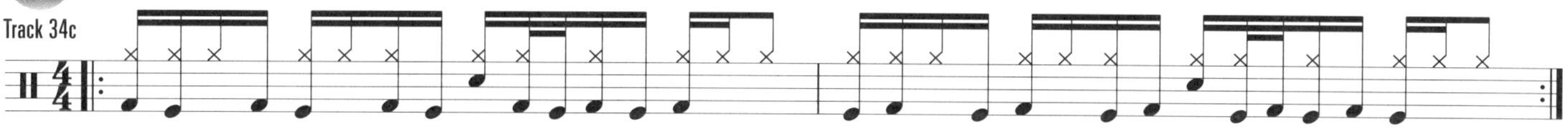

D
Track 34d

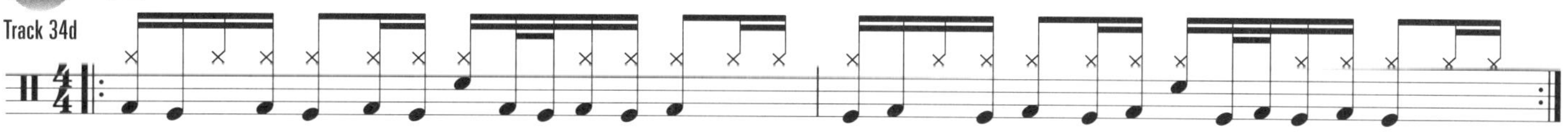

E
Track 34e

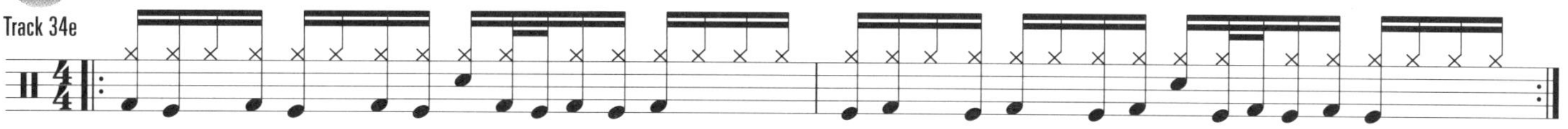

Drumistic Discoveries

Use this page to log your original ideas based on the concepts from this chapter.

1

2

3

4

5

6

7

8

4 8th-Note-Triplet Warm-Ups

In music, a triplet is a series of three evenly-subdivided notes where you would typically find two. For example, three 8th-note triplets occupy the same amount of space as two 8th notes. Similarly, three 16th-note triplets occupy the same amount of space as two 16th notes, and so on.

In double bass, playing consecutive 8th-note triplets will quickly reveal how different they feel than playing consecutive 16th notes. Because of the odd number of notes that 8th-note triplets are built from, every beat will alternate between right and left foot. This will only reinforce the concept of leading with either foot.

To build a strong double bass foundation with 8th-note triplets, the following warm-up exercises utilize the quarter-note triplet to further reveal how the triplet works within the beat. The quarter-note triplet can be thought of the same way we compared 8th-note triplets to 8th notes: three quarter-note triplets occupy the same amount of space as two quarter notes.

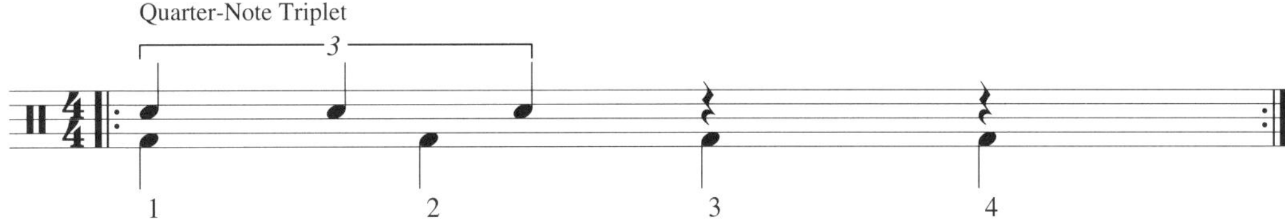

Another way to understand the quarter-note triplet is to think of it as every other 8th-note triplet.

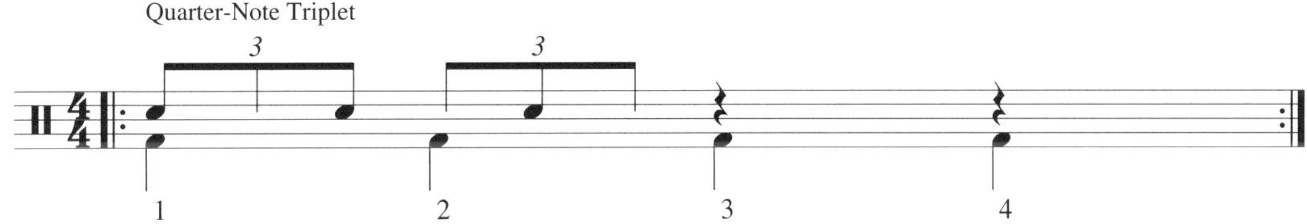

This is how the quarter-note triplet will be notated in this chapter.

Practice Tips:

- Practice to an 8th-note-triplet click and count out loud to ensure an evenly subdivided three-note phrase.
- The quarter-note triplet has a tendency to be felt slower than it is—counting will help prevent this.
- Remember to center yourself on the throne. Triplet may pose a new balance challenge.
- Repeat. Rest. Recall.

"Give me a man who says this one thing I do, and not those fifty things I dabble in."

—Dwight L. Moody

8th-Note-Triplet Progressive Builder

Focus on evenly subdividing the quarter-note triplet within the 8th-note-triplet click at 70–120 BPM.

Dynamic Control Builder

1A

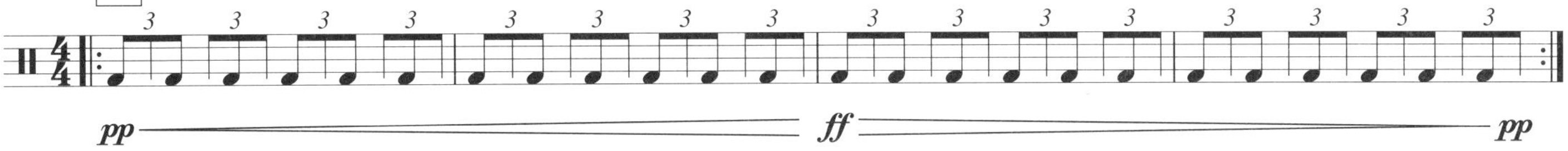
pp
ff
pp

1B

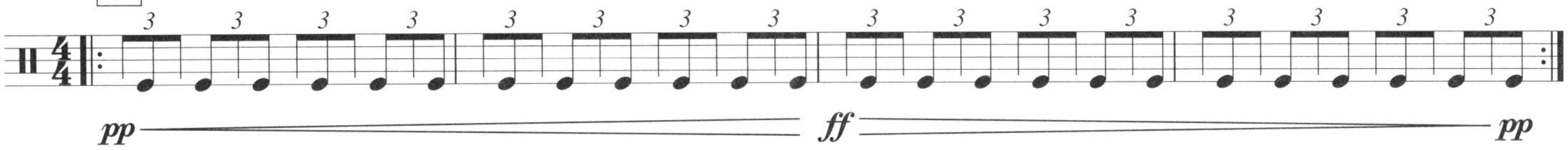
pp
ff
pp

1C

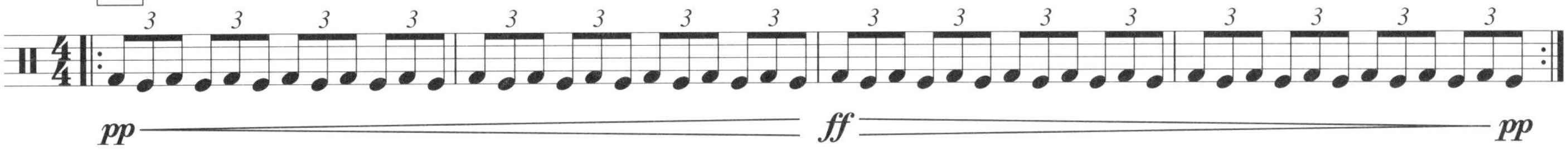
pp
ff
pp

2A

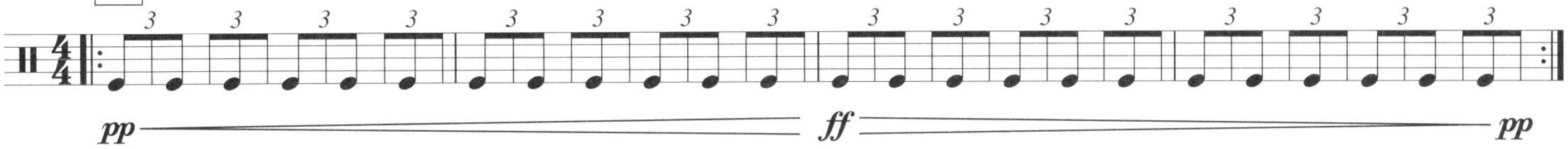
pp
ff
pp

2B

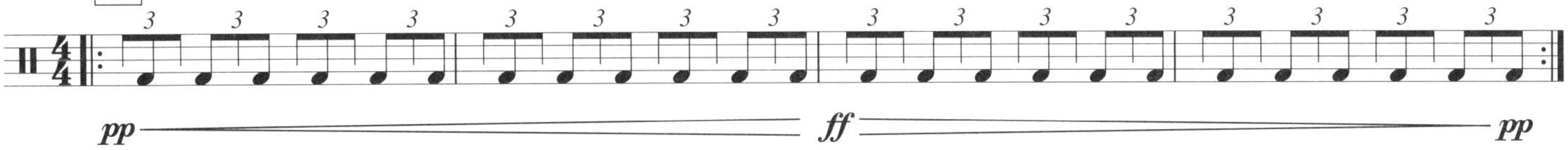
pp
ff
pp

2C

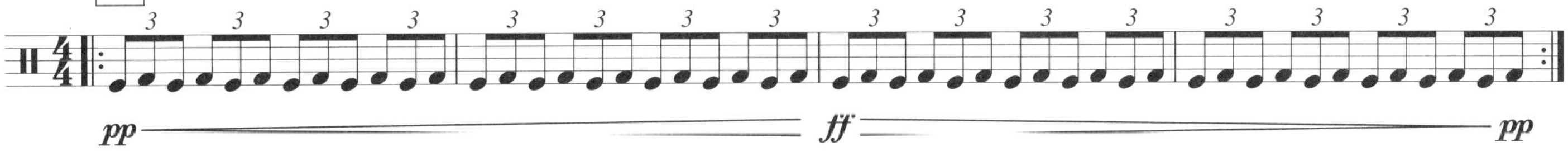
pp
ff
pp

Accent Control Builder

1A

1B

2A

2B

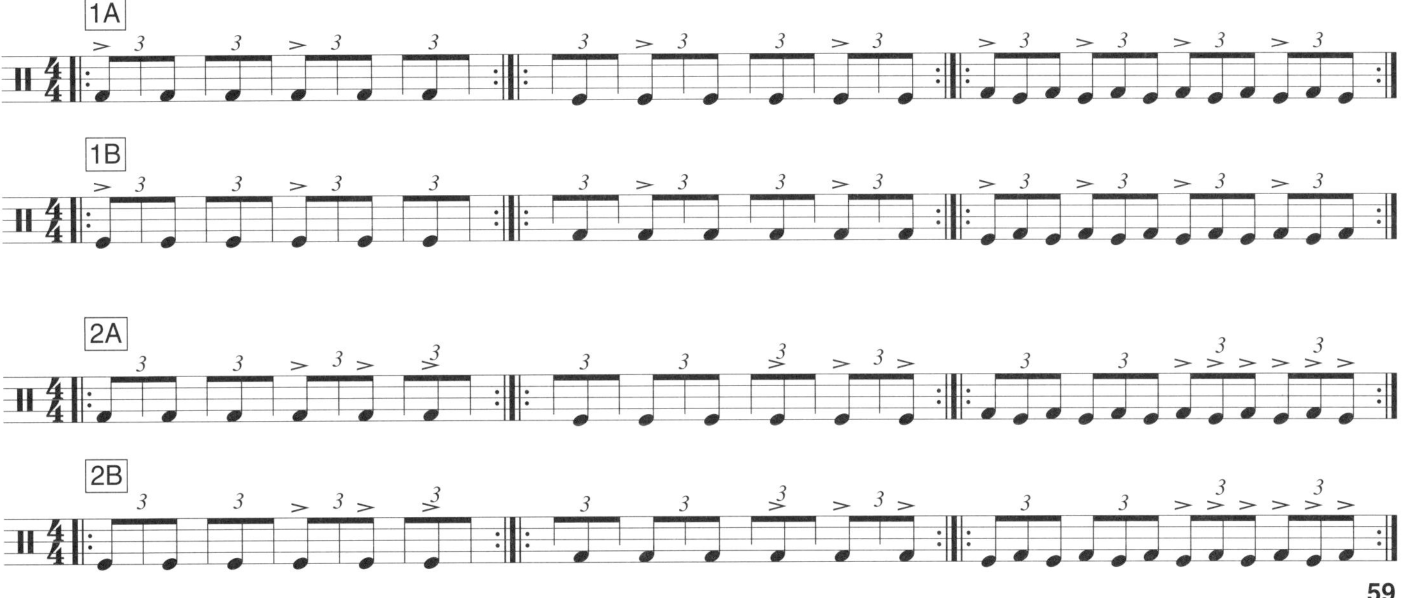

Layered 8th-Note-Triplet Progressive Builder

Layered Accent Control Builder

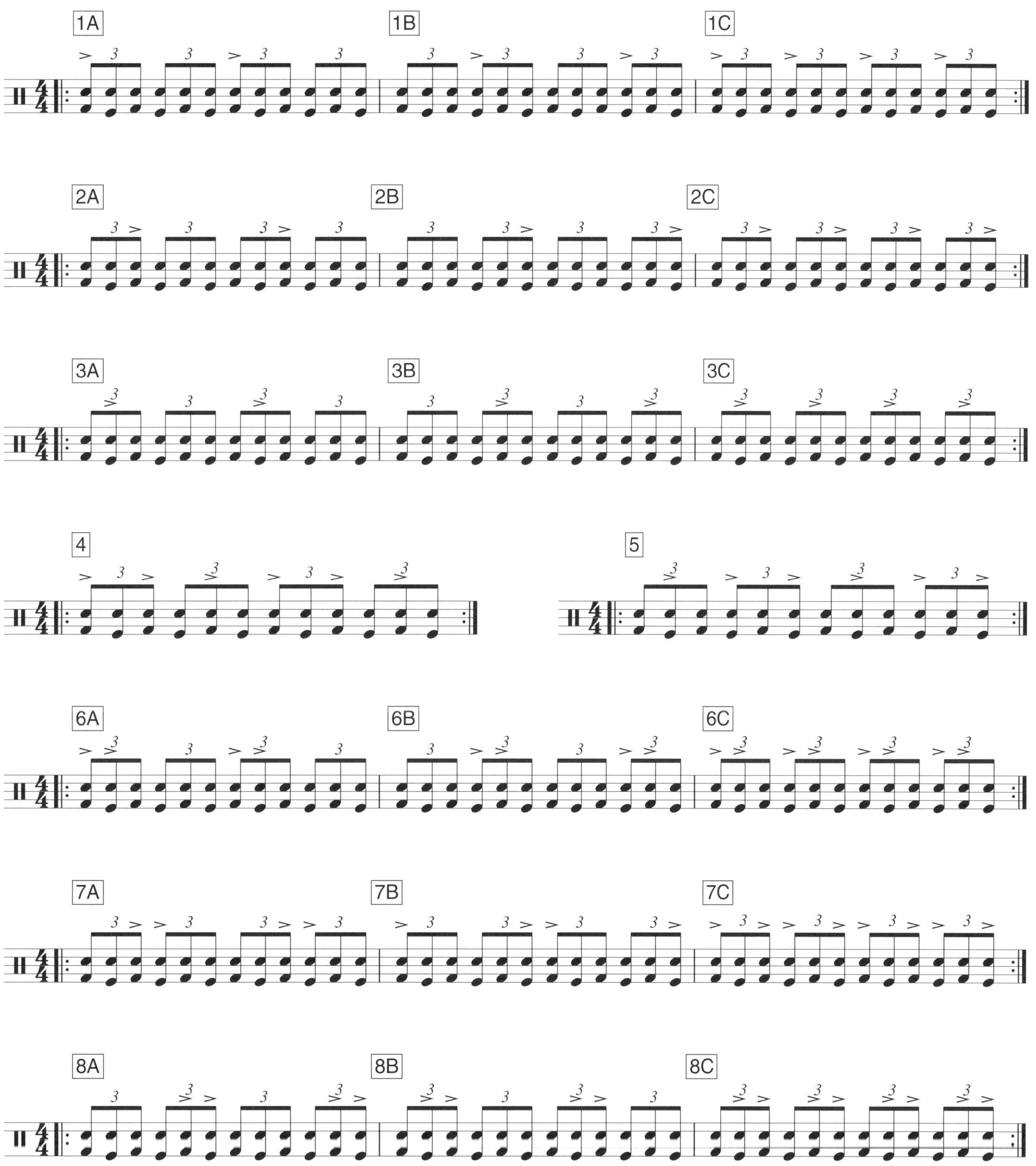

Layered Accent Variations

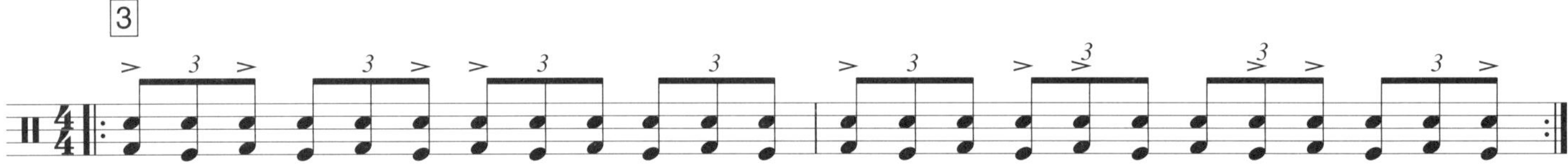

Divided Dynamics

Linear Builders (Singles)

Linear Builders (Doubles)

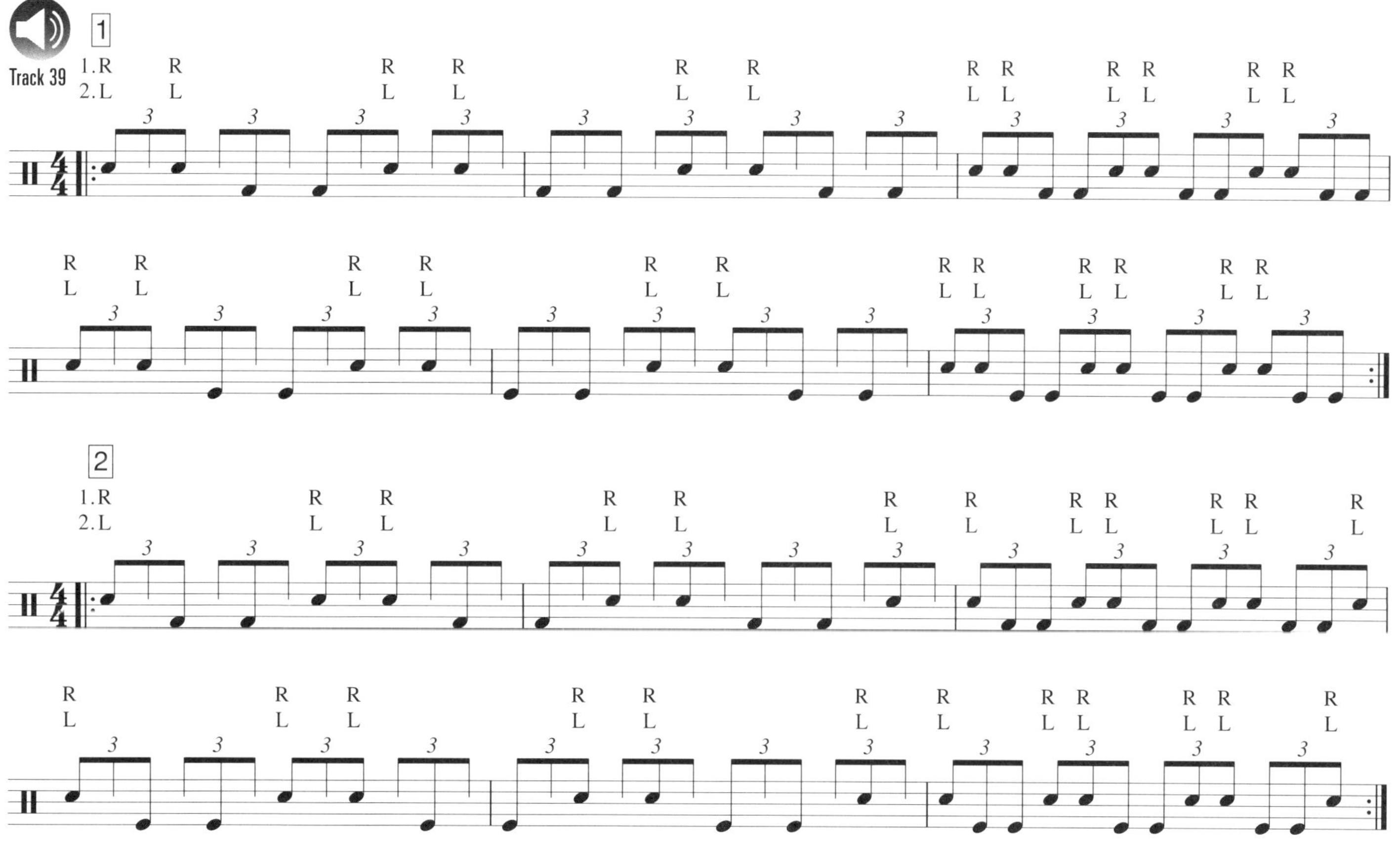

Linear Builders (Double Paradiddle)

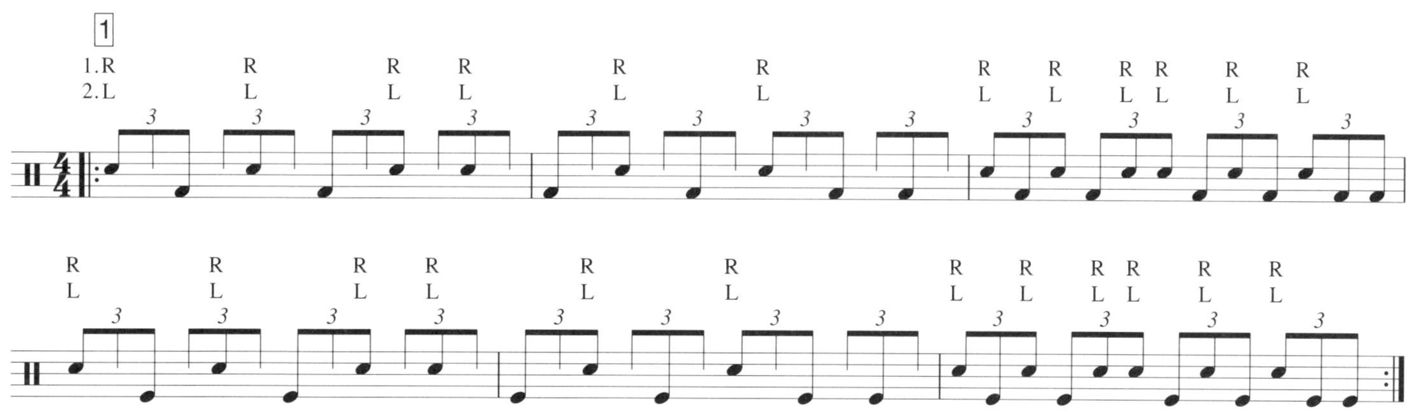

Drumistic Discoveries

Use this page to log your original ideas based on the concepts from this chapter.

1

2

3

4

5

6

7

8

5 8th-Note-Triplet Mirrored Grooves

Continuing with the "mirrored groove" concept from Chapters 2 and 3, the following triplet grooves are based on the same approach. Remember to initially play the alternating bass drum rhythm with your hands, then apply the rhythm to your feet. By involving all of your limbs, the patterns will solidify and internalize more quickly.

Of the following mirrored grooves for this chapter, number 7 is built upon a triplet-based rhythm, referred to as the *shuffle*. Essentially, the shuffle is comprised of the first and last note of the 3-note-triplet pattern.

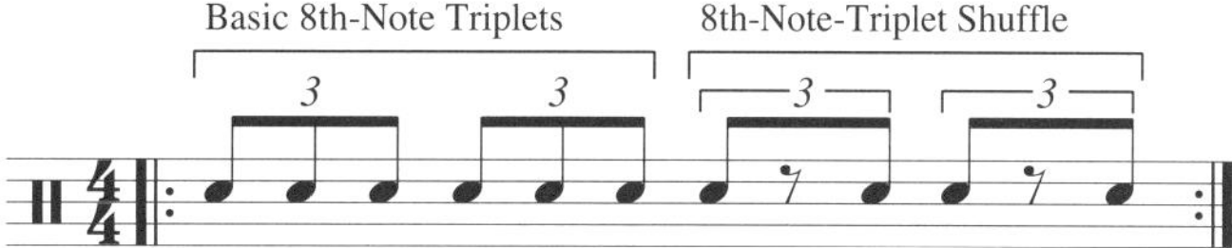

When applying this rhythm to double bass, adding the middle note to the shuffle will automatically switch the feet. This is another example of how developing the ability to lead with either foot offers us more rhythmic freedom.

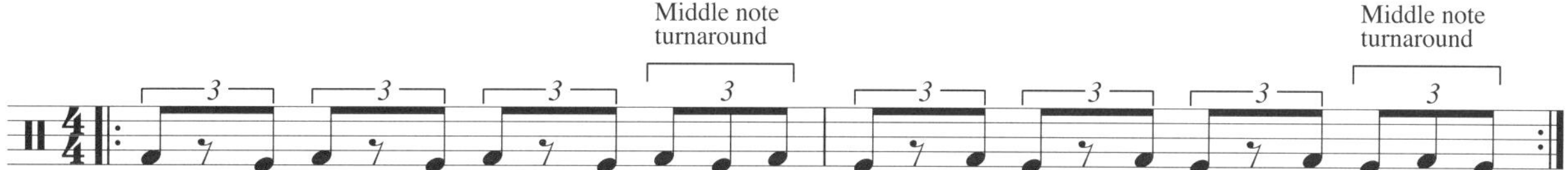

Groove number 7 on pages 67–74 will incorporate this middle note "turnaround."

Practice Tips:

- The primary riding rhythm is now quarter notes.
- Triplets have a more "round" feel compared to 16th notes.
- Play to an 8th-note-triplet click at 80–120 BPM. Play to a shuffle click at 120–160 BPM. Play to a quarter-note click at any tempo above 160 BPM.
- Repeat. Rest. Recall.

"Alleged impossibilities are opportunities for our capacities to be stretched."

—Charles R. Swindoll

8th-Note-Triplet Groove Builders

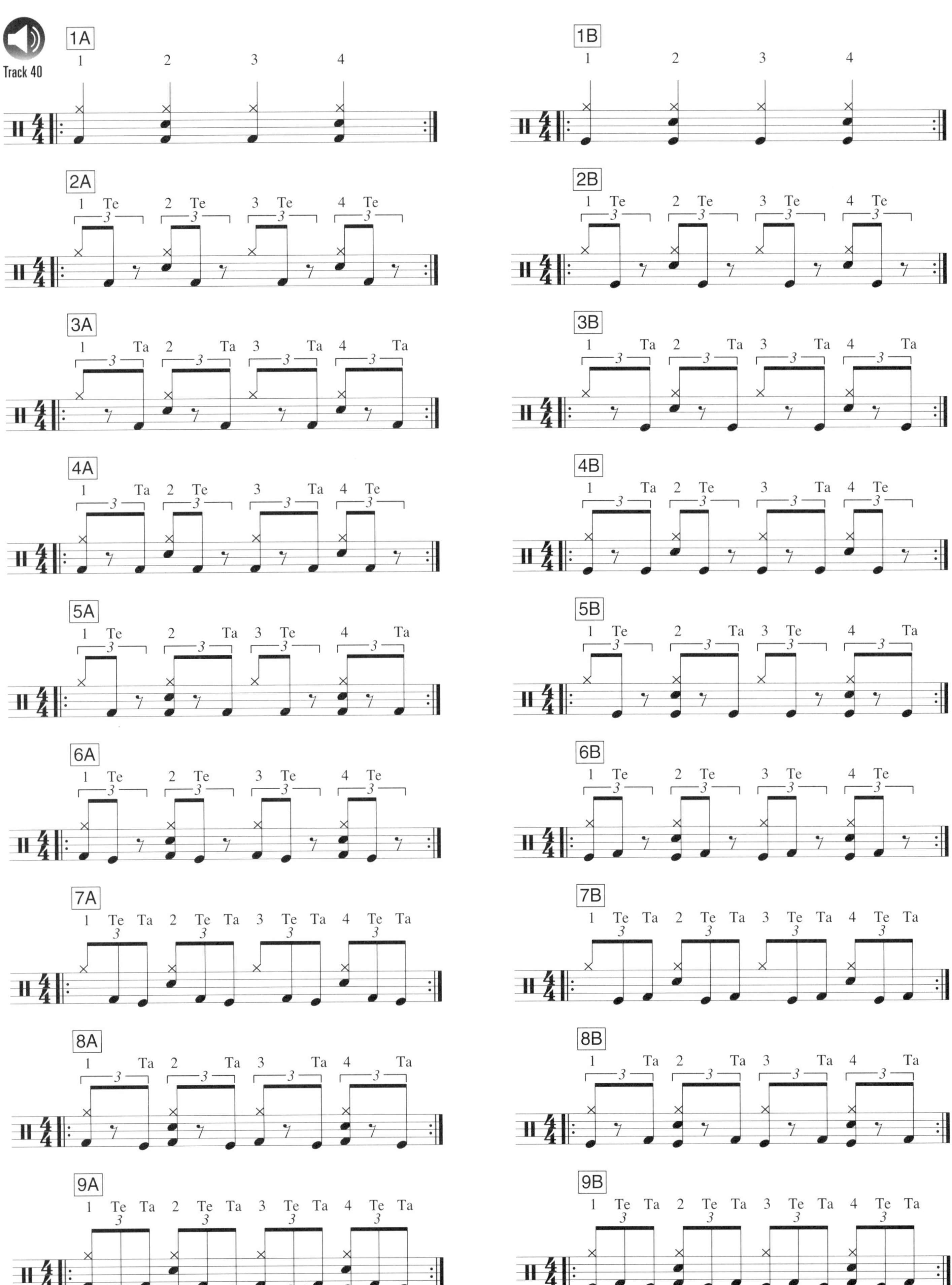

8th-Note-Triplet Mirrored Grooves: Snare on 2 and 4

8th-Note-Triplet Mirrored Grooves: Snare on 3

8th-Note-Triplet Mirrored Grooves: Snare on the "Ta" of 1 and on 4

8th-Note-Triplet Mirrored Grooves: Snare on 2 and the "Ta" of 3

8th-Note-Triplet Mirrored Grooves: Snare on the "Te" of 2 and on 4

8th-Note-Triplet Mirrored Grooves: Snare on 2 and the "Te" of 4

8th-Note-Triplet Mirrored Grooves: Snare on 1, 2, 3, and 4

8th-Note-Triplet Mirrored Grooves: Snare Combinations

Ride Variations

Apply all of the following ride variations to the previous mirrored grooves. By doing this, you will discover how various ride patterns can alter the entire character of the groove. They may pose some new coordination challenges; in that case, take it slow and count out loud... but you already know this!

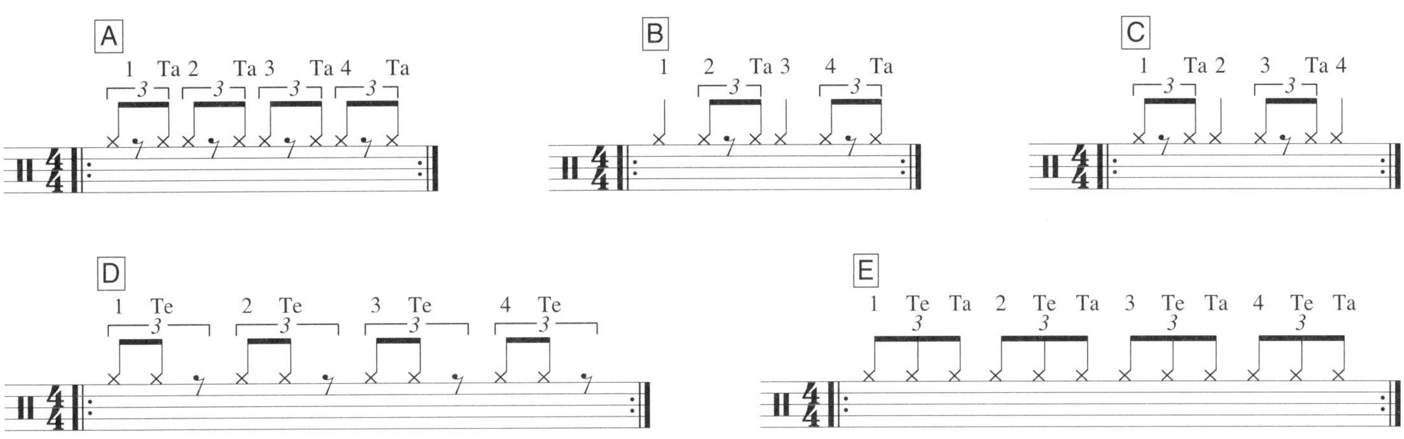

Groove Variations

This is what the notation looks like when applying all of the ride variations to one mirrored groove from this chapter.

A
Track 49a

B
Track 49b

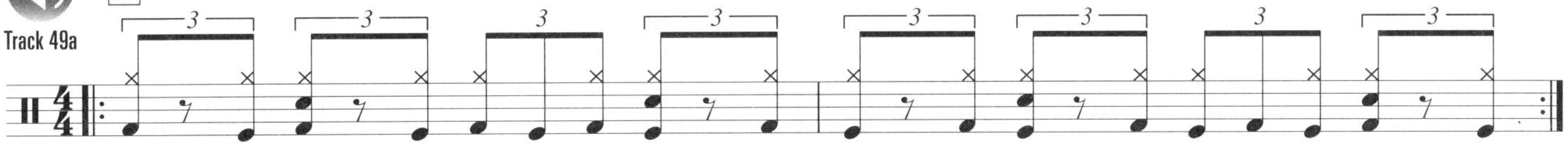

C
Track 49c

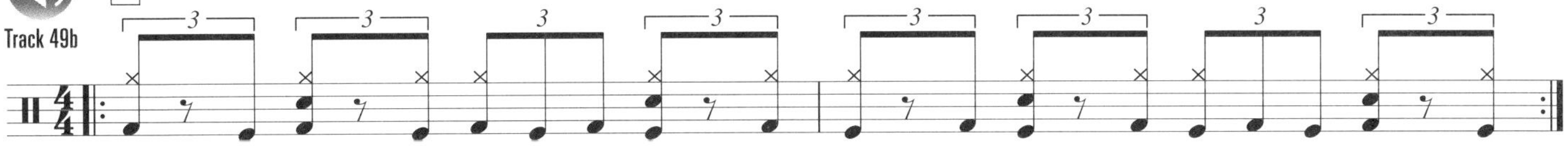

D
Track 49d

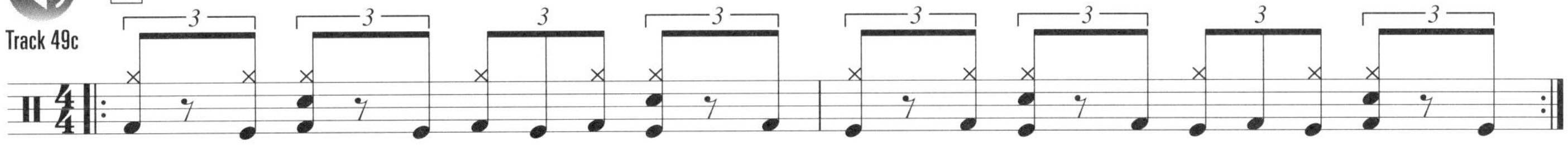

E
Track 49e

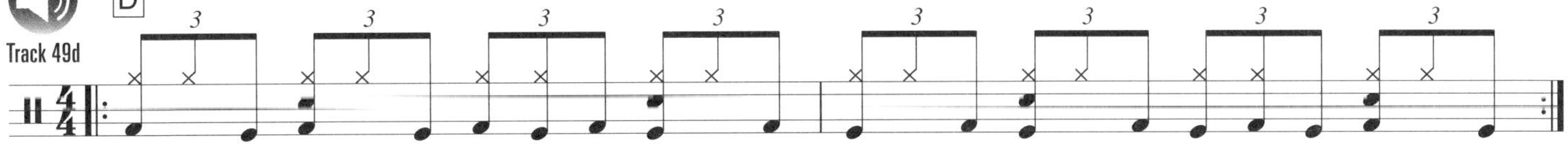

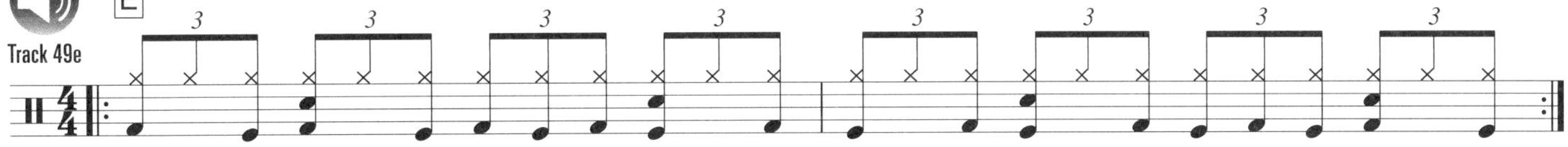

Drumistic Discoveries

Use this page to log your original ideas based on the concepts from this chapter.

1

2

3

4

5

6

7

8

6 8th/16th-Note-Triplet and Sextuplet Mirrored Grooves

Subdividing 16th-note triplets can be approached in two ways. In this chapter, the first approach is "doubling" each 8th-note triplet. By grouping each 8th-note triplet as two 16th-note triplets, one beat will contain three groups of two 16th-note triplets. This is notated as shown below:

When every note of an 8th-note triplet within a beat is doubled it can also be called a "sextuplet." Counting the subdivisions can be tricky. To assign a name to each note in this approach, one could count like this:

As you can see, it's a bit of a mouthful. My suggestion is to count one 8th-note triplet while playing two 16th-note triplets. This will allow you to breathe, which is a good thing.

The mixed note value section at the end of this chapter explores the second approach, which is based on straight 8th notes. By taking one eighth note (which has the same value as two 16th notes) and assigning three 16th notes to its value, there will be a 16th-note triplet. This is notated as shown below:

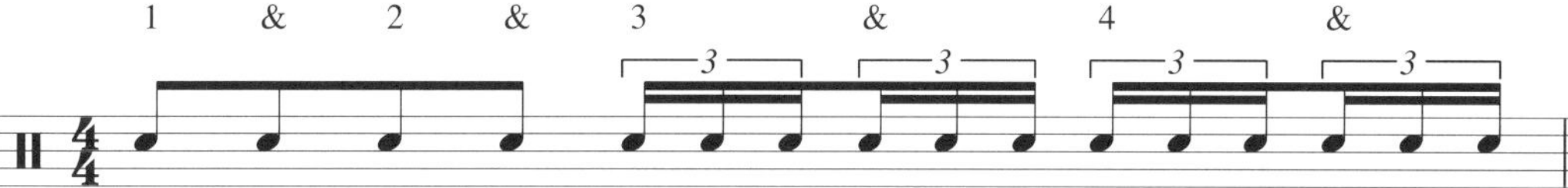

There is a counting system that names all of the notes with this approach as well. See the following:

Once again, it's kind of a mouthful. I would suggest counting one 8th note while playing three 16th-note triplets (as notated in the previous example). Your lungs will thank you.

Both approaches are equally valid, subjective only to the music in which they are used. Applying the mirrored groove method to these two approaches will provide you with a thorough understanding and vocabulary within the exciting world of 16th-note triplets and sextuplets!

Practice Tips:

- Remember to apply the appropriate counting system.
- Use Ride Variation E on page 91 with the groove builders on pages 79–82 to give you a stronger sense of the 8th-note-triplet pulse from which they're built.
- Challenge yourself to create your own grooves and write them down on the Drumistic Discoveries page.
- Repeat. Rest. Recall.

"By perseverance the snail reached the ark."

—Charles Haddon Spurgeon

Ride/Snare Patterns

Some of these mirrored grooves may inintially be rhythmically challenging. These 16th-Note-Triplet groove builders will provide a thorough primer in preparing you for the ensuing double bass adventure.

First, play each bass drum pattern with your hands to help understand the rhythm, then try to play it with your feet. Next, add the quarter-note ride pattern, and finally, add the the following ride/snare drum patterns.

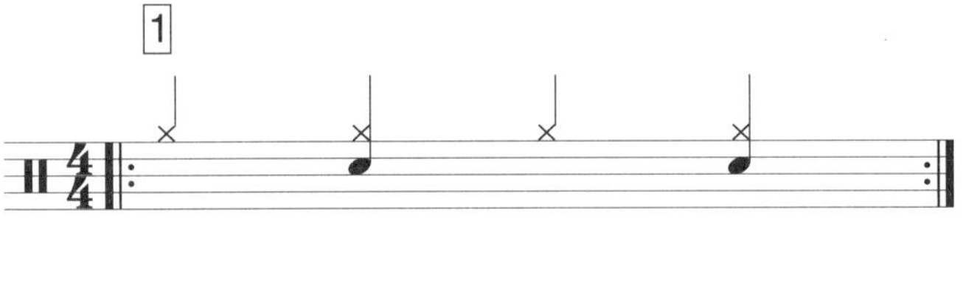

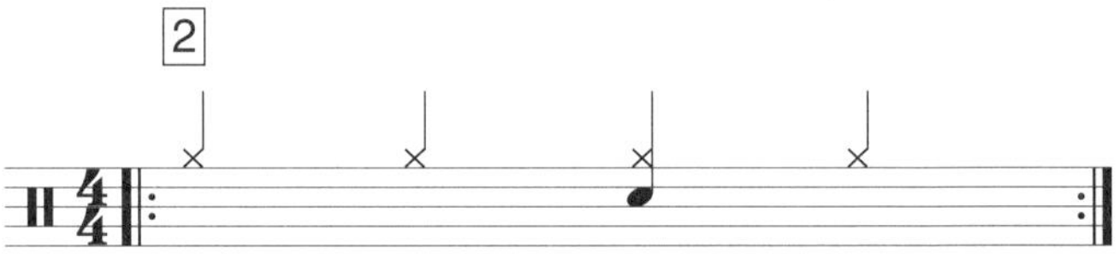

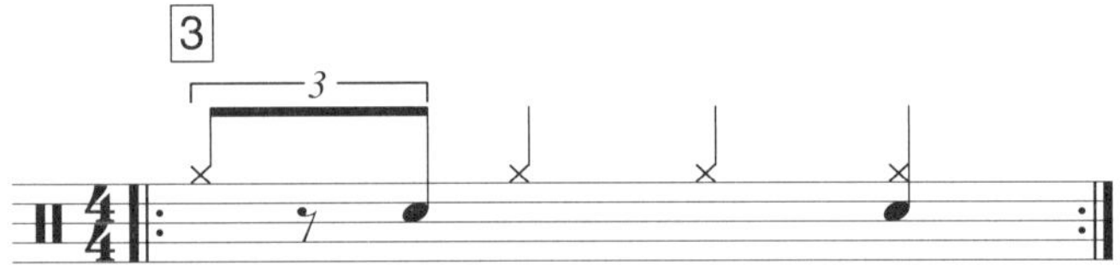

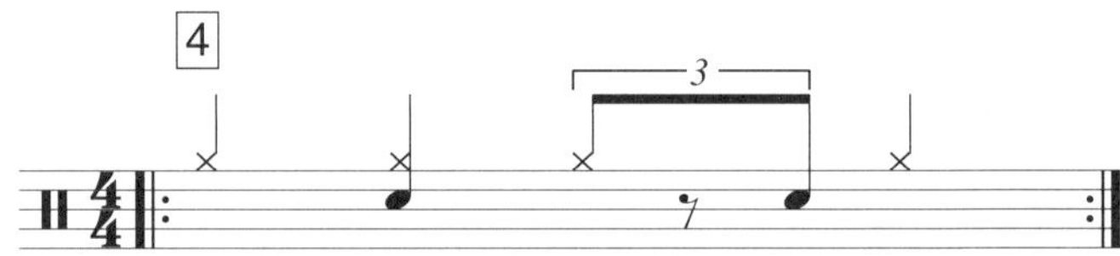

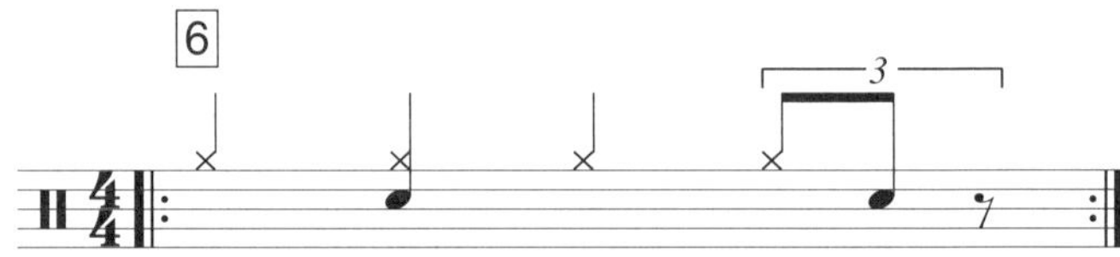

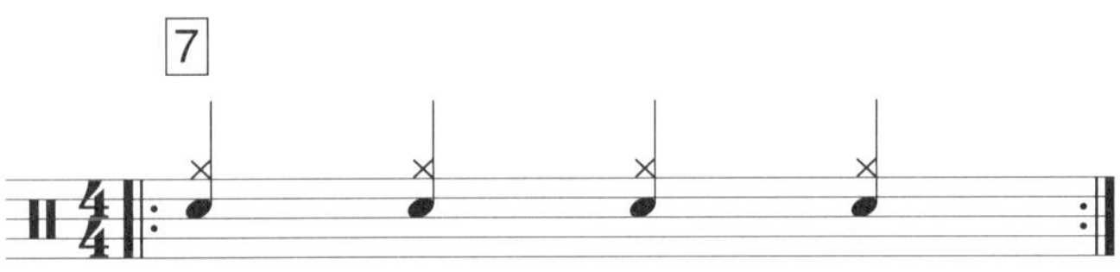

16th-Note-Triplet Groove Builders: 2-Note

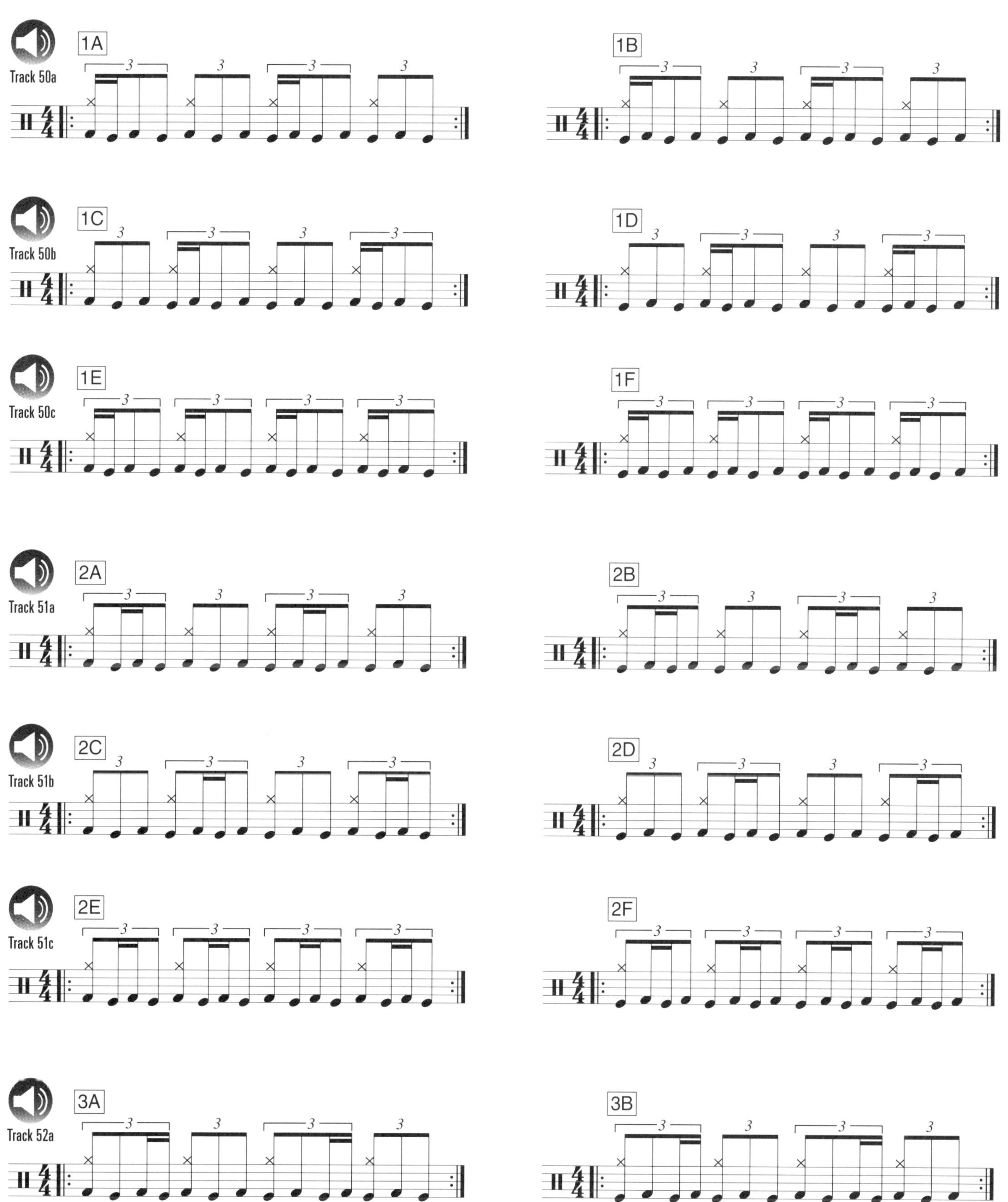

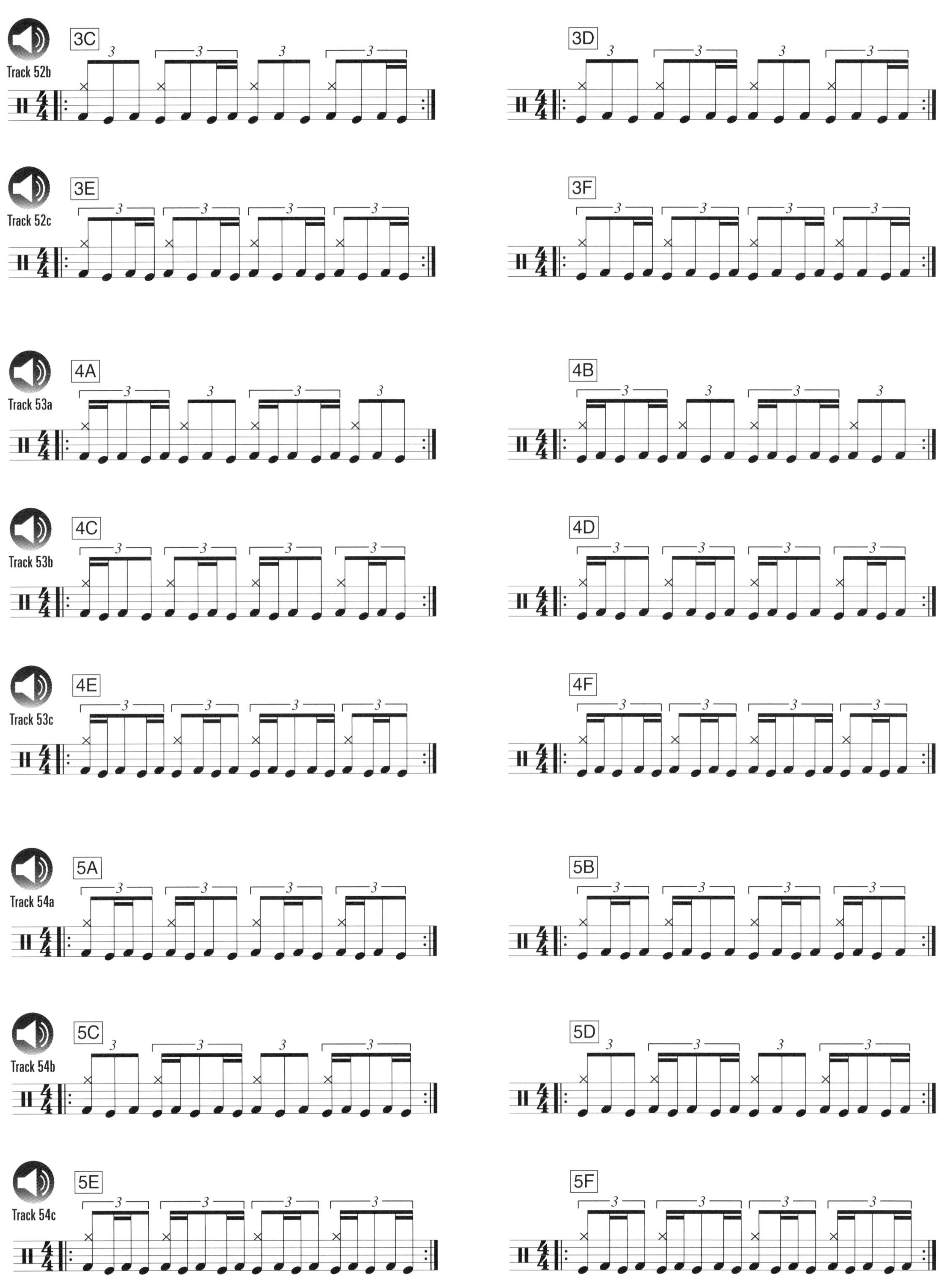

Track 52b
3C
3D
Track 52c
3E
3F
Track 53a
4A
4B
Track 53b
4C
4D
Track 53c
4E
4F
Track 54a
5A
5B
Track 54b
5C
5D
Track 54c
5E
5F

16th-Note-Triplet Groove Builders: 4-Note

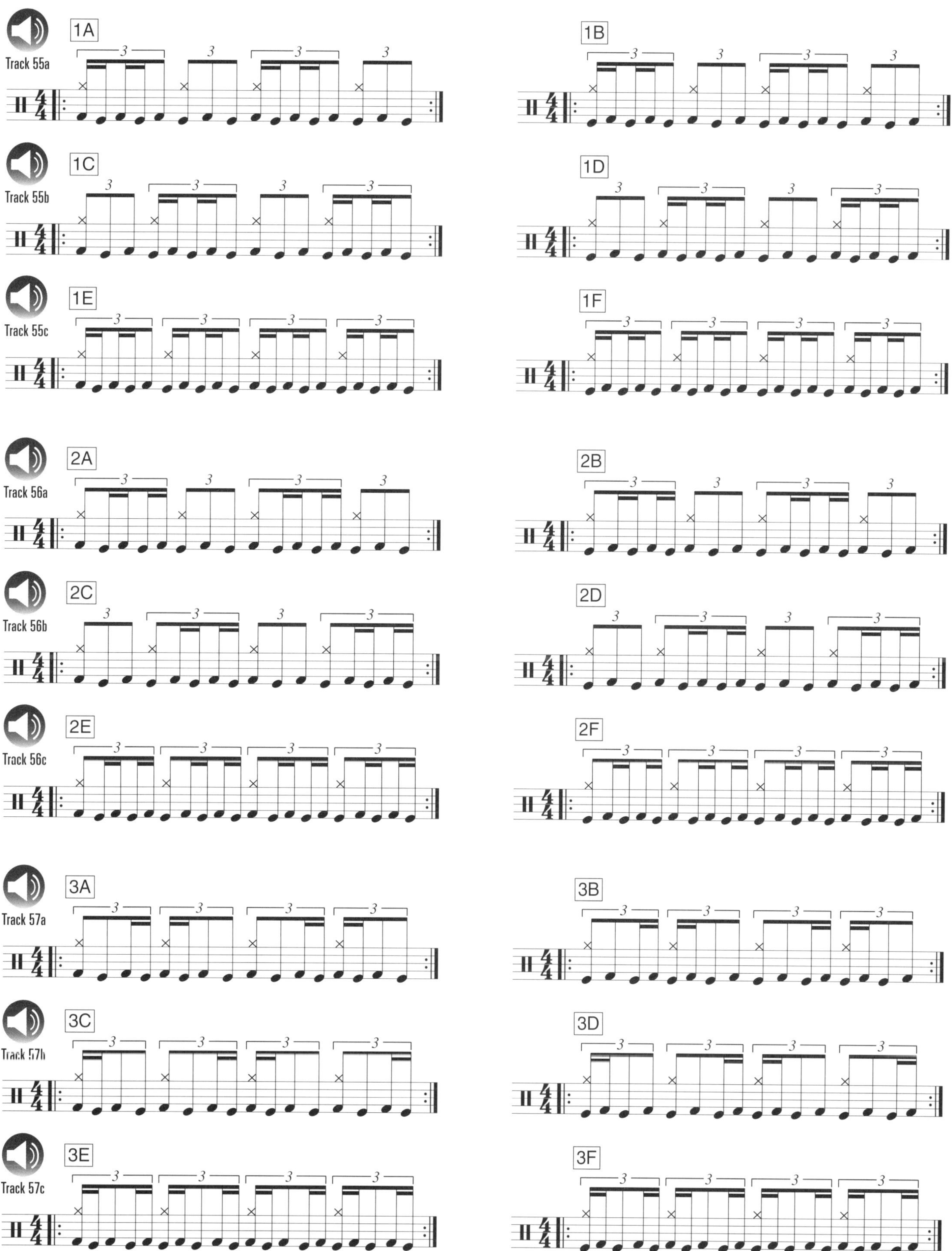

Progressive Groove Builder: 8th-Note and 16th-Note Triplets (Sextuplets)

The main objective for this exercise is to play measure 1A to measure 12 without stopping. However, as with most exercises, feel free to repeat any measure as long as it takes before moving on; that is practicing with a "quality over quantity" mindset.

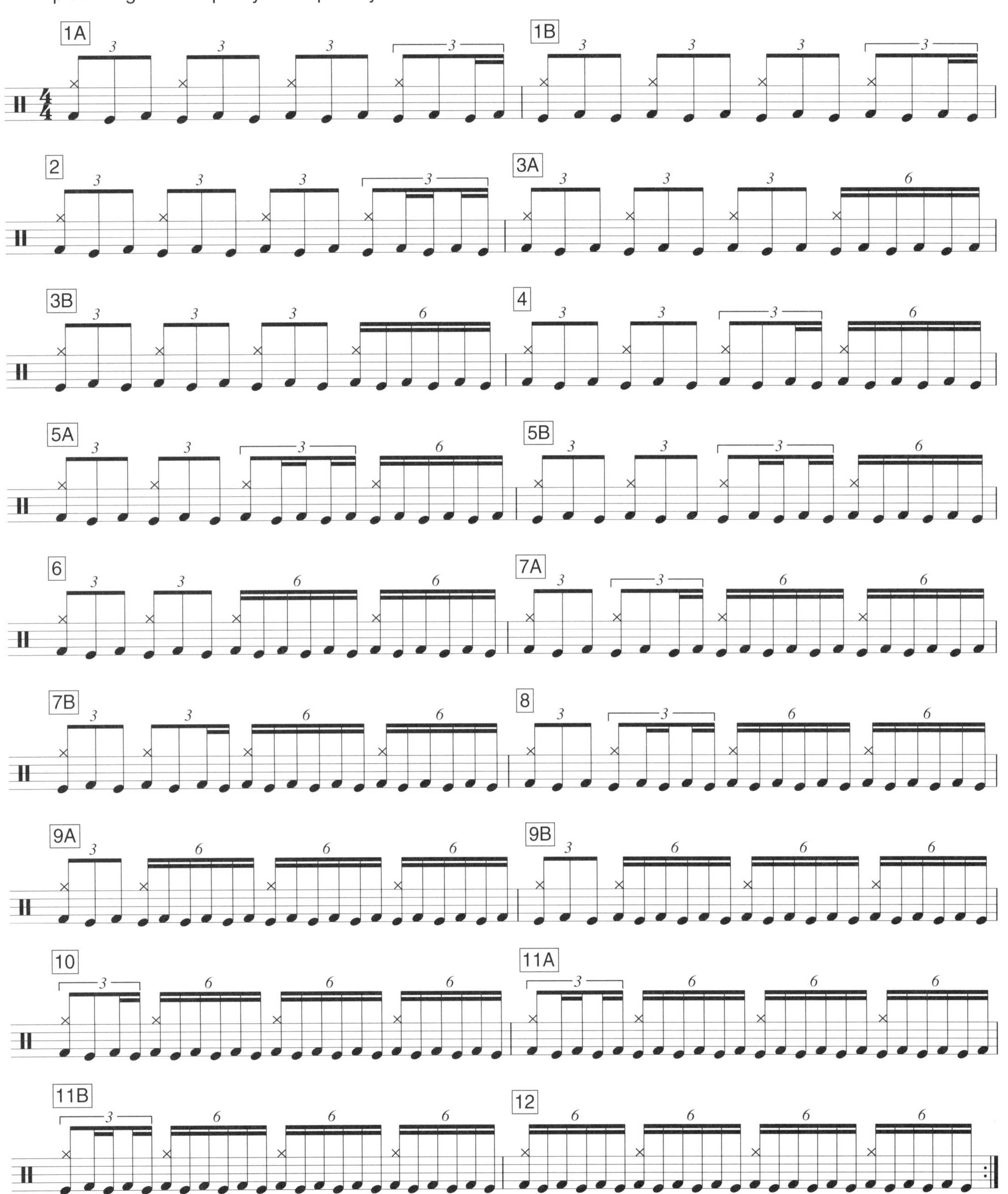

8th/16th-Note-Triplet Mirrored Grooves: Snare on 2 and 4

8th/16th-Note-Triplet Mirrored Grooves: Snare on 3

8th/16th-Note-Triplet Mirrored Grooves: Snare on the "Ta" of 1 and on 4

8th/16th-Note-Triplet Mirrored Grooves: Snare on 2 and the "Ta" of 3

8th/16th-Note-Triplet Mirrored Grooves: Snare on the "Te" of 2 and on 4

8th/16th-Note-Triplet Mirrored Grooves: Snare on 2 and the "Te" of 4

8th/16th-Note-Triplet Mirrored Grooves: Snare on 1, 2, 3, and 4

8th/16th-Note-Triplet Mirrored Grooves: Snare Combinations

Ride Variations

A

B

C

D

E

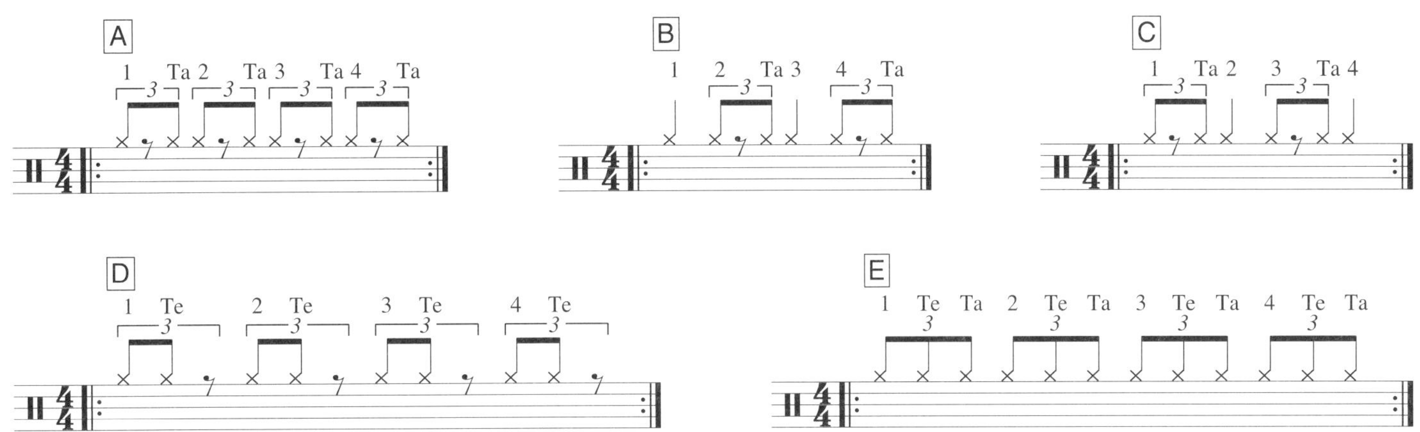

Groove Variations

Track 64a

A

Track 64b

B

Track 64c

C

Track 64d

D

Track 64e

E

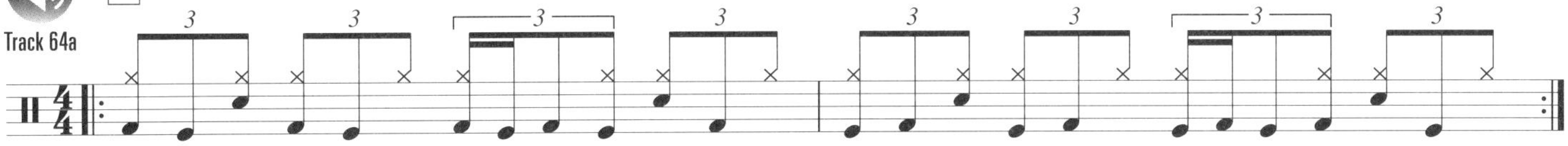

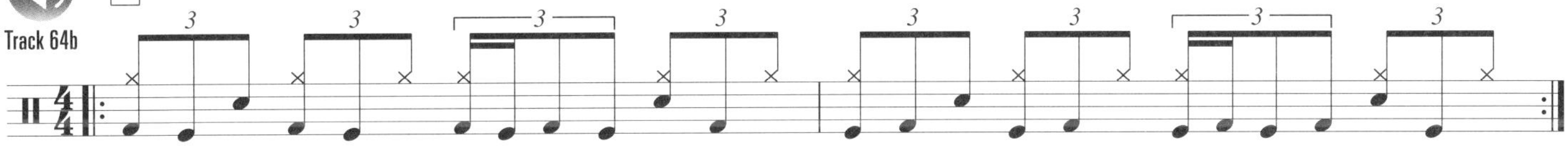

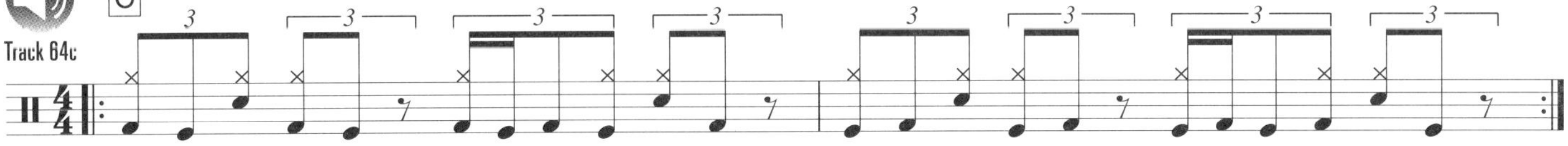

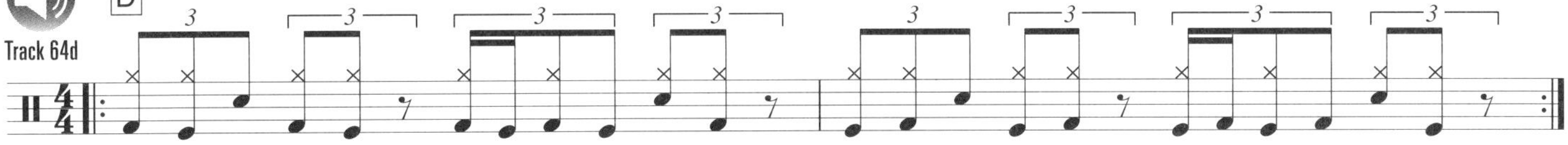

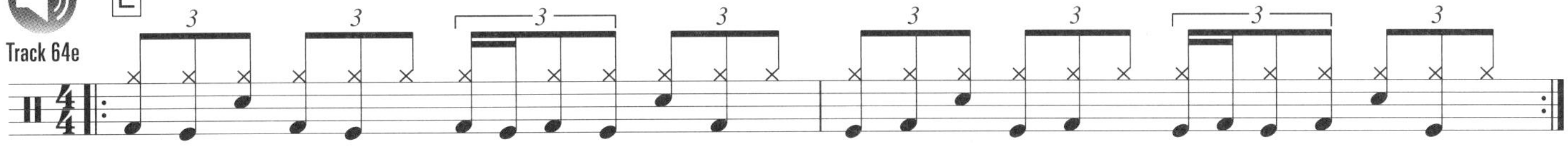

Ride/Snare Patterns

Some of these mirrored grooves may inintially be rhythmically challenging. These 16th-Note-Triplet and Sextuplet Groove Builders will provide a thorough primer in preparing you for the ensuing double bass adventure.

First, play each bass drum pattern with your hands to help understand the rhythm, then try to play it with your feet. Next, add the eighth-note ride pattern and, finally, add the the following snare drum patterns.

Mixed Note Values Groove Builders: 8th Notes, 16th-Note Triplets, and Sextuplets

Mixed Note Values Groove Builders: 16th Notes, 16th-Note Triplets and Sextuplets

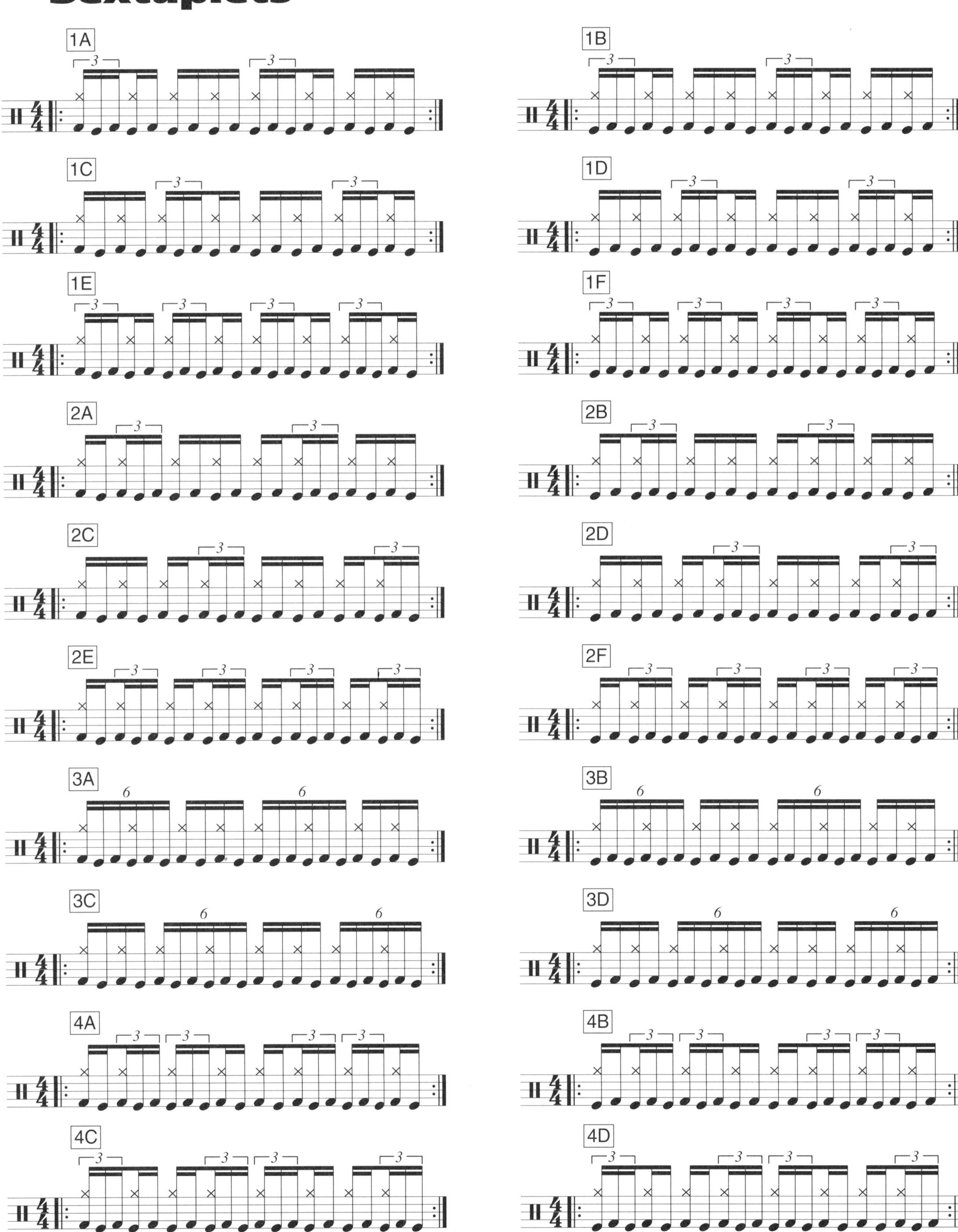

Progressive Groove Builder: 16th Notes, 16th-Note Triplets and Sextuplets

The main objective for this exercise is to play measure 1A to measure 8 without stopping. However, as with most exercises, feel free to repeat any measure as long as it takes before moving on; that is practicing like a master craftsman.

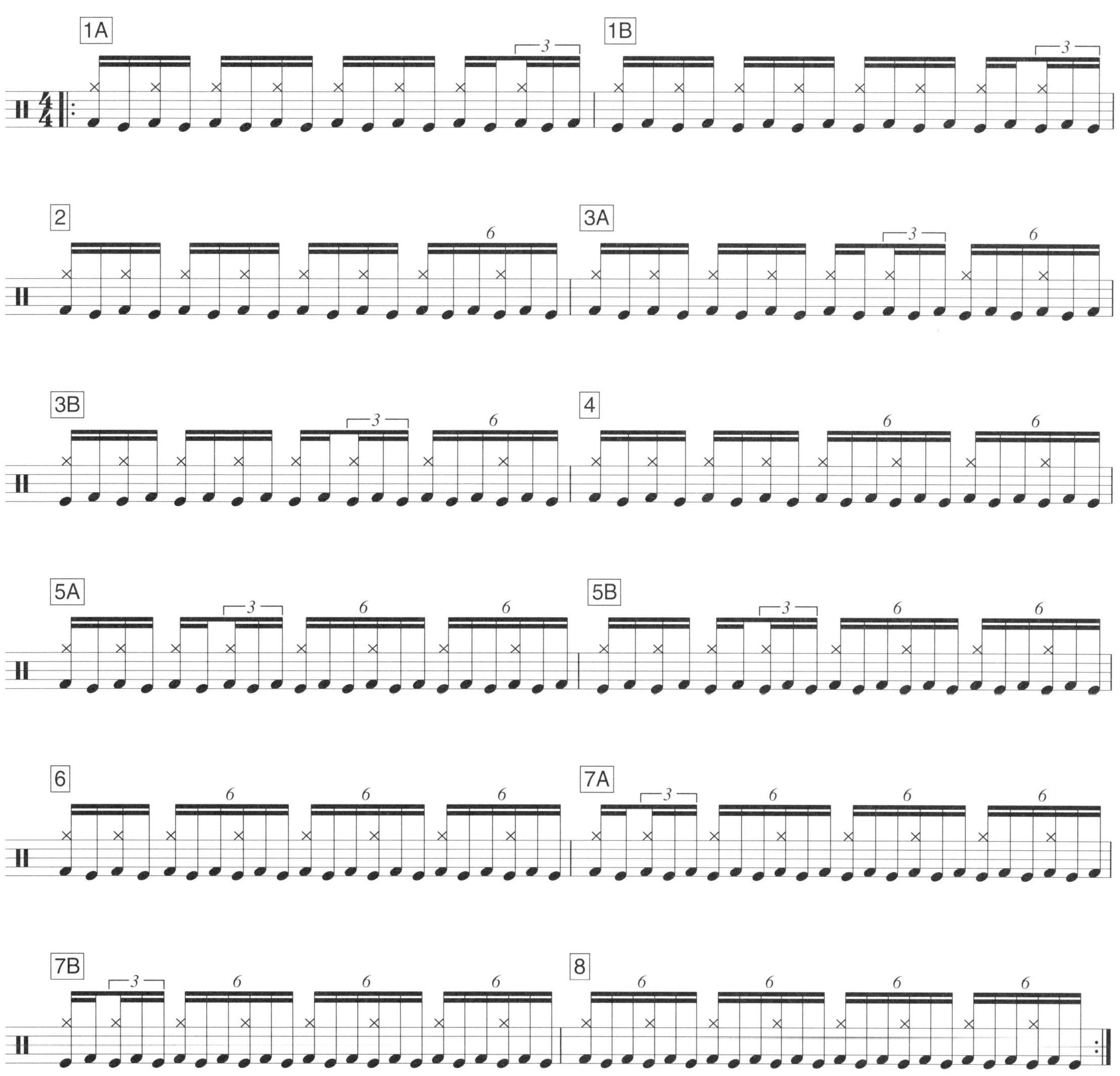

Mixed Note Value Mirrored Grooves: Snare on 2 and 4

Mixed Note Value Mirrored Grooves: Snare on 3

Mixed Note Value Mirrored Grooves: Snare on "&" of 2 and on 4

Mixed Note Value Mirrored Grooves: Snare on 2 and on the "&" of 4

Mixed Note Value Mirrored Grooves: Snare on 1, 2, 3, and 4

Mixed Note Value Mirrored Grooves: Snare on the "&s" of 1, 2, 3, and 4

Mixed Note Value Mirrored Grooves: Snare Combinations

Drumistic Discoveries

Use this page to log your original ideas based on the concepts from this chapter.

1

2

3

4

5

6

7

8

7 16th/32nd-Note Fills

One of the most effective and powerful ways to incorporate double bass technique is within your fill vocabulary. Double bass fills can range from very simple to quite complex. Regardless, both applications require a strong foundation to be able to play with conviction.

Many times, double bass fills only incorporate two single notes—one from each foot. This may lead you to think, why use double bass at all when the same effect can be achieved with one foot? In this case, I challenge you to play the following rhythm as loud as you can, with your hands alternating right-left-right-left. Continue to increase the tempo with each repeat.

Now try playing the same rhythm with your right hand only, as loud as possible, and faster with each repeat.

Was it the same? Could you maintain the same dynamic level as the speed increased? The laws of physics do not always allow this to be so. We use double bass when it is needed, not when it's an easy alternative. The goal of this experiment is to reveal that each technique has its own unique value. Make sure your ego doesn't prevent you from being the best drummer you can be.

The main focus for these fills is evenly subdividing them at the same rate as your hands. It is very easy to play the bass drum notes faster—especially when it's only two notes. Focus on the space between the notes; this will bring articulation to your fills. Playing evenly and articulately will allow the listener to hear and appreciate everything you play. Don't rob them of your amazing musical statement!

Practice Tips:

- Fills are primarily linear. Focus on every limb giving each note its equal value.
- There are many hand/foot combinations here. Don't rush through all of them. Spend time on just one and explore the endless orchestrations.
- Maintain a 16th-note count even if you're playing 32nd notes
- Repeat. Rest. Recall.

"Life is not accumulation, it is about contribution."

—Stephen Covey

Progressive Fill Builders: 16th Notes

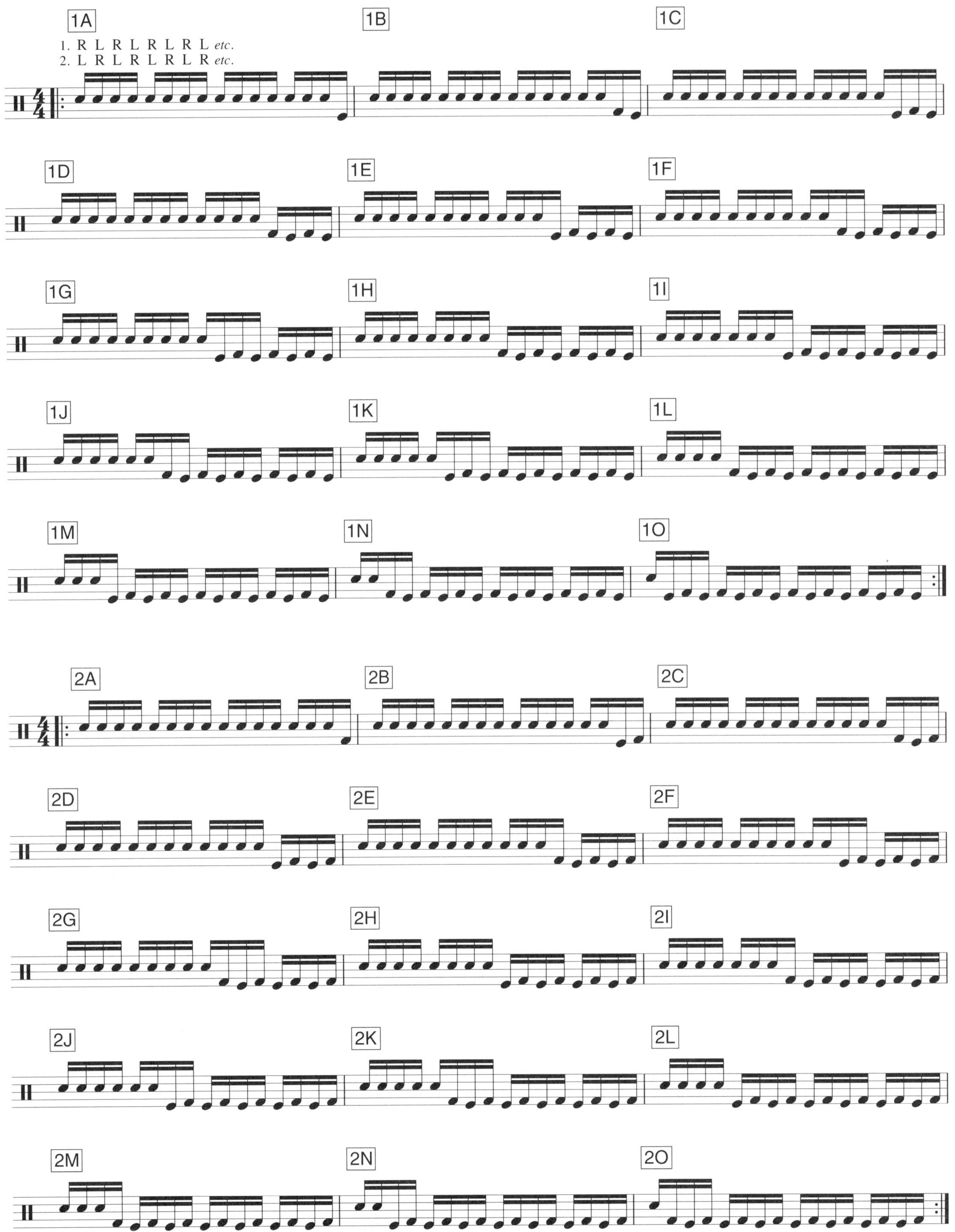

16th-Note Combinations

2 + 2 Variations

4 + 2; 4 + 2; 2 + 2 Variations

4 + 4 Variations

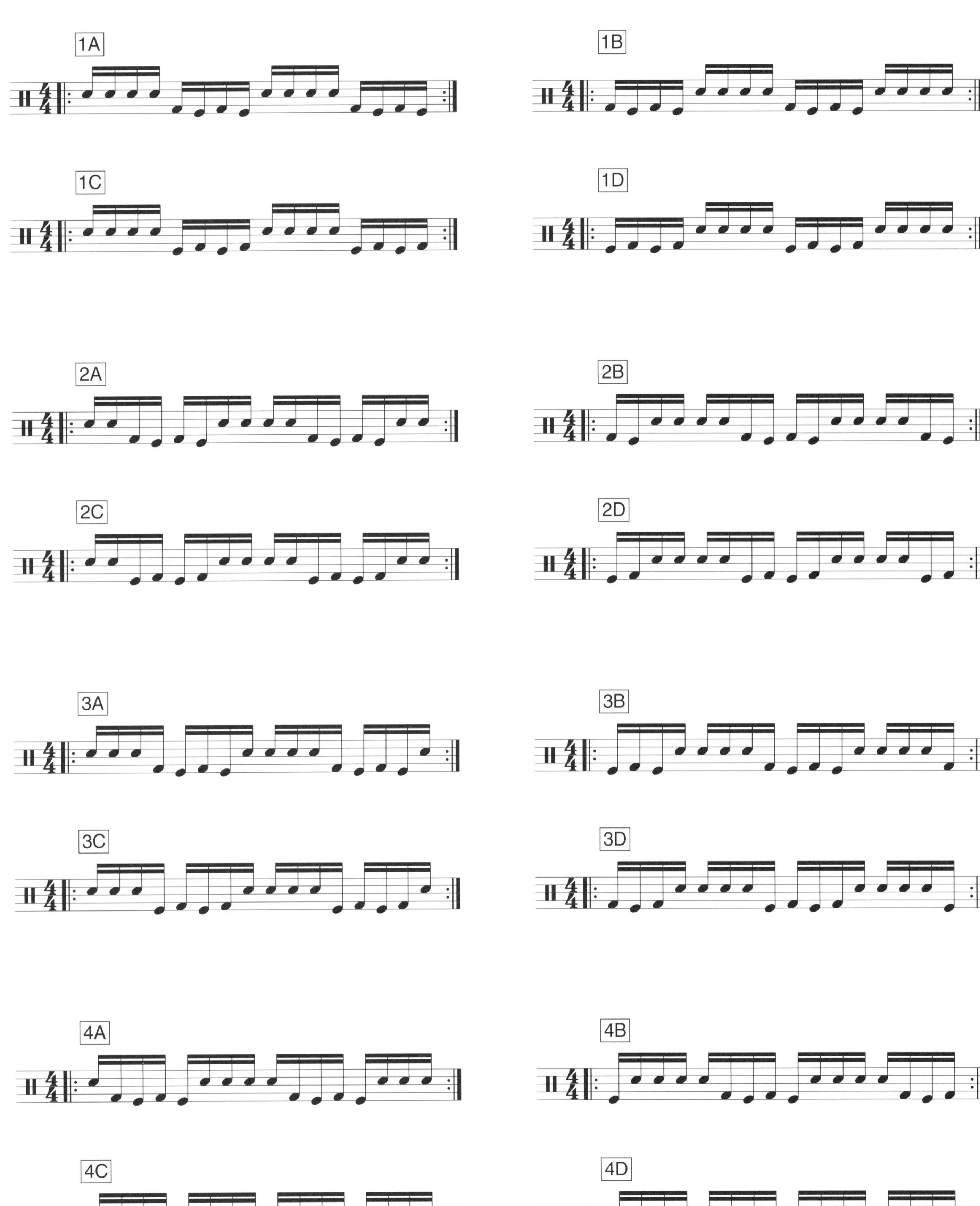

2 + 2; 2 + 2; 4 + 4 Variations

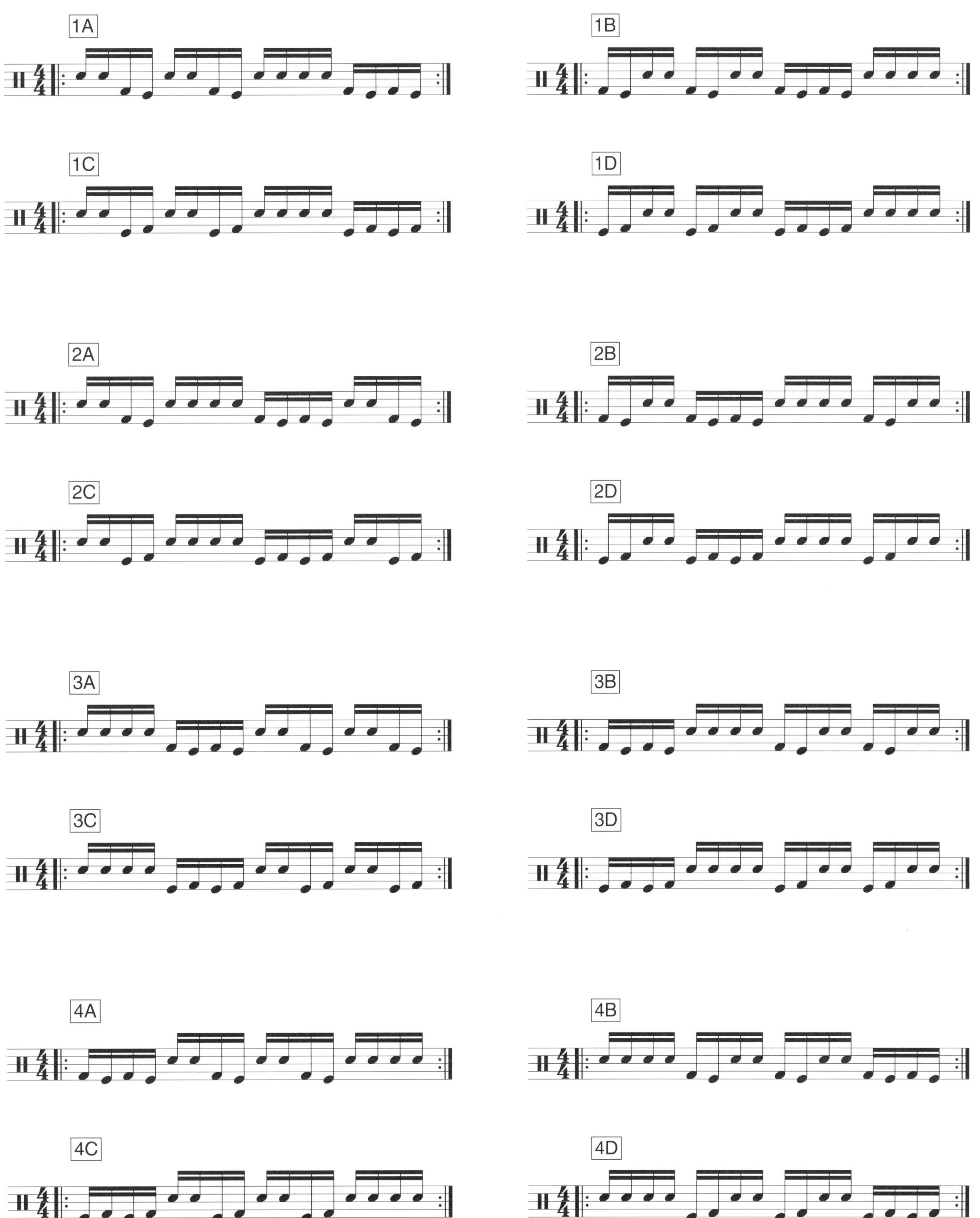

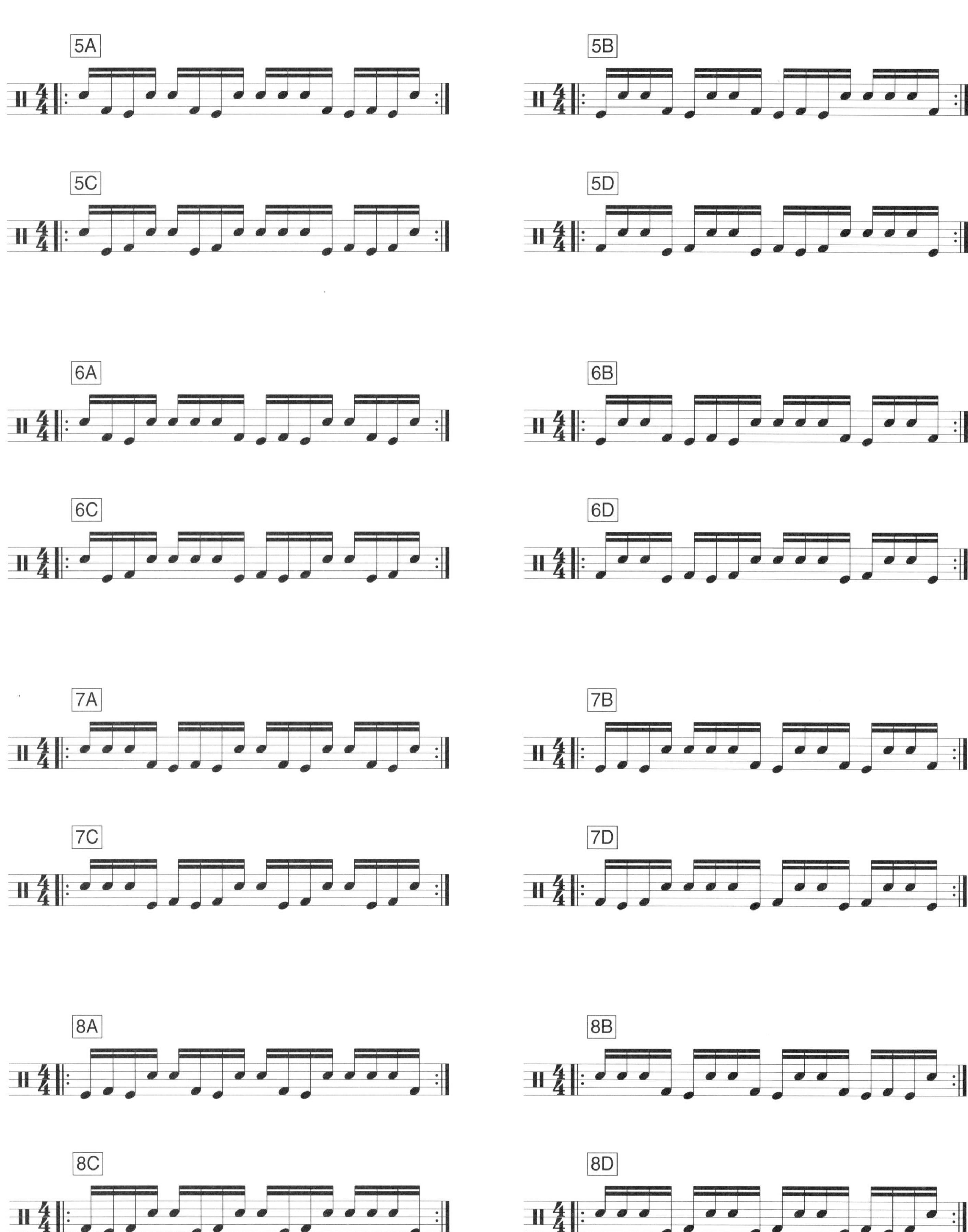
5A
5B
5C
5D
6A
6B
6C
6D
7A
7B
7C
7D
8A
8B
8C
8D

16th-Note Fills

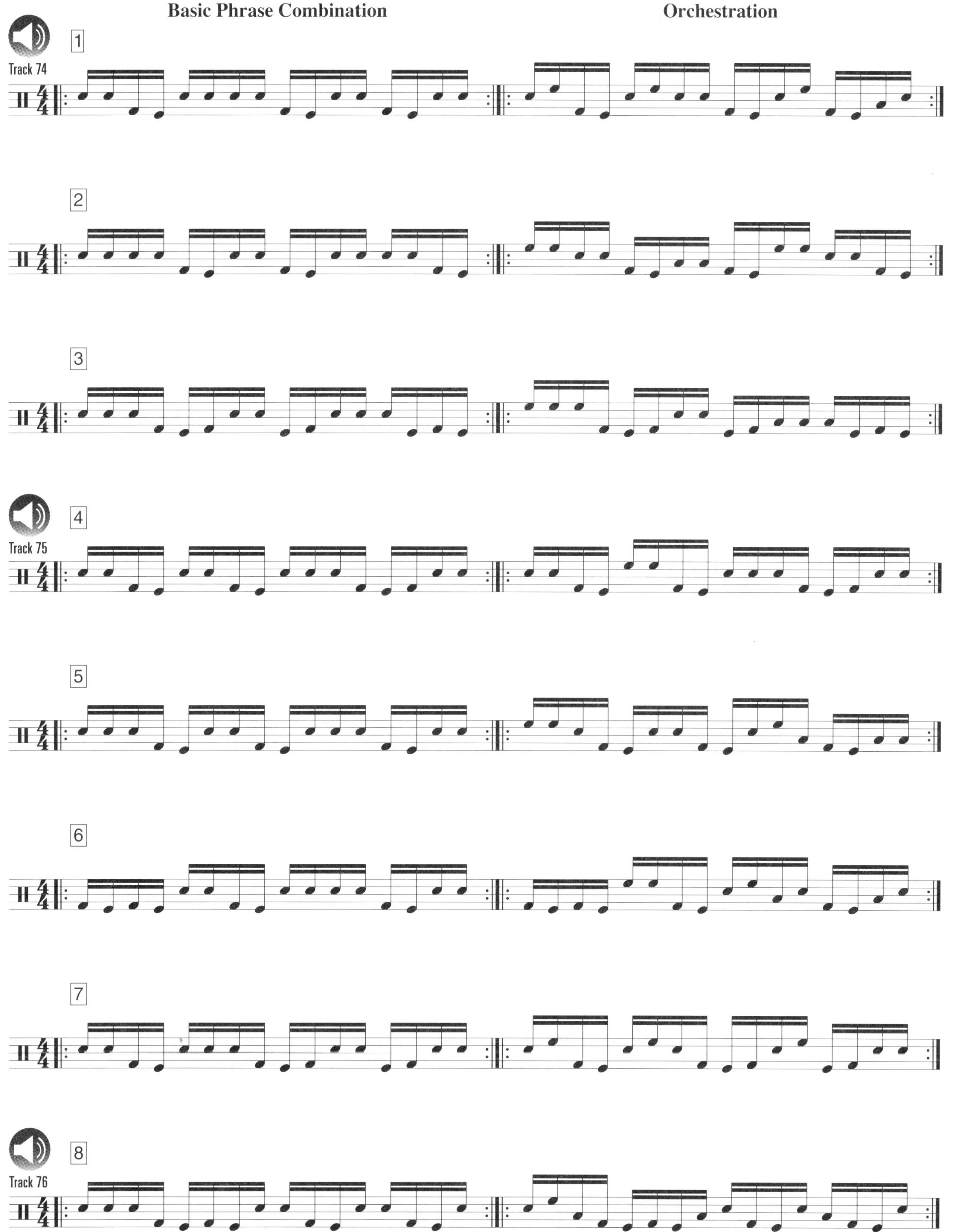

16th/32nd-Note Progressive Builders

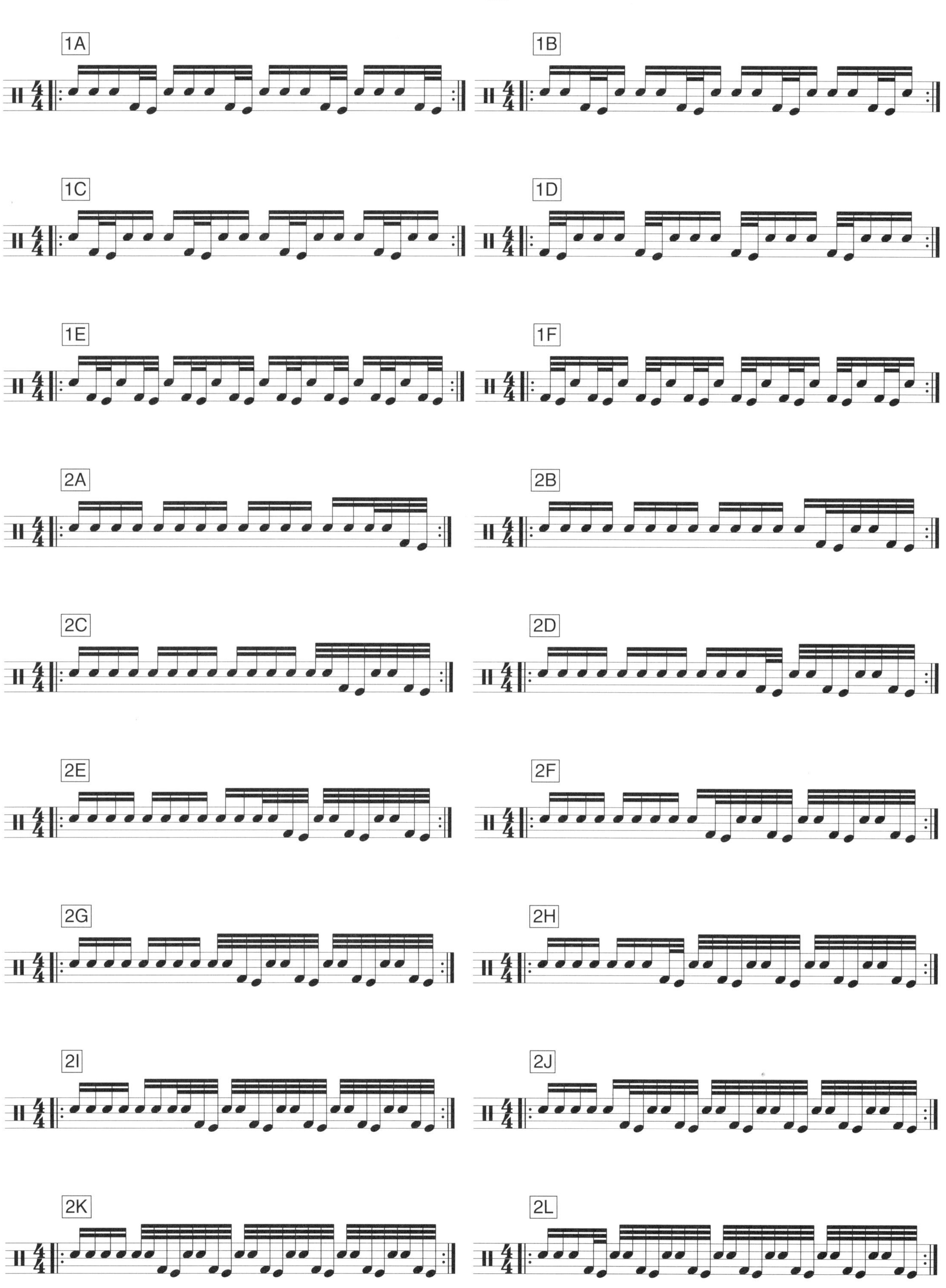

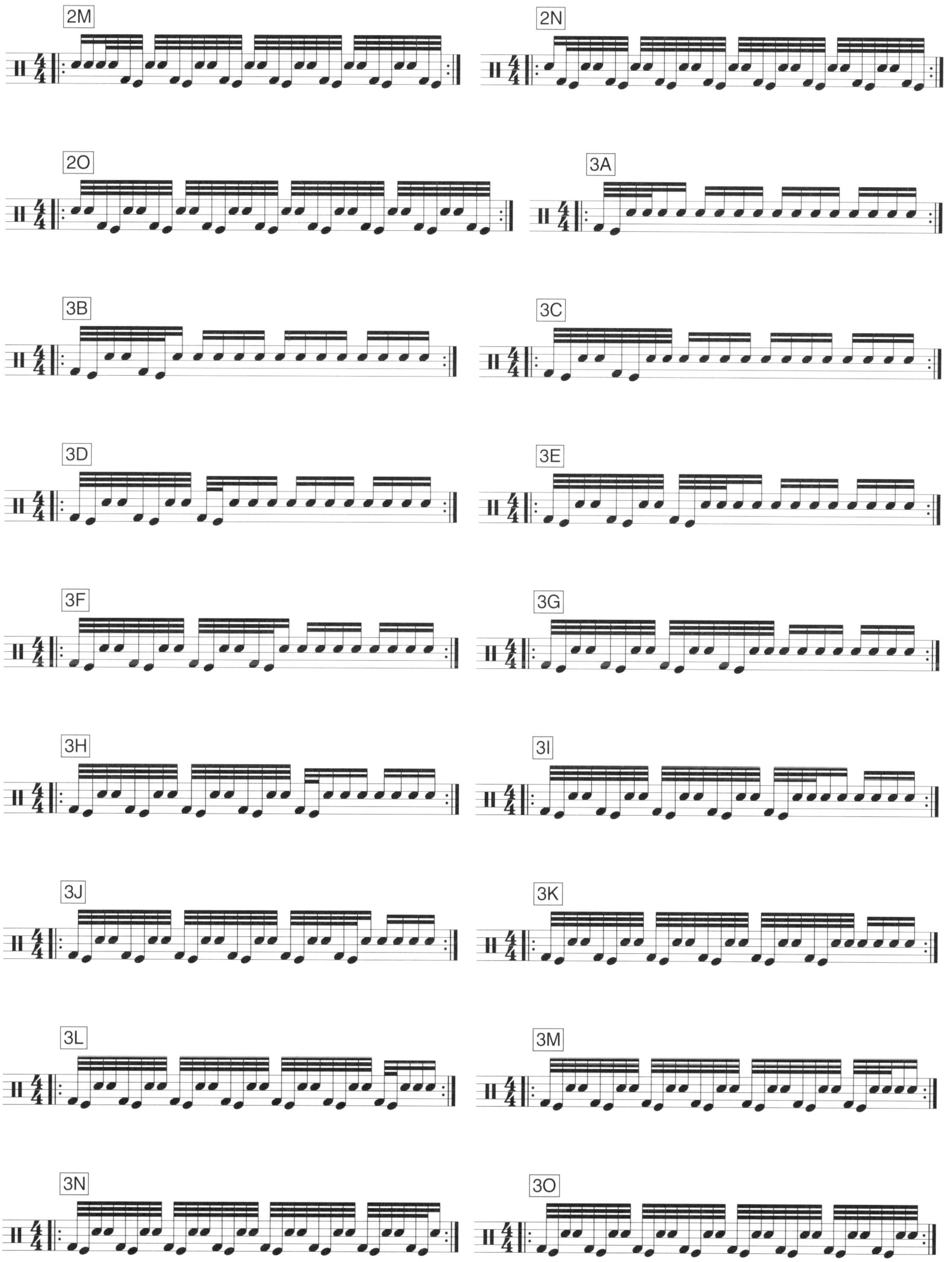
2M
2N
2O
3A
3B
3C
3D
3E
3F
3G
3H
3I
3J
3K
3L
3M
3N
3O

16th/32nd-Note Combinations

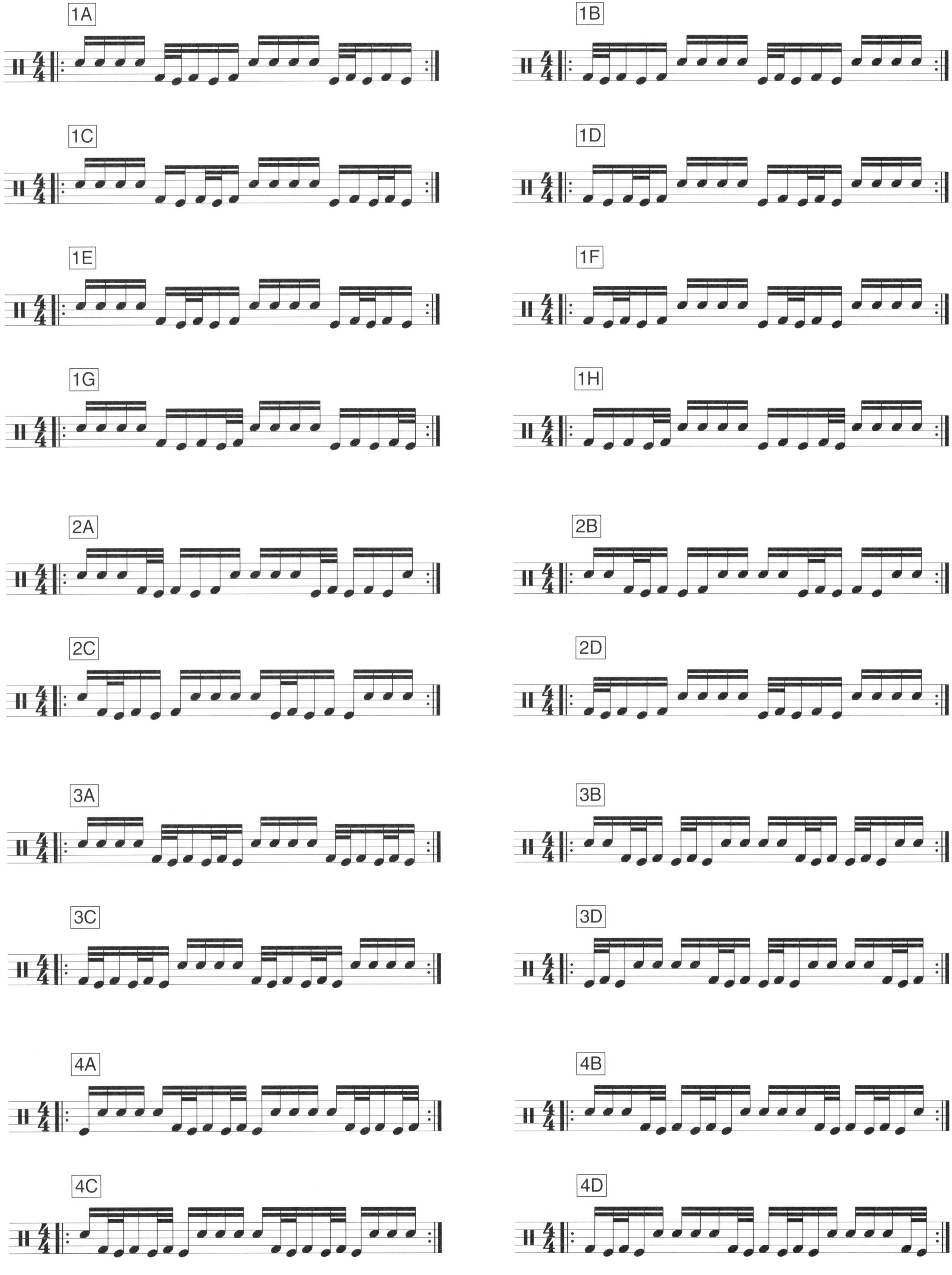

16th/32nd-Note Fills

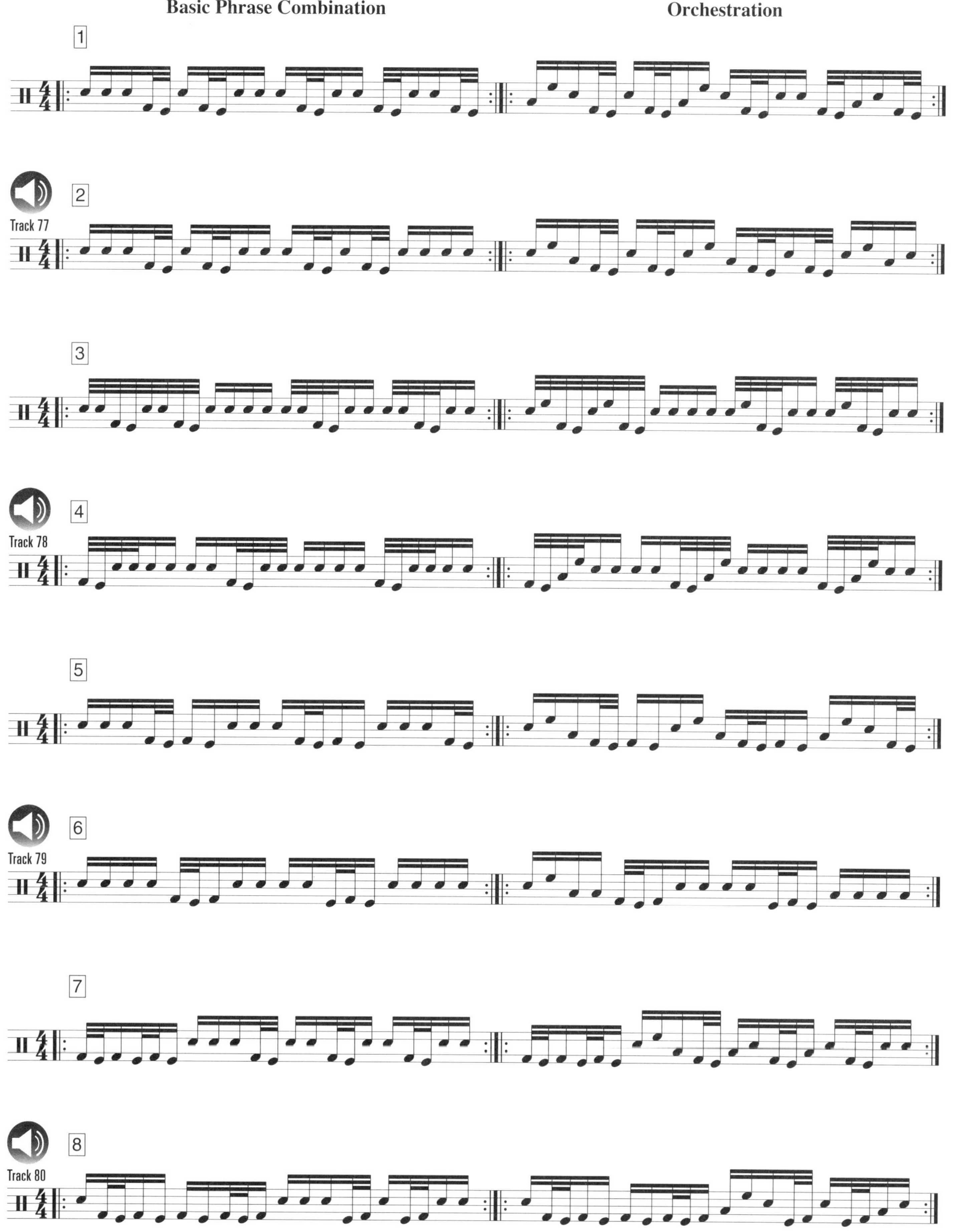

Drum-to-Cymbal Builders

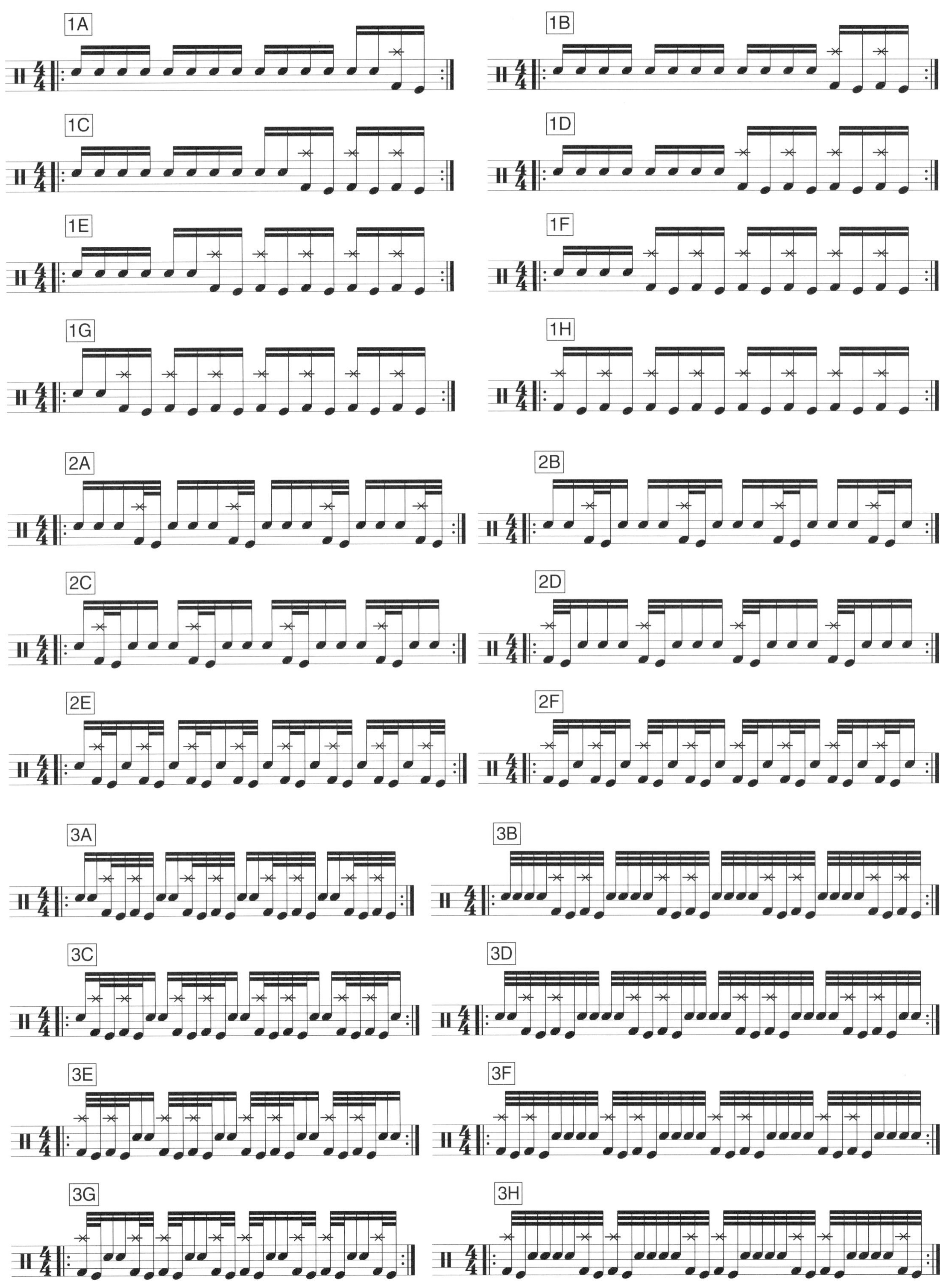

16th/32nd-Note Fills with Cymbals

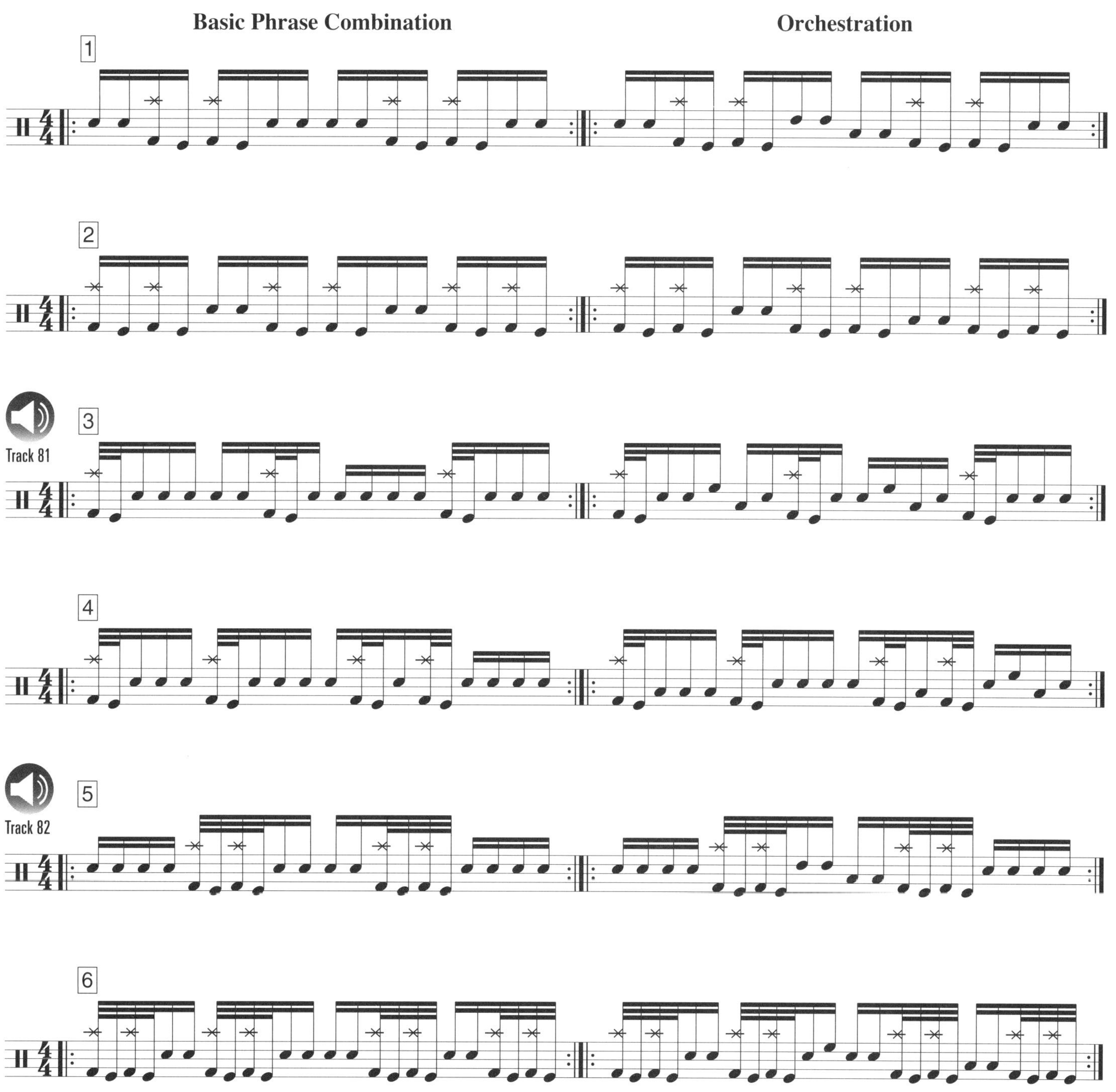

Drumistic Discoveries

Use this page to log your original ideas based on the concepts from this chapter.

1

2

3

4

5

6

7

8

8 8th-Note-Triplet and Mixed Note Value Fills

In the previous chapter, we used various techniques to explore the basic components of 16th/32nd-note fills. This chapter will incorporate those same techniques in applying them to the various triplet-based fills that are essential to your double bass arsenal. Using progressive builders, exploring the basic combinations, incorporating mixed note values, and integrating various cymbals applications will provide an exhaustive resource to help in the development of a triplet-based fill vocabulary.

As you may have noticed from the previous chapter, many of the combinations are presented with both the right and left foot leading. At the risk of sounding redundant, this is to aid in equal development of both feet. Surely, there are combinations that feel better one way, but I challenge you to break out of your comfort zone and try the alternate version. This will help strengthen your weaker foot and, ultimately, your courage to always keep an open mind in trying something new. Your drumming journey is only limited by your mindset. Be brave and explore those uncharted rhythmic worlds!

Practice Tips:

- Count 8th-note triplets even if you're playing 16th-note triplets.
- When playing two notes with the bass drum, be careful not to flam them. Maintain even subdivision throughout the phrase.
- Practice all of the combinations with various stickings. Ultimately, the orchestration will help determine what sticking to use.
- Repeat. Rest. Recall.

"Ever since I was a child I have had this instinctive urge for expansion and growth. To me, the function and duty of a quality human being is the sincere and honest development of one's potential."

—Bruce Lee

Progressive Fill Builders: 8th-Note Triplet

8th-Note-Triplet Combinations

1 + 2 Variations

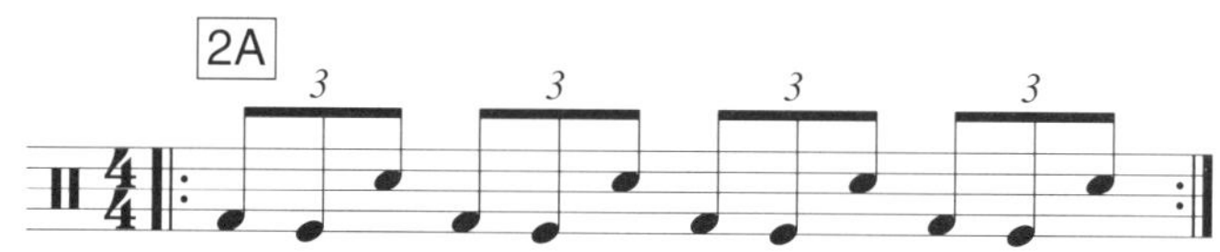

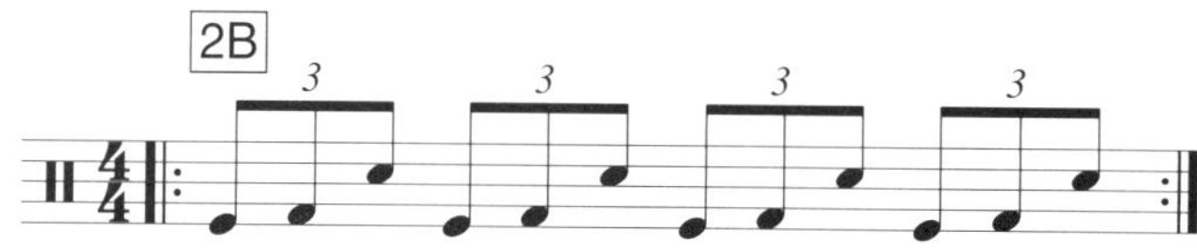

2 + 2 Variations

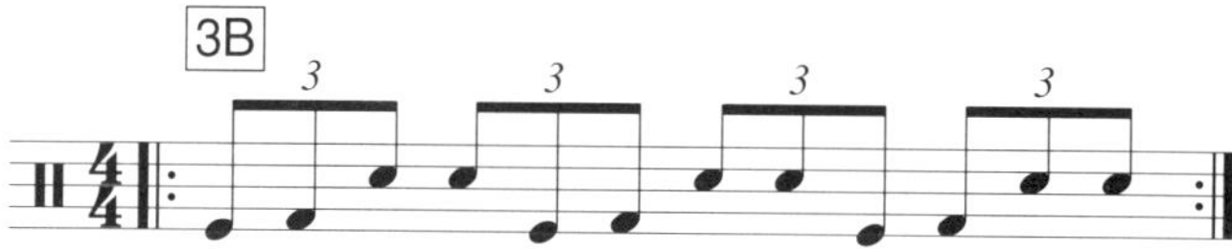

4 + 2 Variations

1A

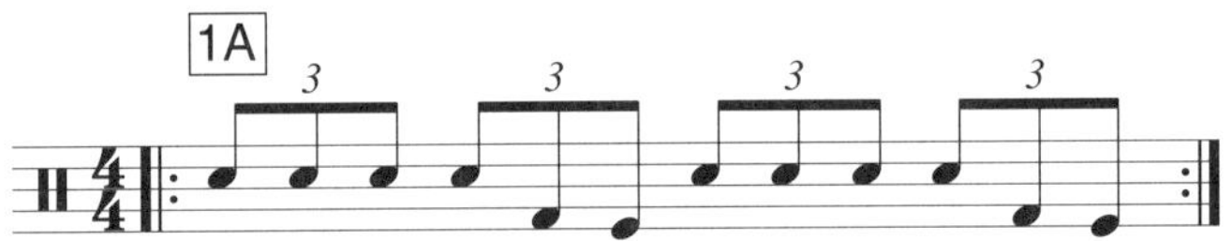

1B

2A

2B

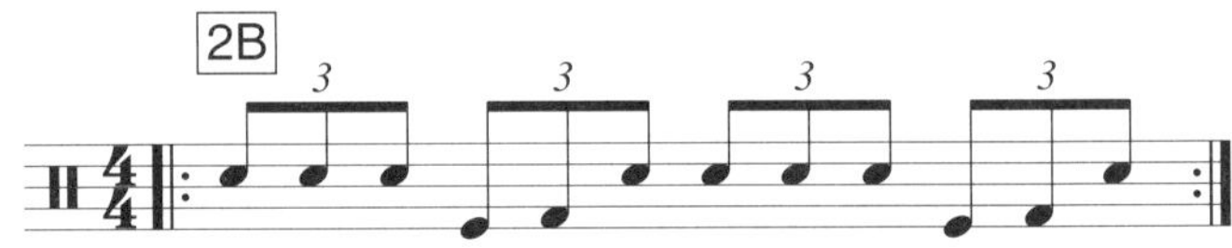

3A

3B

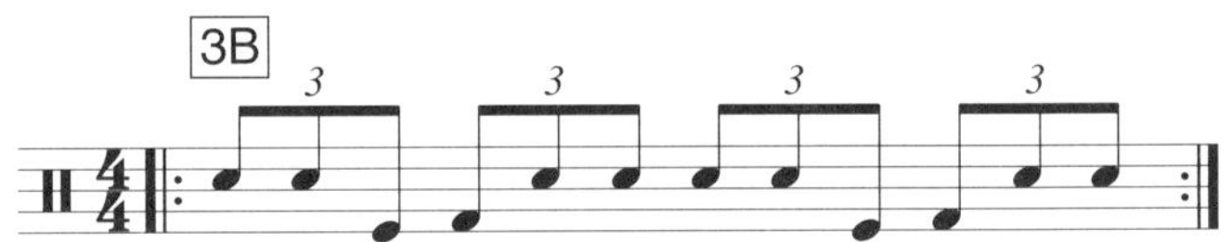

4A

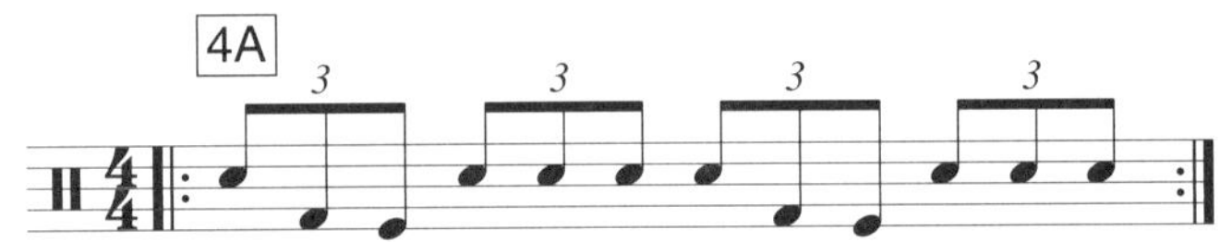

4B

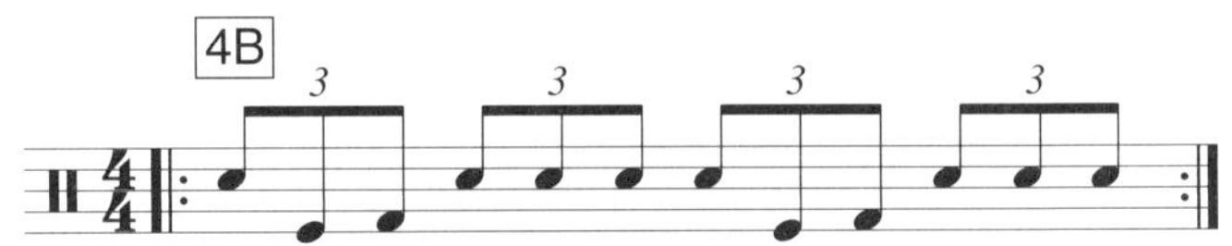

5A

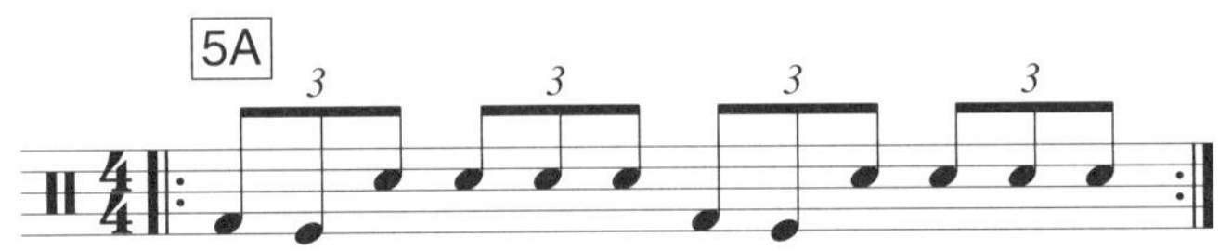

5B

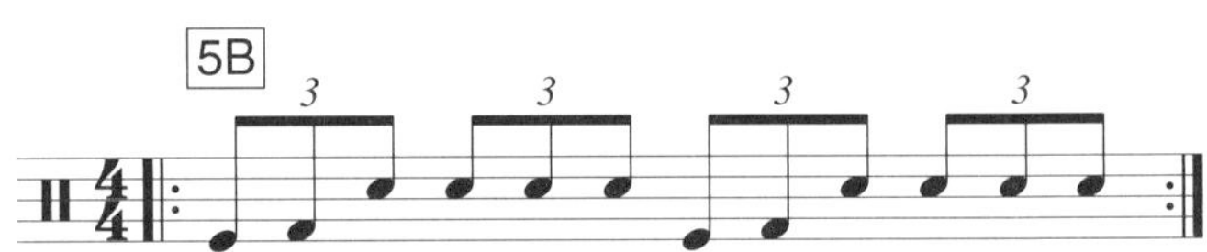

6A

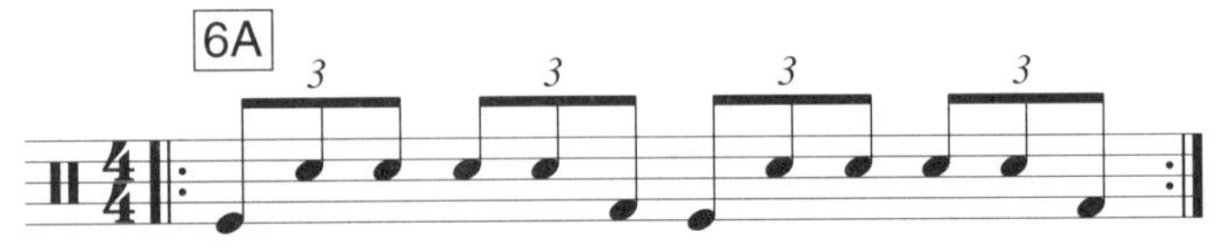

6B

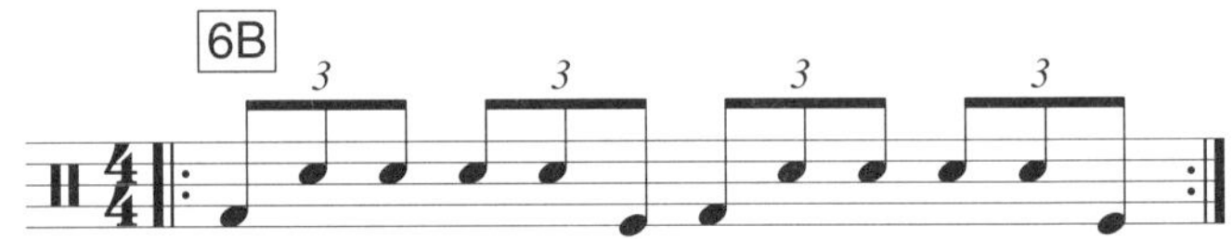

4 + 2; 1 + 2; 1 + 2 Variations

1A

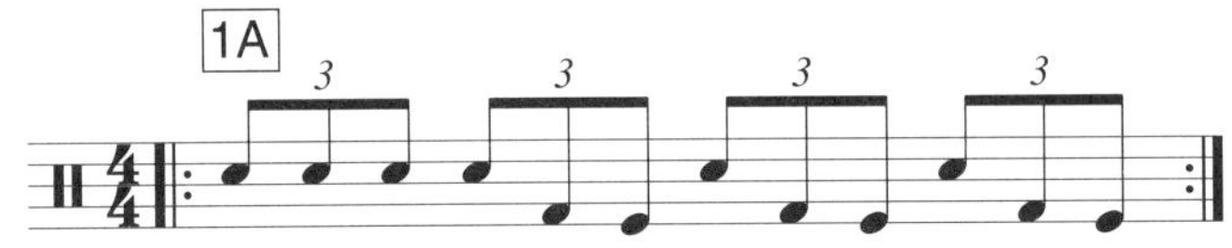

1B

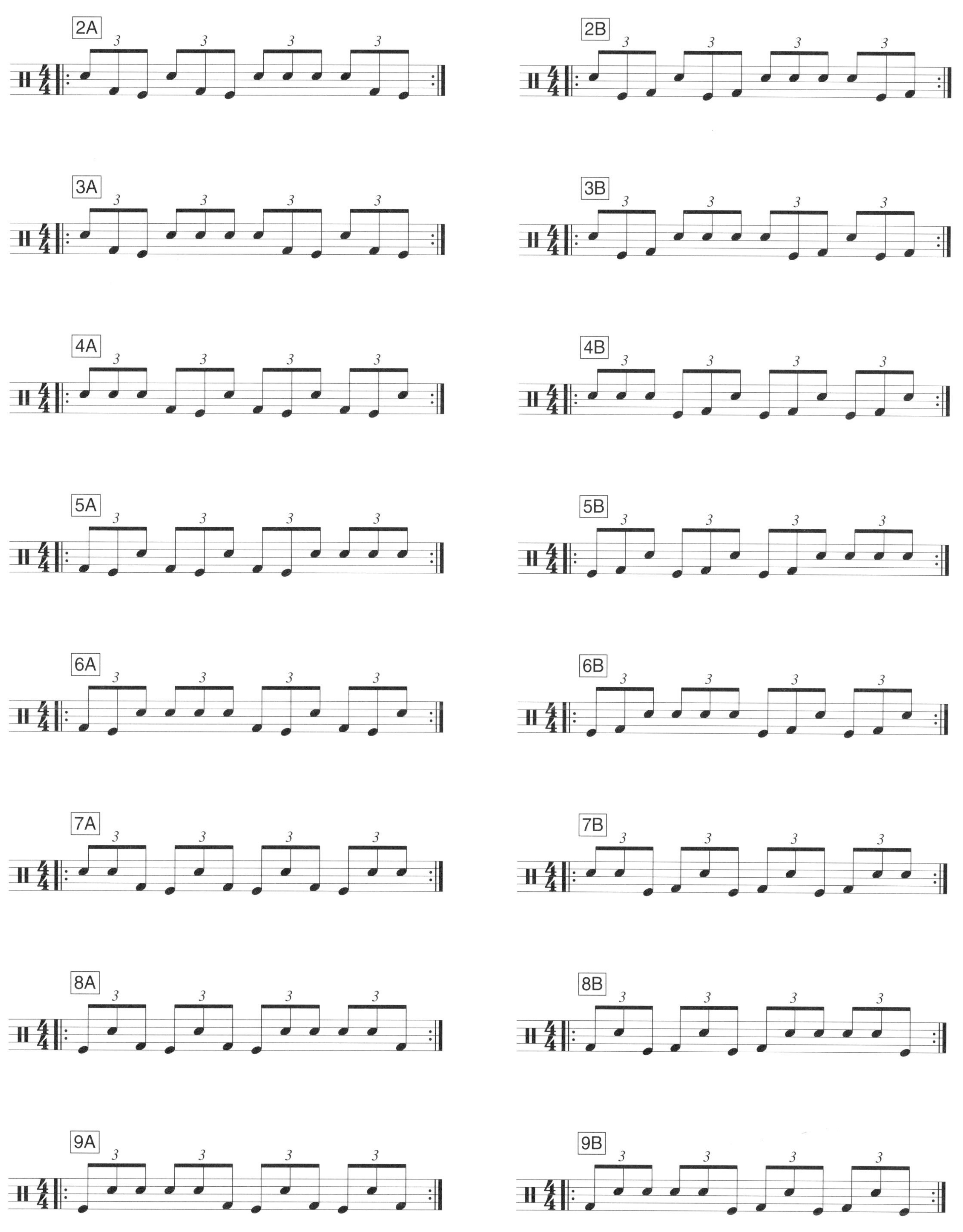
2A
2B
3A
3B
4A
4B
5A
5B
6A
6B
7A
7B
8A
8B
9A
9B

4 + 2; 2 + 2 + 2 Variations

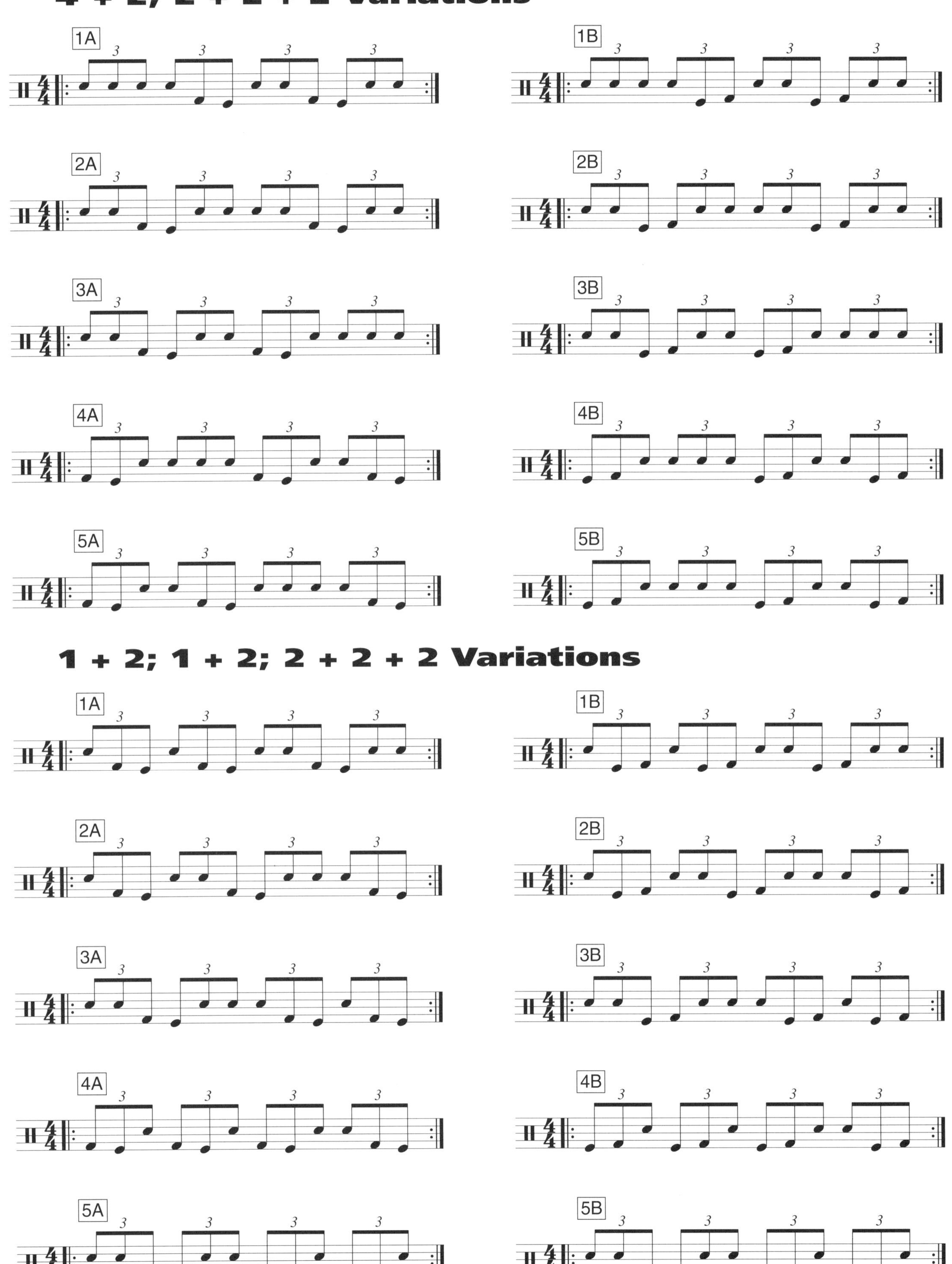

8th-Note-Triplet Fills

8th/16th-Note-Triplet and Sextuplet Progressive Builders

3A

3B

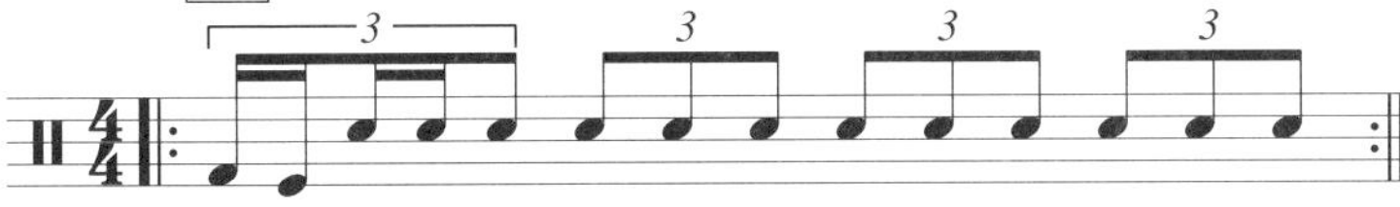

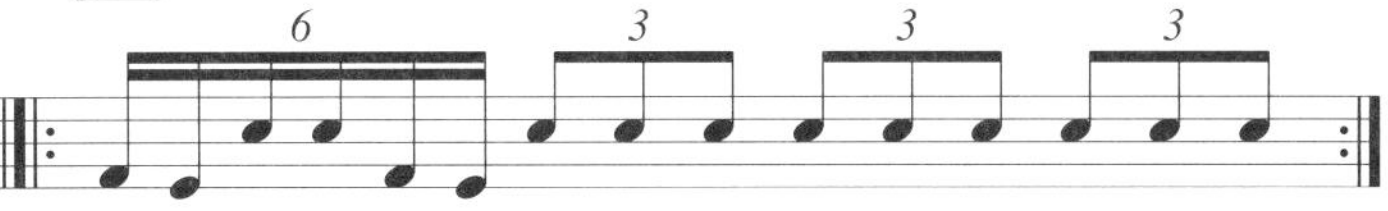

3C

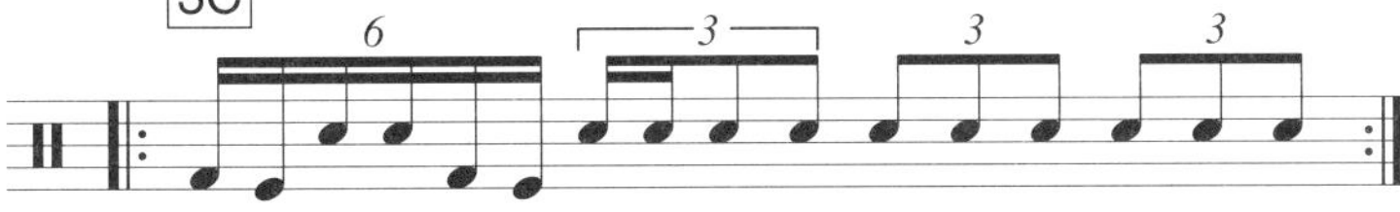

3D

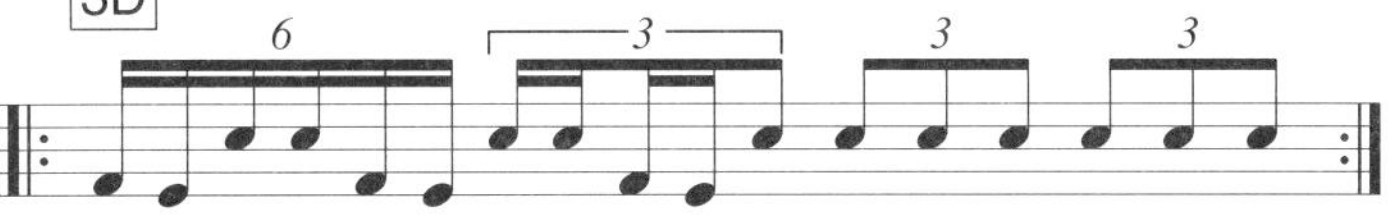

3E

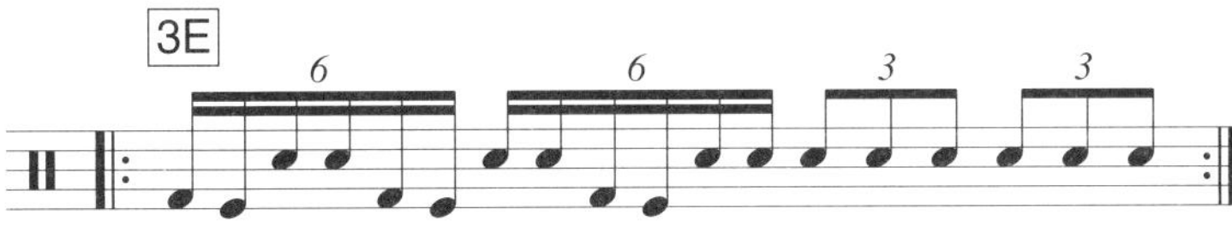

3F

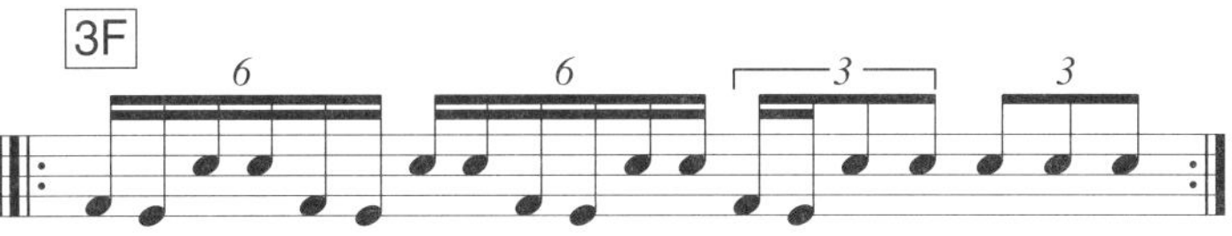

3G

3H

3I

3J

3K

8th/16th-Note-Triplet Combinations

1A

1B

1C

1D

1E

1F

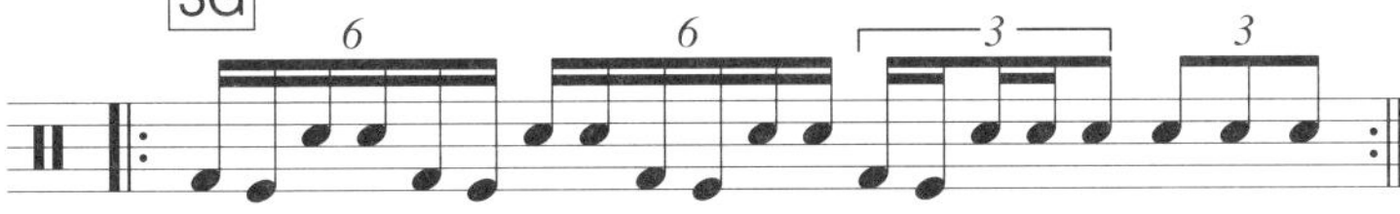

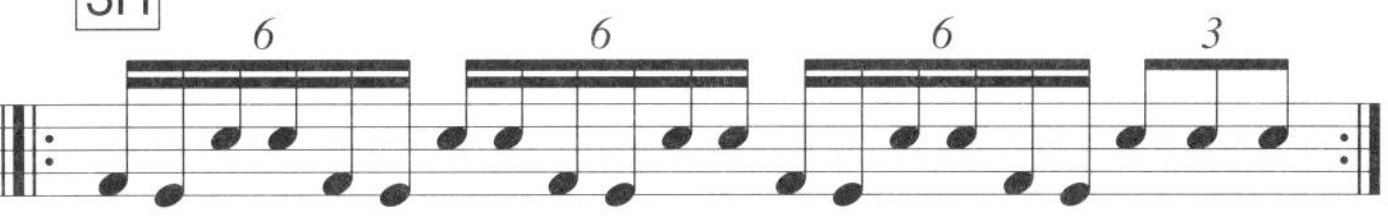

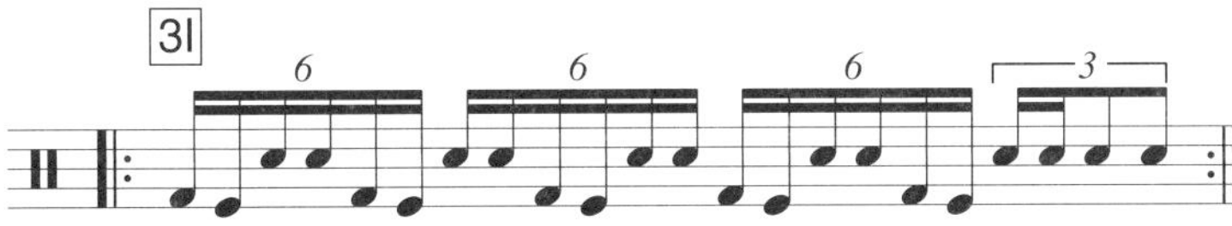

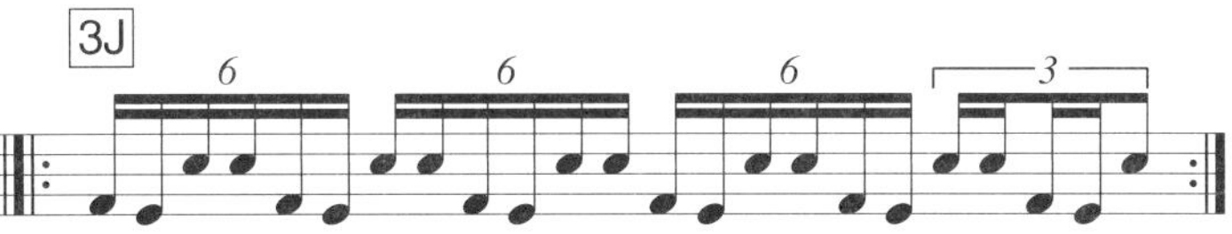

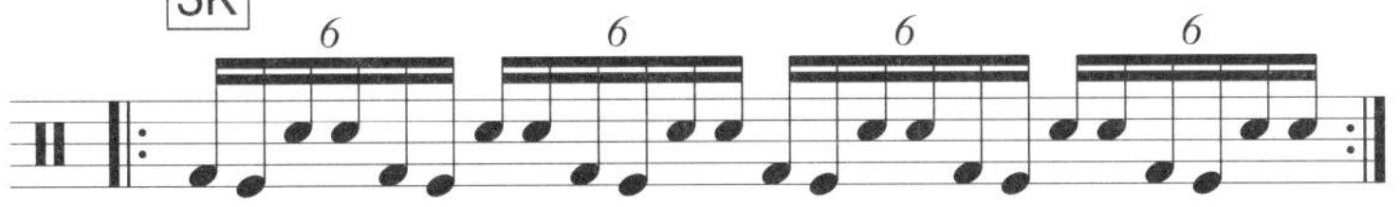

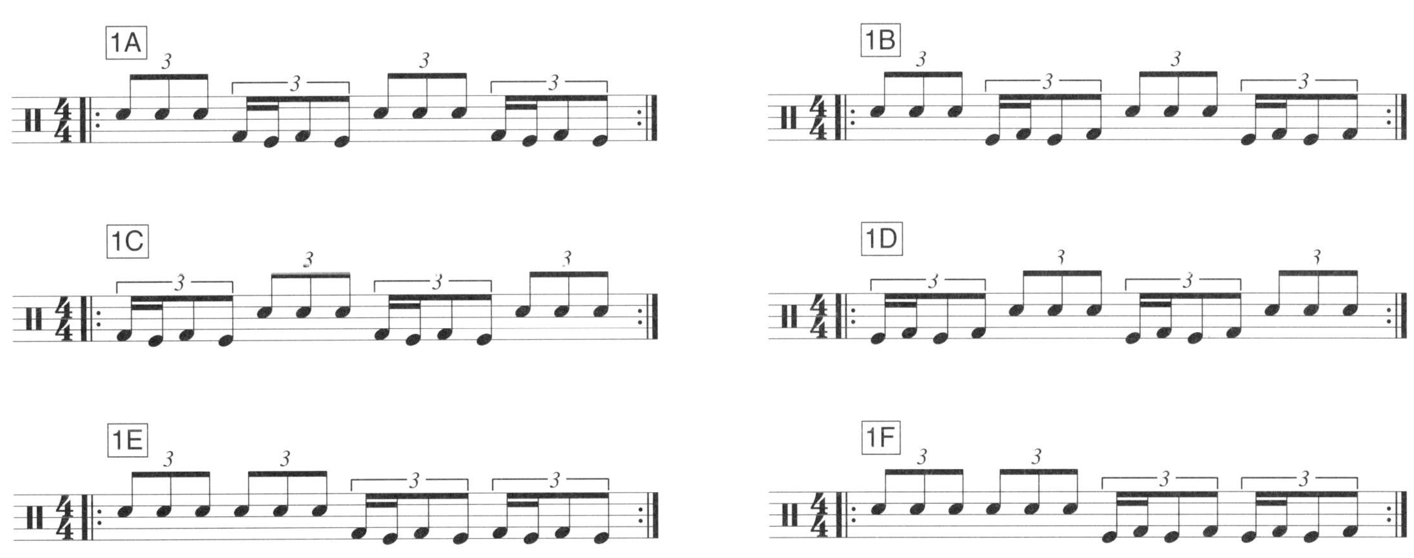

1G
1H
1I
1J
1K
1L
2A
2B
2C
2D
2E
2F
2G
2H
2I
2J
2K
2L
3A
3B
3C
3D

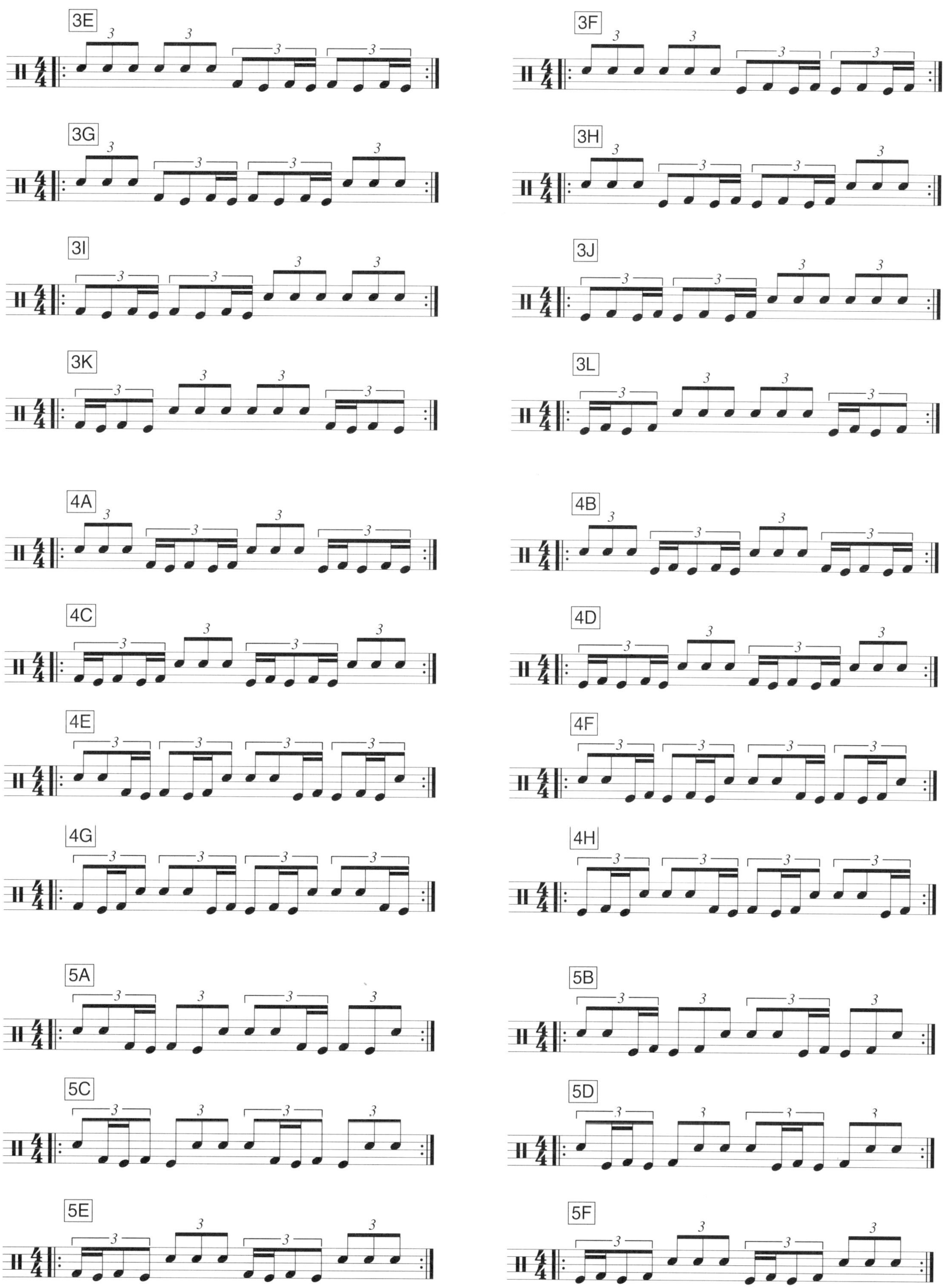
3E
3F
3G
3H
3I
3J
3K
3L
4A
4B
4C
4D
4E
4F
4G
4H
5A
5B
5C
5D
5E
5F

8th/16-Note-Triplet and Sextuplet Fills

Drum-to-Cymbal Builders

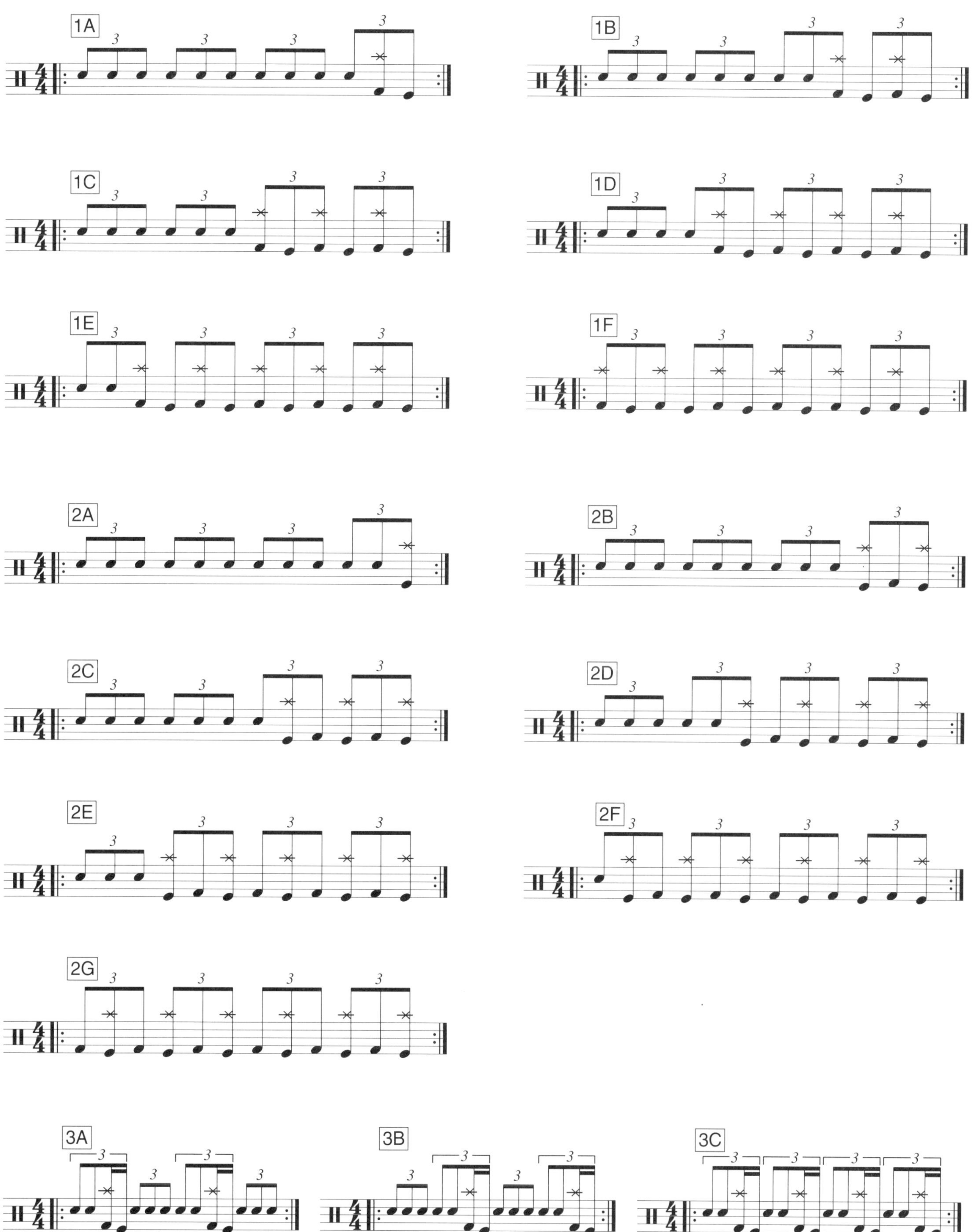

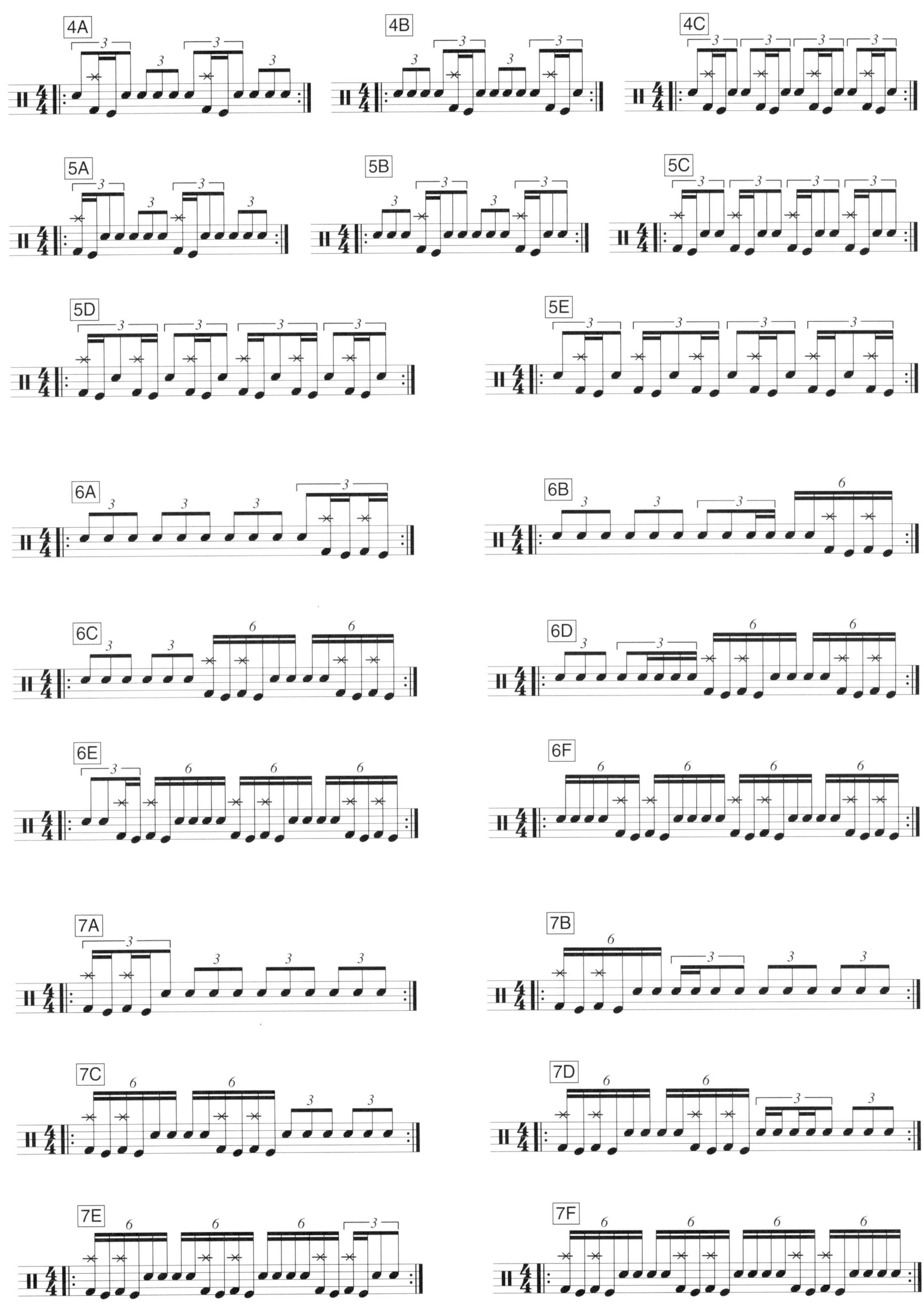
4A
4B
4C
5A
5B
5C
5D
5E
6A
6B
6C
6D
6E
6F
7A
7B
7C
7D
7E
7F

8th/16th-Note-Triplet and Sextuplet Fills with Cymbals

16th-Note and 8th-Note-Triplet Fills

16th/32nd-Note, 8th/16th-Note-Triplet and Sextuplet Fills

16th/32nd-Note, 8th/16th-Note-Triplet and Sextuplet Fills with Cymbals

Drumistic Discoveries

Use this page to log your original ideas based on the concepts from this chapter.

1

2

3

4

5

6

7

8

9 Phrasing Concepts—Grooves

Developing the ability to group phrases of notes that don't resolve within the beat or the bar can open up an endless world of rhythmic opportunity. Typically, 16th notes are phrased in groupings of two or four, but creating a repetitive phrase of three or five 16th notes will change the feel and the rhythmic architecture tremendously. This is an extremely valuable concept to understand, whether or not it is applied to double bass. If these concepts are new to you, this chapter will give you a strong foundation in approaching these techniques with or without double bass.

As with almost every aspect of rhythm, there are endless ways to apply phrasing concepts; this chapter will explore the most common. Phrasing 16th notes in groupings of three and five as well as phrasing 8th-note triplets in groups of four and five will be the focus. You will encounter how these phrases lay the foundation for "implied metric modulation" opportunities. For a deeper understanding of the difference between "implied metric modulation" and "metric modulation," I will refer you to my book *Essential Rock Drumming Concepts*. For now, the applications in this chapter will be an exhaustive resource regarding implied metric modulation.

The Basic Phrase at the beginning of each section is crucial. Internalize and memorize this rhythm by playing it slow, counting out loud, and repeating it multiple times. Recognize how and where the phrase begins and ends. This rhythm lays the groundwork for the applications to come.

These concepts may be new to you. Take it slow, be patient, and enjoy the journey.

Practice Suggestions:

- Play to a click track or metronome. These are advanced concepts that need to be played with an objective time source. Don't try to feel them.
- Play quarter notes on the bass drum and/or hi-hat when internalizing the Basic Rhythm. This will help you understand how the phrase works against the primary pulse.
- Practice/play these grooves live only with rhythmically-advanced musicians.
- Repeat. Rest. Recall.

"To play a wrong note is insignificant; to play without passion is inexcusable."

—Ludwig Van Beethoven

Three-Note Phrasing: Variation 1

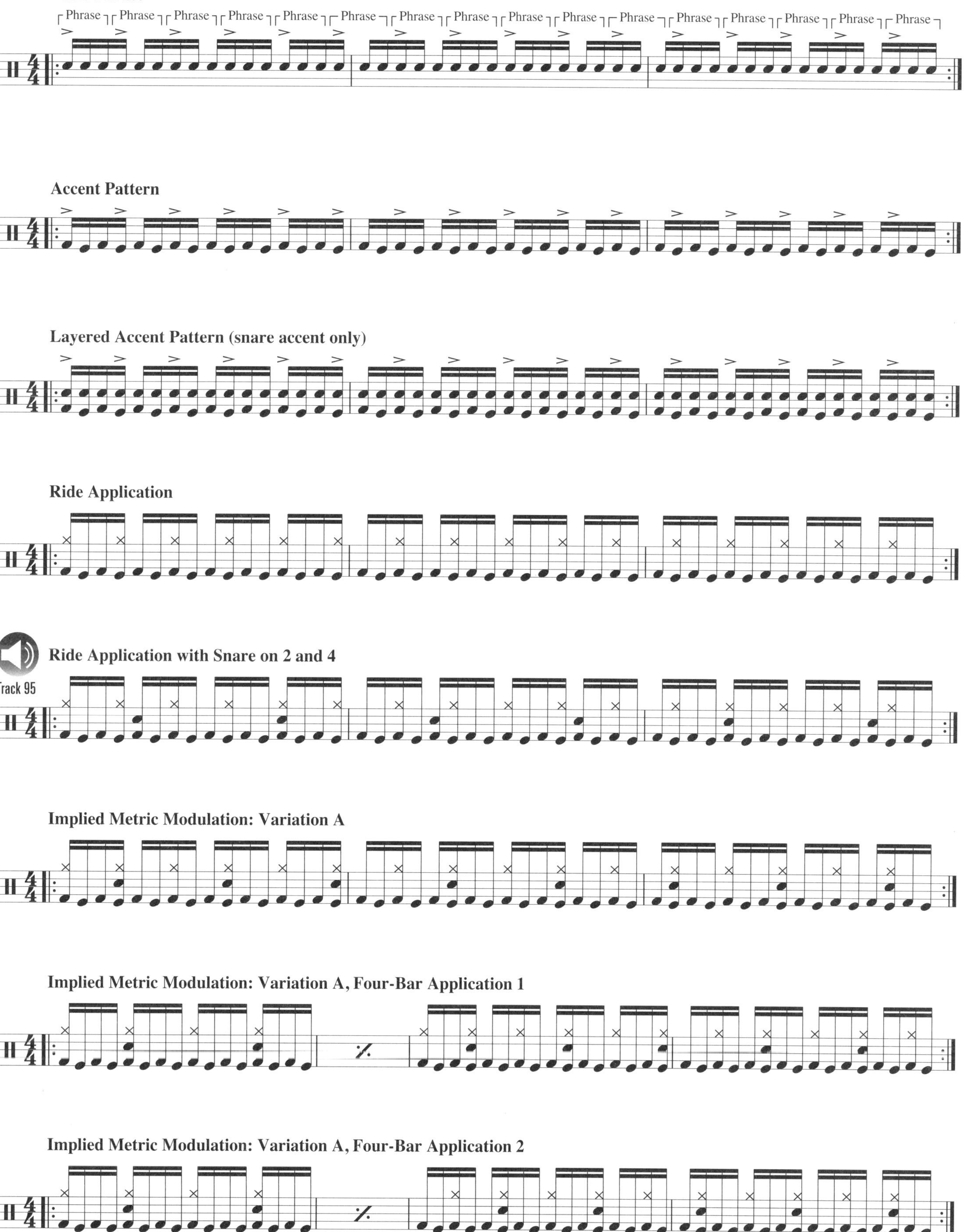

Implied Metric Modulation: Variation A, Four-Bar Application 3

Implied Metric Modulation: Variation B

Implied Metric Modulation: Variation B, Four-Bar Application 1

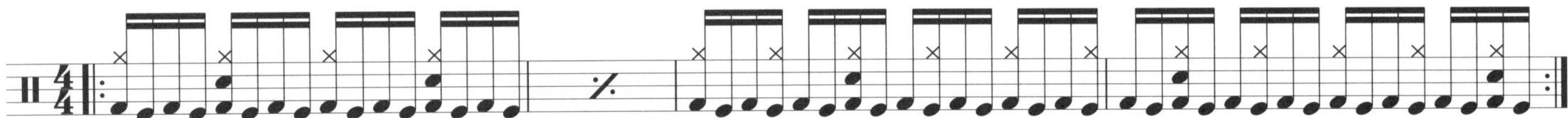

Implied Metric Modulation: Variation B, Four-Bar Application 2

Track 96

Implied Metric Modulation: Variation B, Four-Bar Application 3

Three-Note Phrasing: Variation 2

Basic Phrase

Accent Pattern

Layered Accent Pattern (snare accent only)

Ride Application

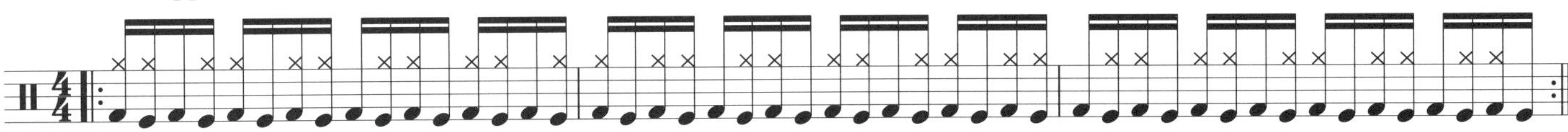

Ride Application with Snare on 2 and 4

Implied Metric Modulation: Variation A

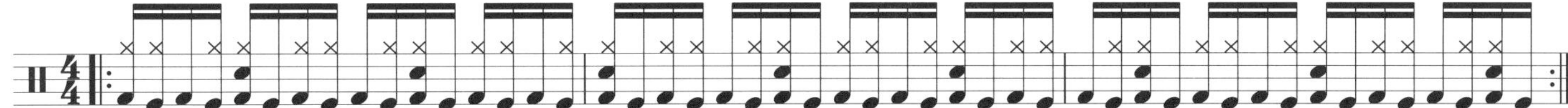

Implied Metric Modulation: Variation A, Four-Bar Application 1

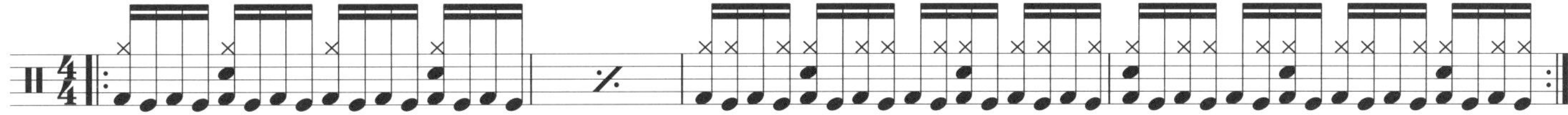

Track 97

Implied Metric Modulation: Variation A, Four-Bar Application 2

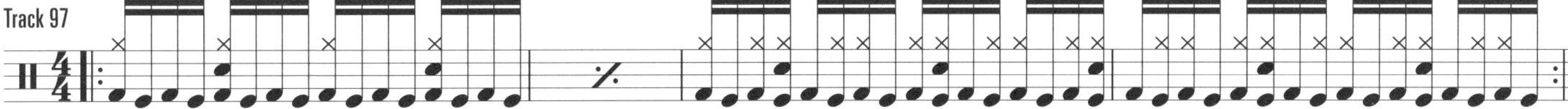

Implied Metric Modulation: Variation A, Four-Bar Application 3

Implied Metric Modulation: Variation B

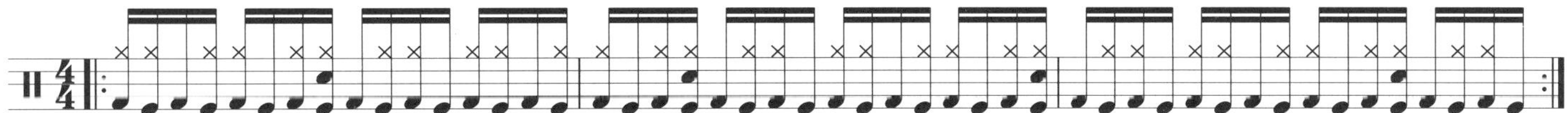

Implied Metric Modulation: Variation B, Four-Bar Application 1

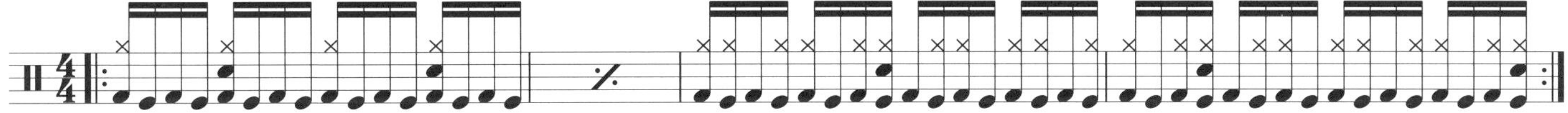

Implied Metric Modulation: Variation B, Four-Bar Application 2

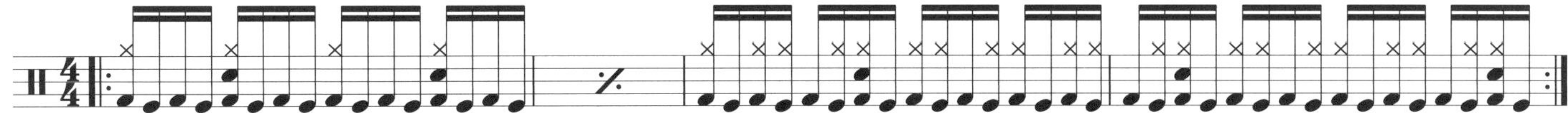

Implied Metric Modulation: Variation B, Four-Bar Application 3

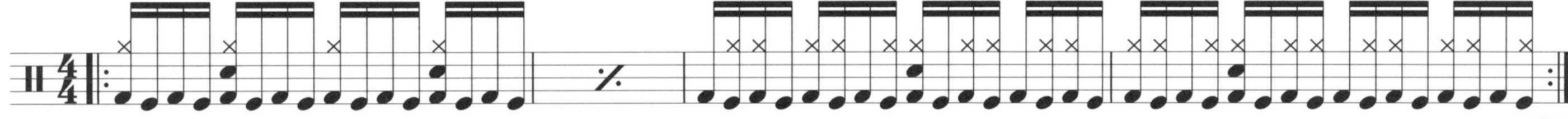

Three-Note Phrasing Groove Applications

4A Snare on 2 and 4
Track 98
4B Snare on 3
4C Snare on Fill in
5A Snare on 2 and 4
5B Snare on 3

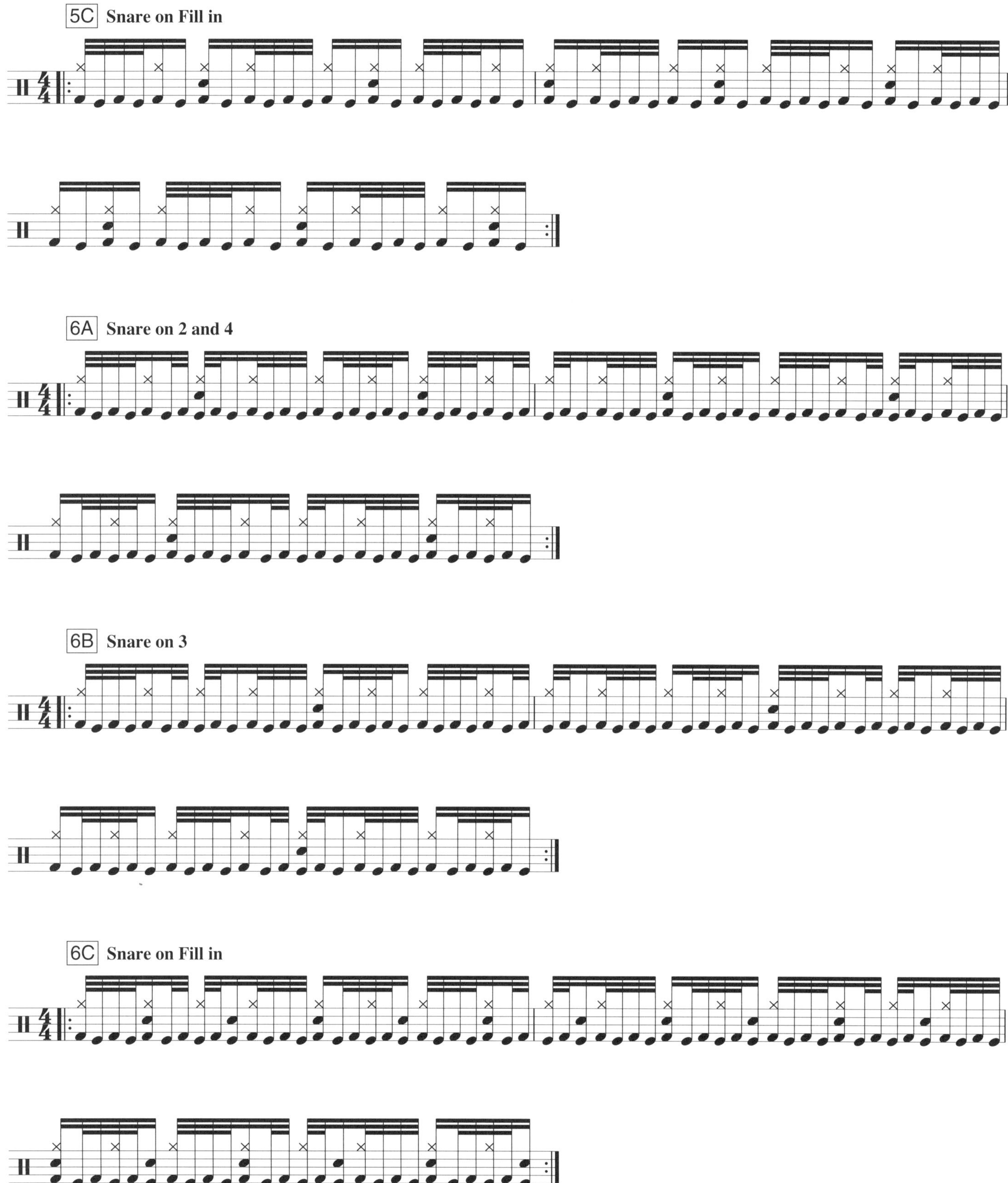

5C Snare on Fill in
6A Snare on 2 and 4
6B Snare on 3
6C Snare on Fill in

Five-Note Phrasing: Variation 1

Implied Metric Modulation

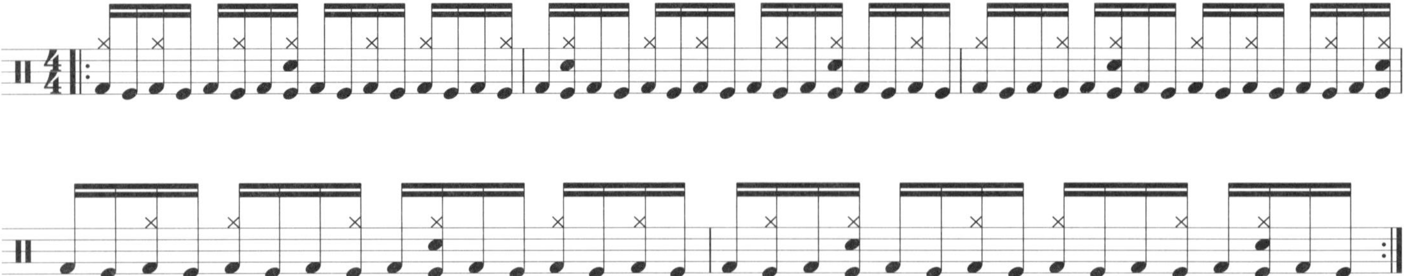

Implied Metric Modulation: Four-Bar Application 1

Implied Metric Modulation: Four-Bar Application 2

Implied Metric Modulation: Four-Bar Application 3

Implied Metric Modulation: Four-Bar Application 4

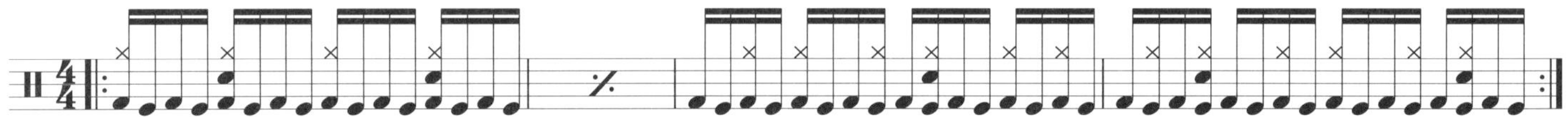

Implied Metric Modulation: Four-Bar Application 5

Five-Note Phrasing: Variation 2

Basic Phrase

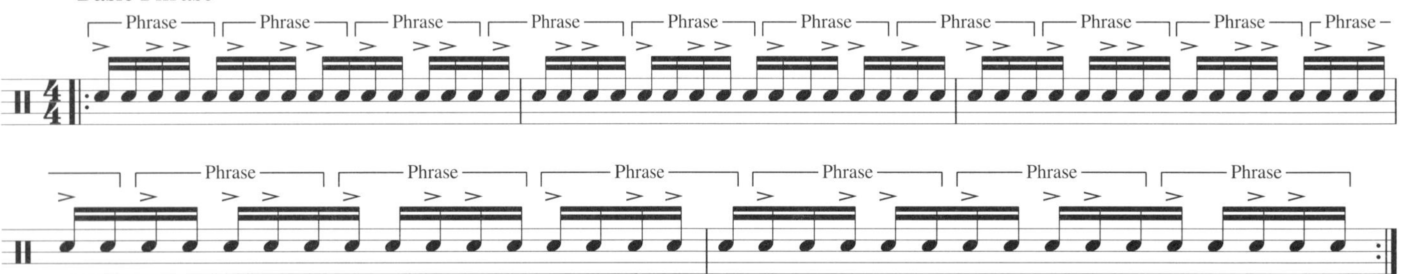

Accent Pattern

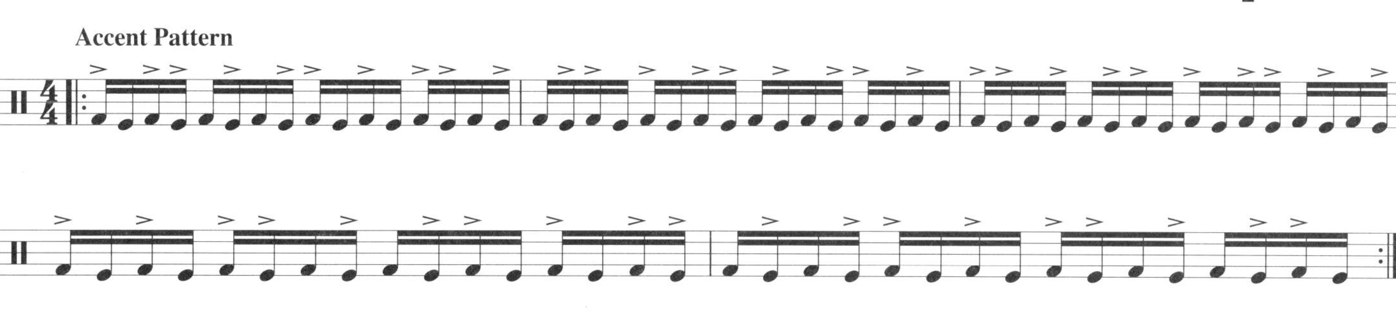

Layered Accent Pattern (snare accent only)

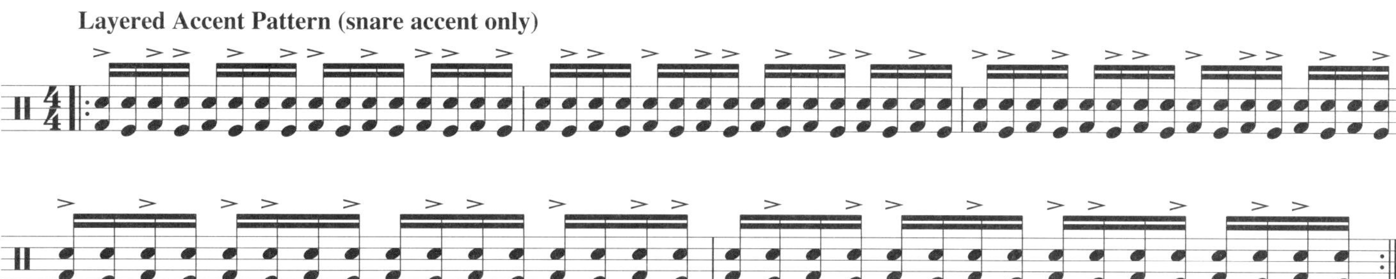

Ride Application

Ride Application with Snare on 2 and 4

Track 101

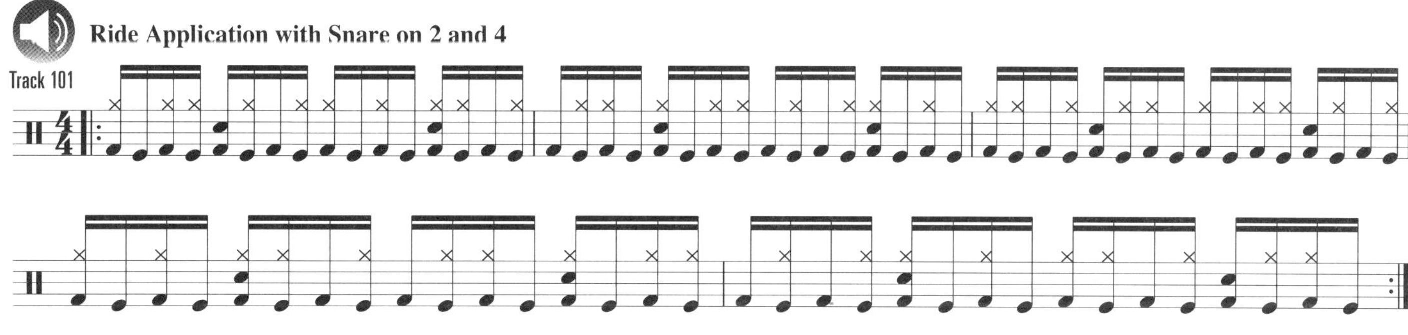

Implied Metric Modulation

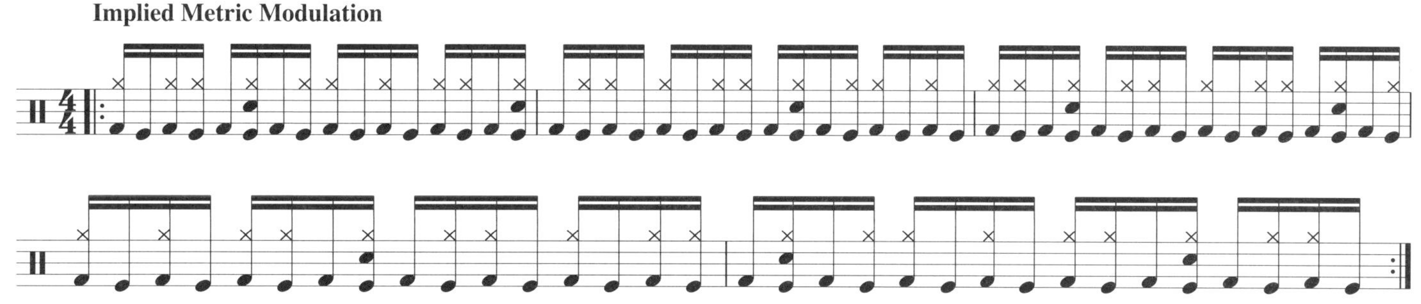

Track 102

Implied Metric Modulation: Four-Bar Application 1

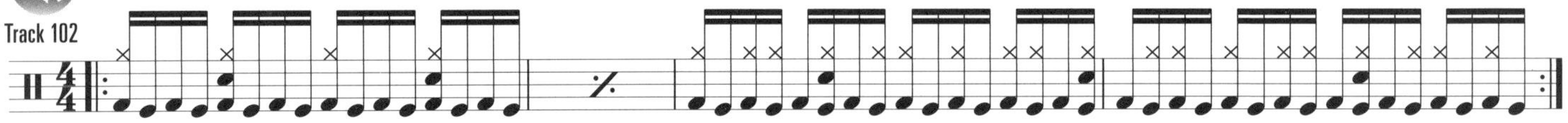

Implied Metric Modulation: Four-Bar Application 2

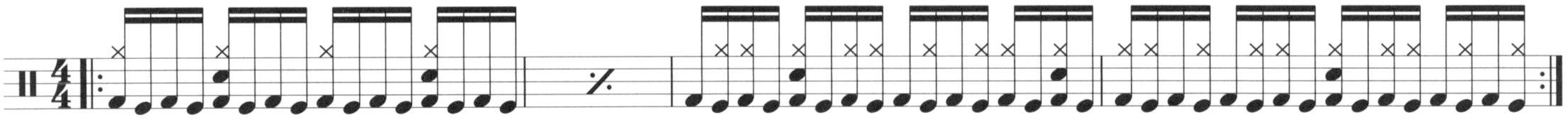

Implied Metric Modulation: Four-Bar Application 3

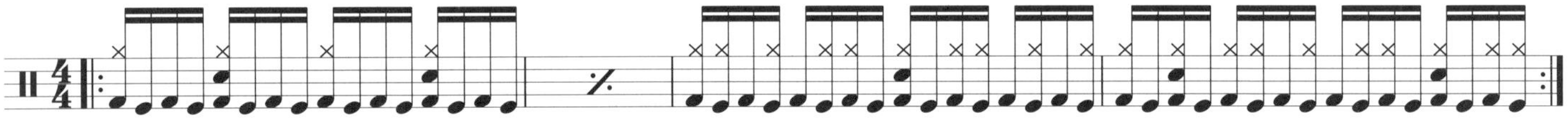

Implied Metric Modulation: Four-Bar Application 4

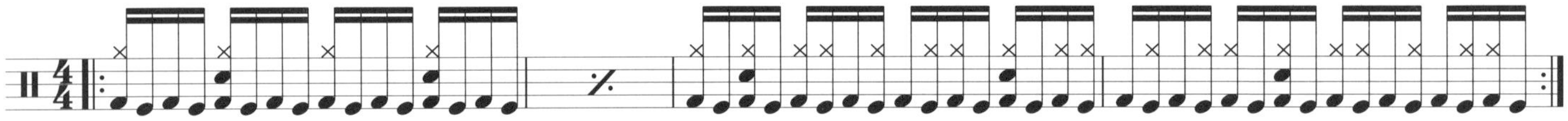

Implied Metric Modulation: Four-Bar Application 5

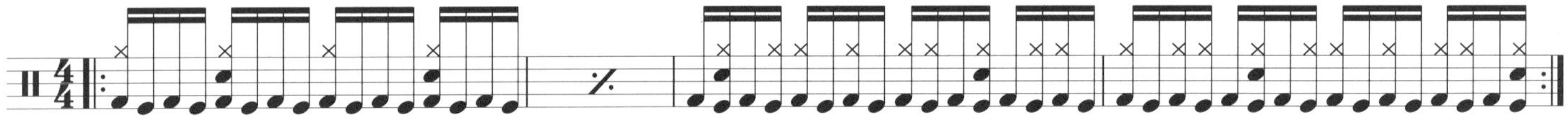

Five-Note Phrasing Groove Applications

1A Snare on 2 and 4

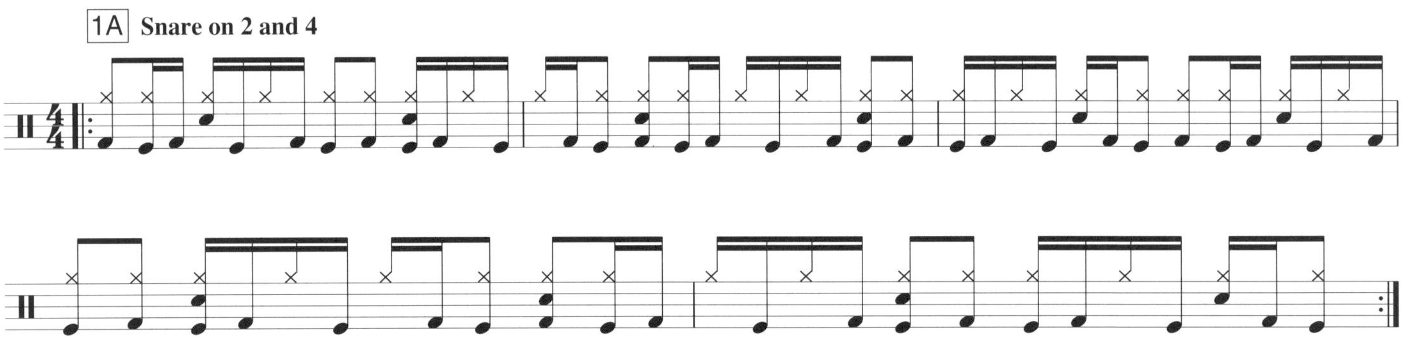

1B Snare on 3
1C Snare on Fill in
2A Snare on 2 and 4
Track 103
2B Snare on 3
2C Snare on Fill in

3A Snare on 2 and 4

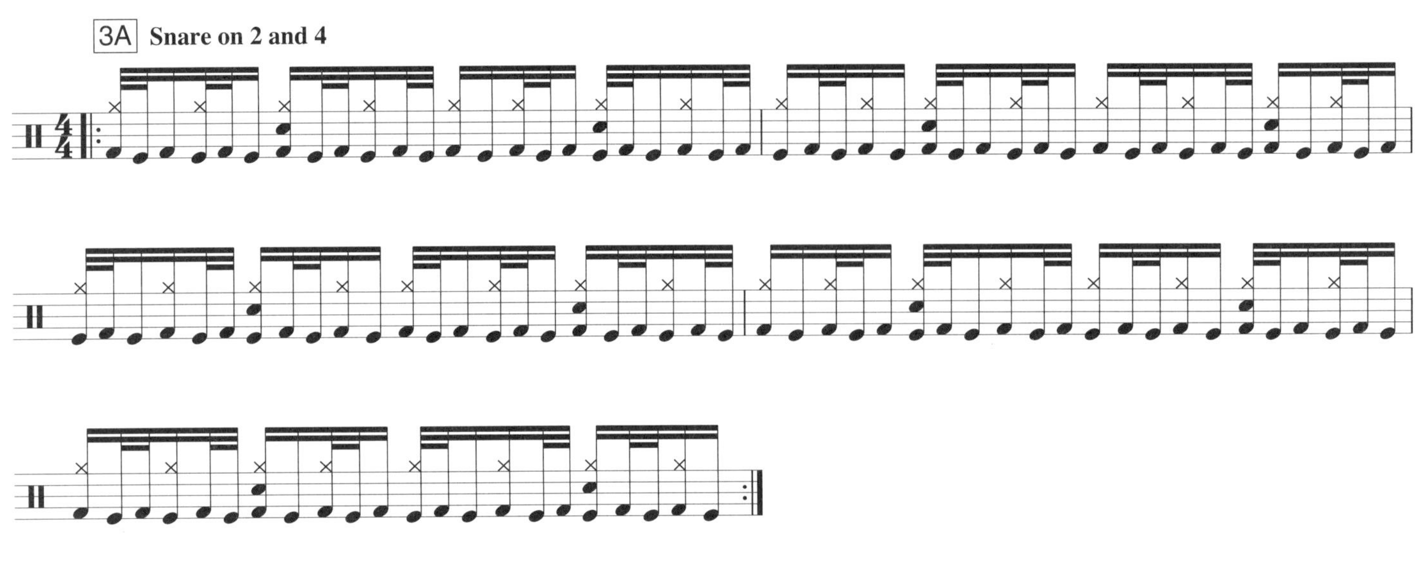

3B Snare on 3

3C Snare on Fill in

Track 104
4A Snare on 2 and 4
4B Snare on 3
4C Snare on Fill in

Four-Note-Triplet Phrasing

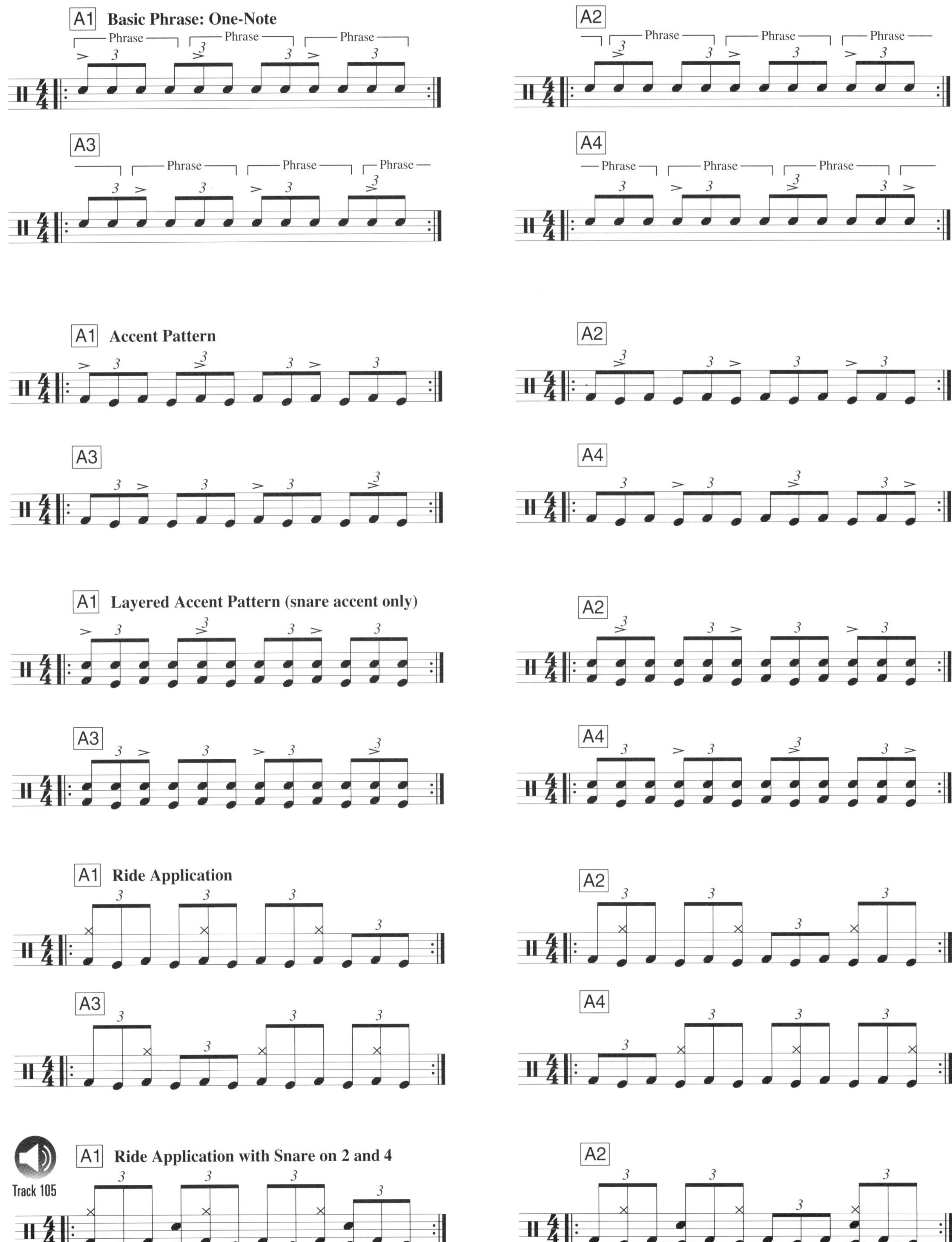

A3

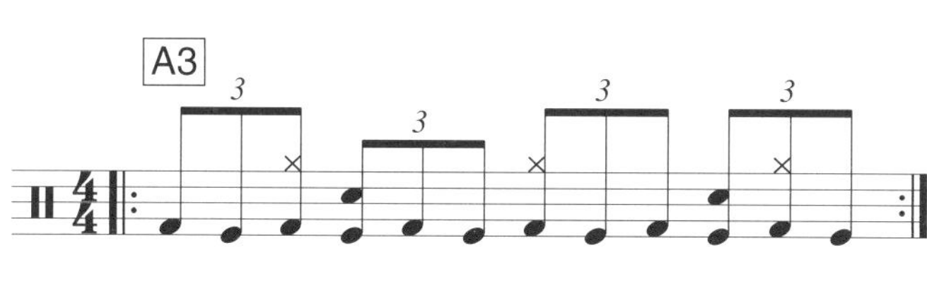

A4

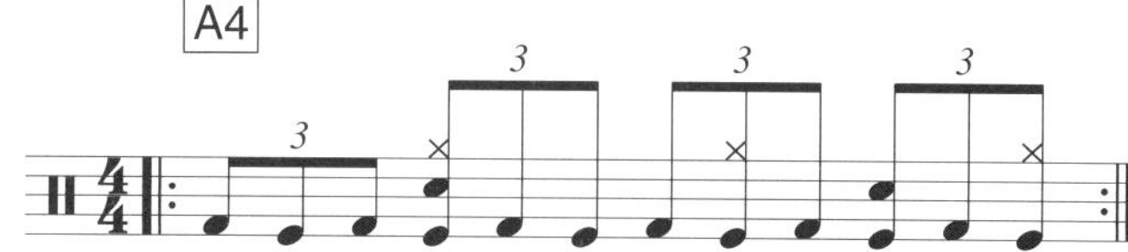

1 **Implied Metric Modulation**

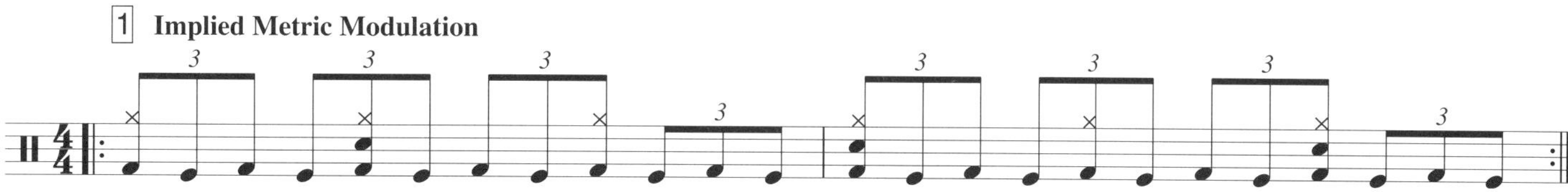

2 **Implied Metric Modulation**

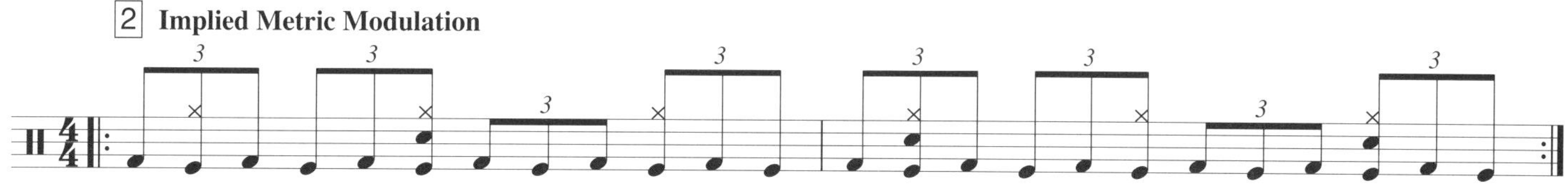

3 **Implied Metric Modulation**

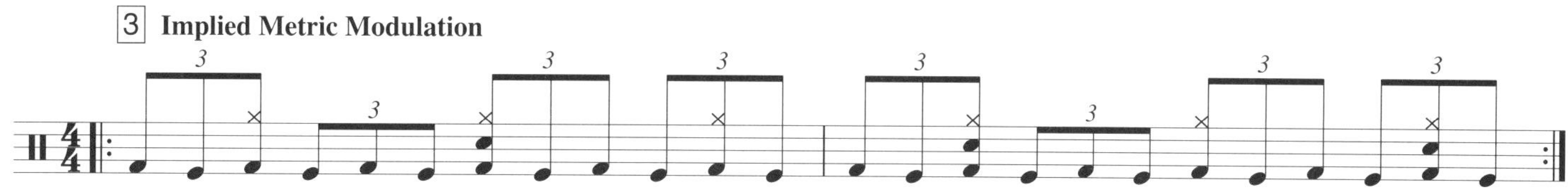

4 **Implied Metric Modulation**

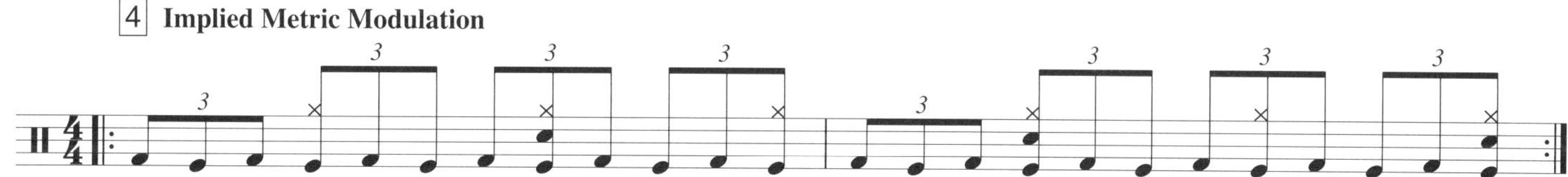

B1 **Basic Phrase: Two-Note**

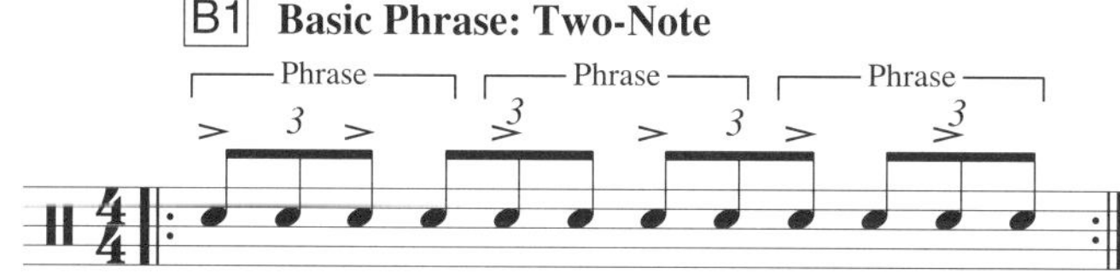

B2

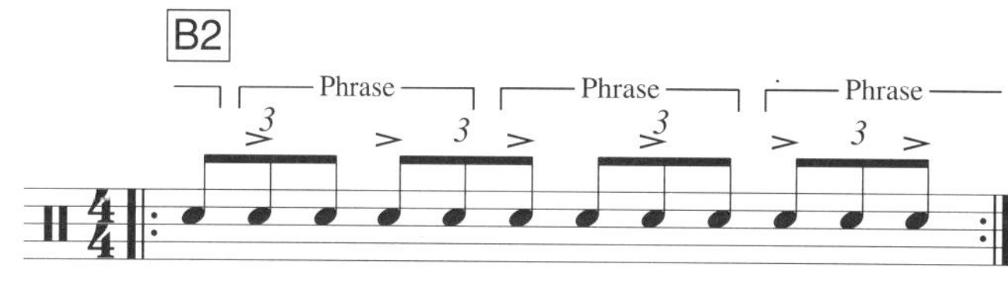

B1 **Accent Pattern**

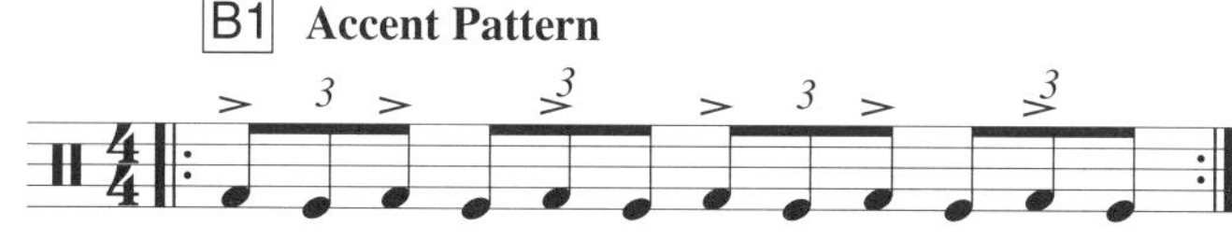

B2

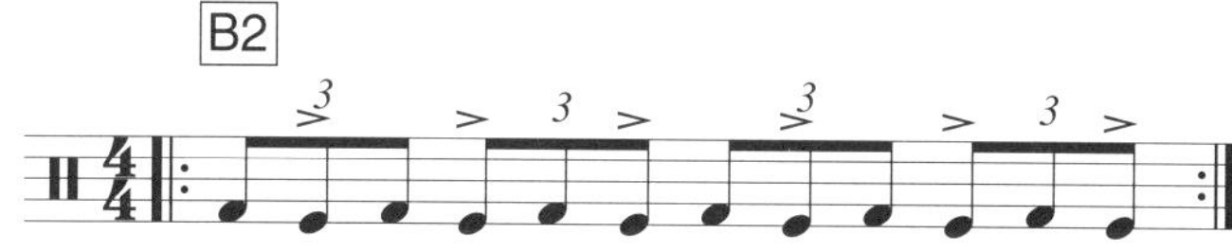

B1 **Ride Application**

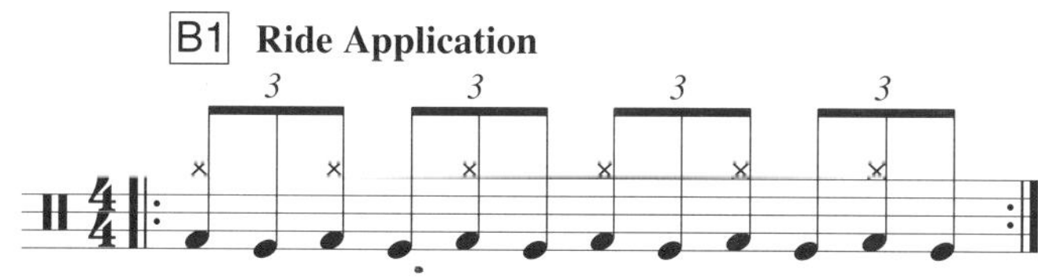

B2

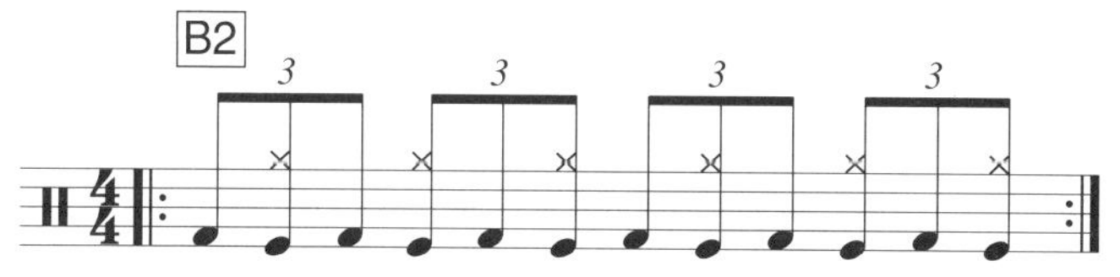

B1 **Ride Application with Snare on 2 and 4**

B2

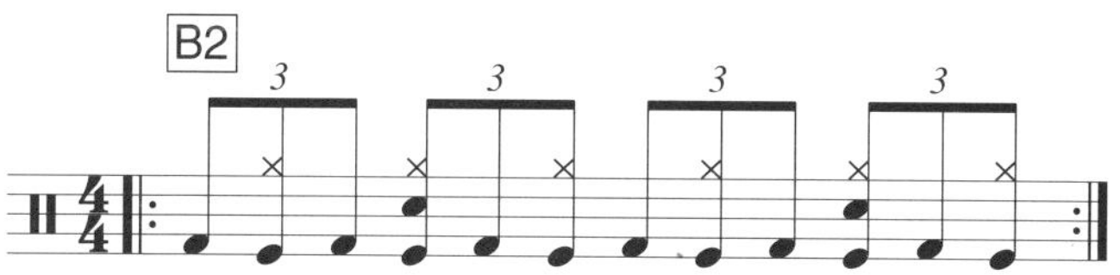

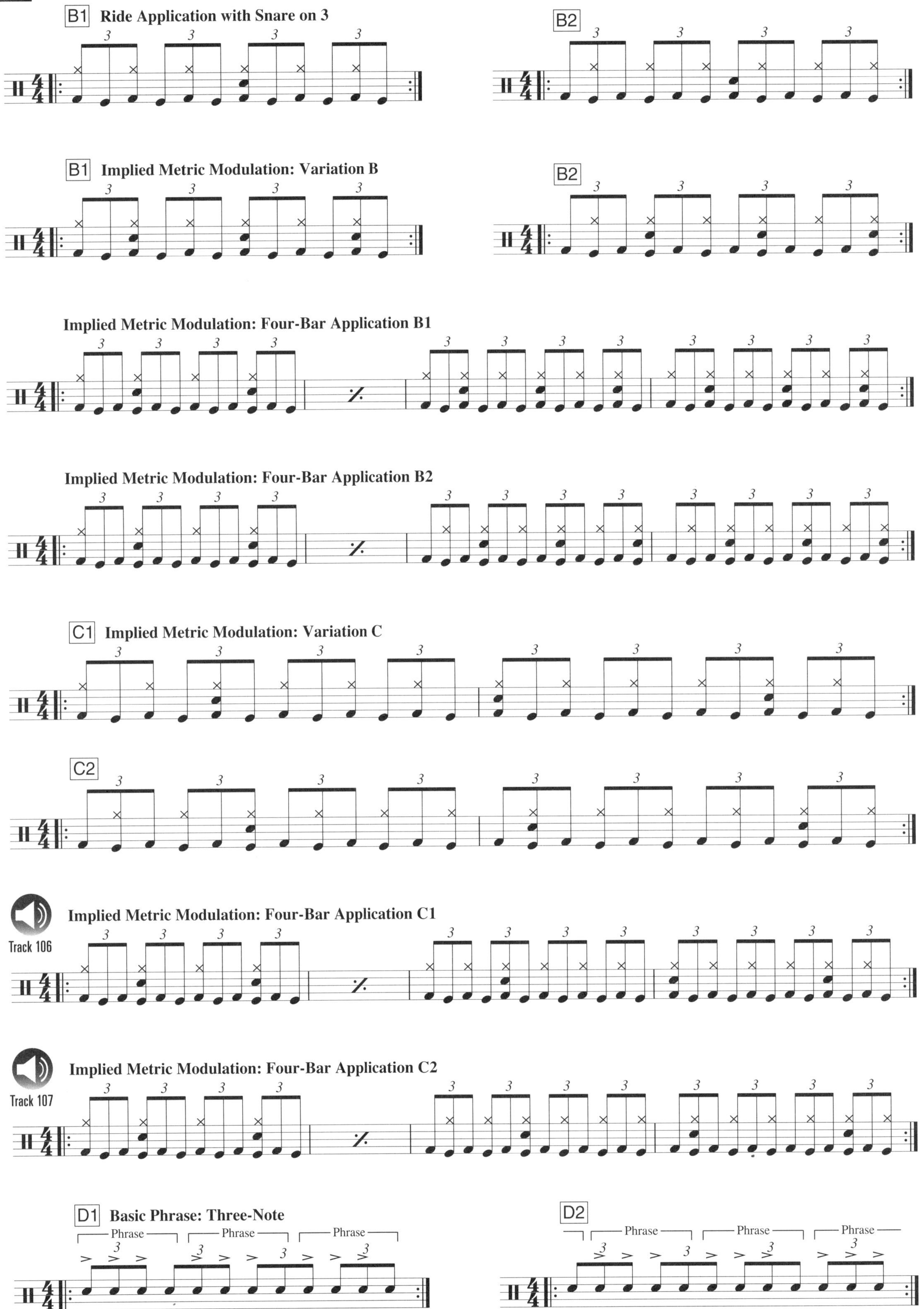
B1 Ride Application with Snare on 3
B2
B1 Implied Metric Modulation: Variation B
B2
Implied Metric Modulation: Four-Bar Application B1
Implied Metric Modulation: Four-Bar Application B2
C1 Implied Metric Modulation: Variation C
C2
Track 106
Implied Metric Modulation: Four-Bar Application C1
Track 107
Implied Metric Modulation: Four-Bar Application C2
D1 Basic Phrase: Three-Note
Phrase
Phrase
Phrase
D2
Phrase
Phrase
Phrase

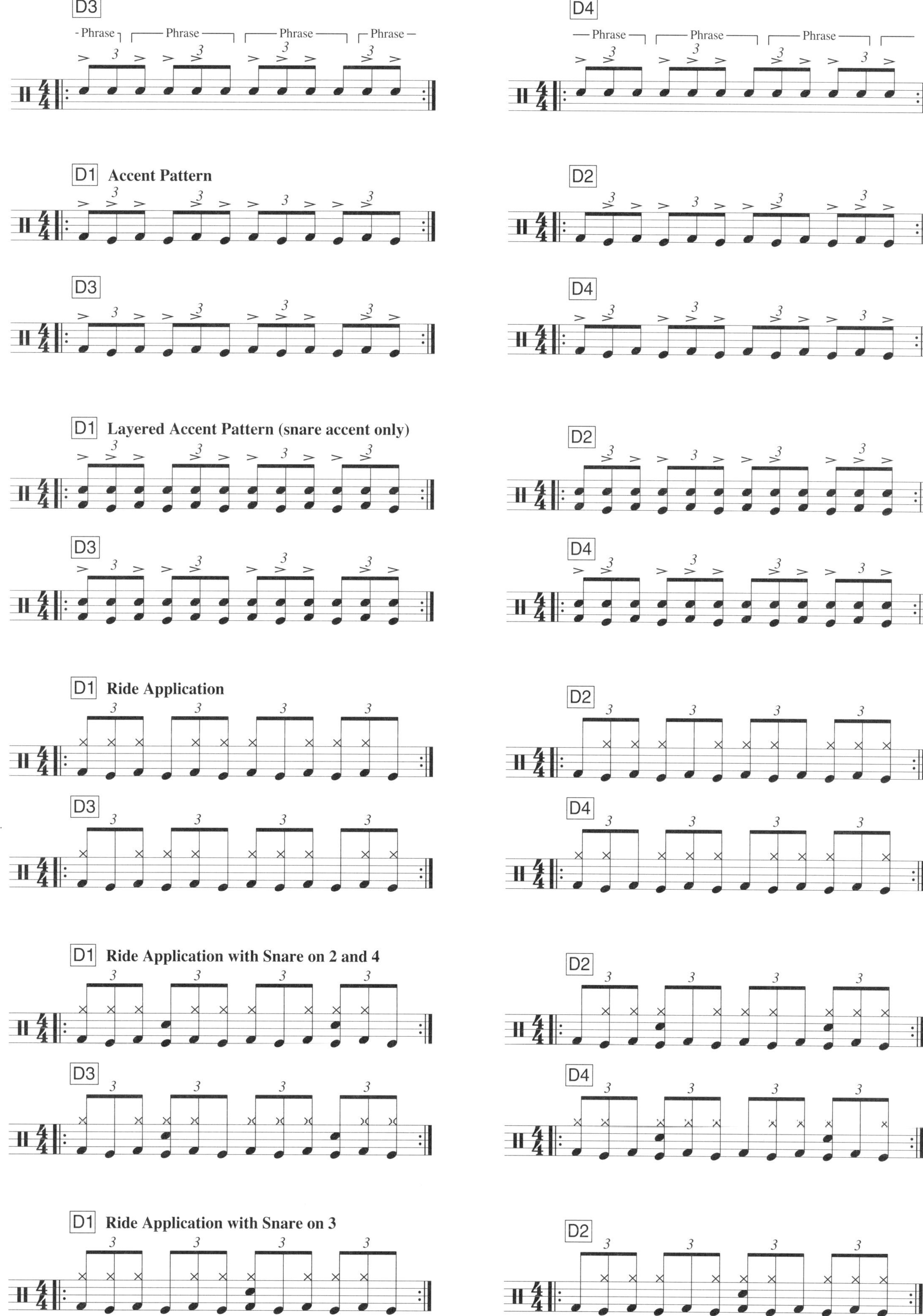
D3
Phrase
Phrase
Phrase
Phrase
D4
Phrase
Phrase
Phrase
D1 Accent Pattern
D2
D3
D4
D1 Layered Accent Pattern (snare accent only)
D2
D3
D4
D1 Ride Application
D2
D3
D4
D1 Ride Application with Snare on 2 and 4
D2
D3
D4
D1 Ride Application with Snare on 3
D2

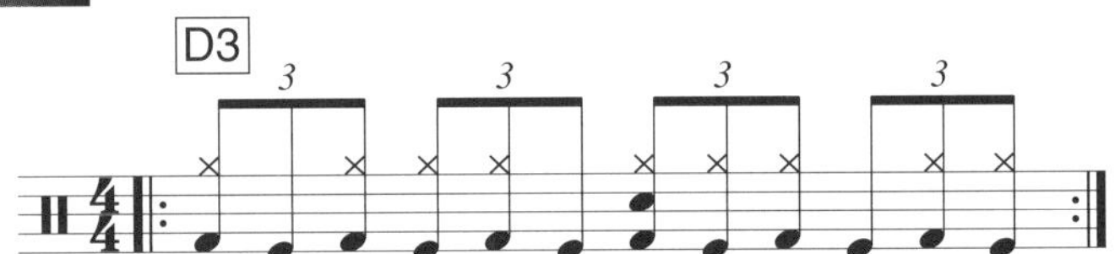

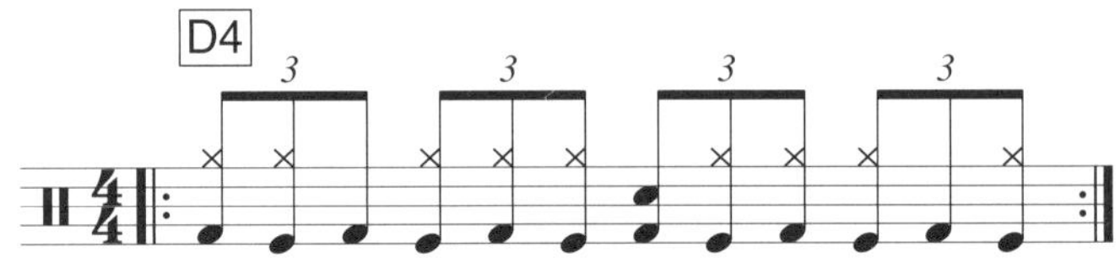

Implied Metric Modulation: Four-Bar Application D1

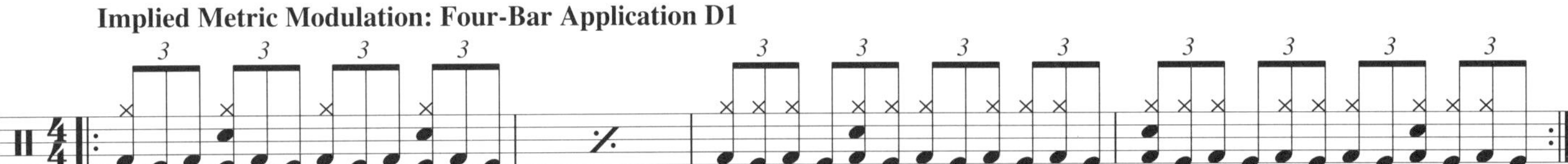

Implied Metric Modulation: Four-Bar Application D2

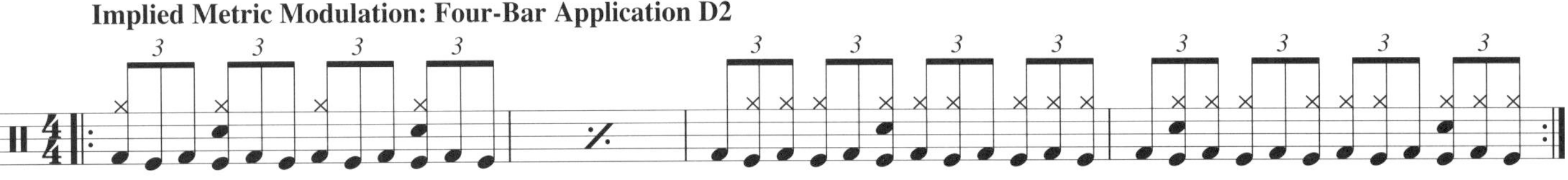

Track 108

Implied Metric Modulation: Four-Bar Application D3

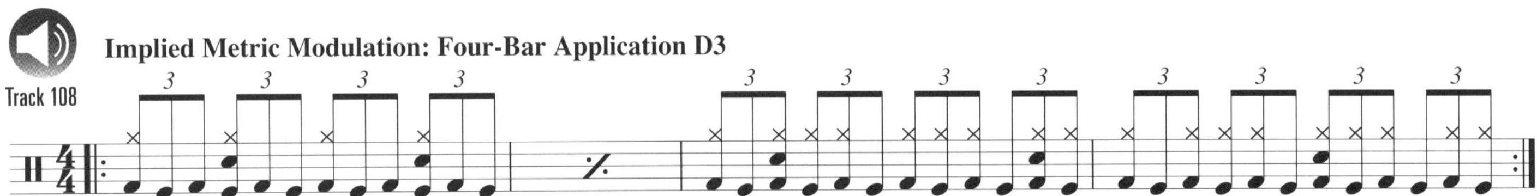

Implied Metric Modulation: Four-Bar Application D4

Four-Note-Triplet Phrasing: Groove Applications

1B-a Snare on 3
1B-b
1B-c
1B-d
2A-a Snare on 2 and 4
2A-b
2A-c
2A-d
Track 110
2B-a Snare on 3
2B-b

2B-c

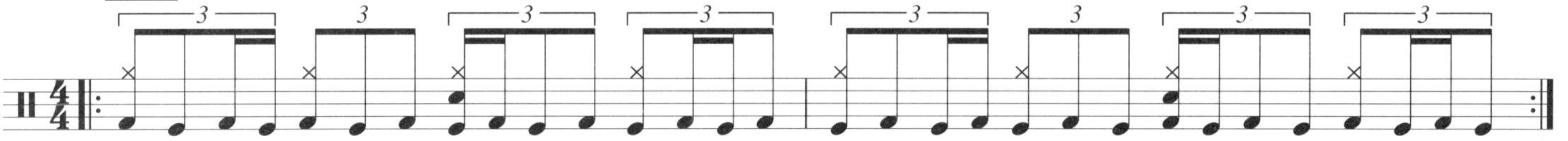

2B-d

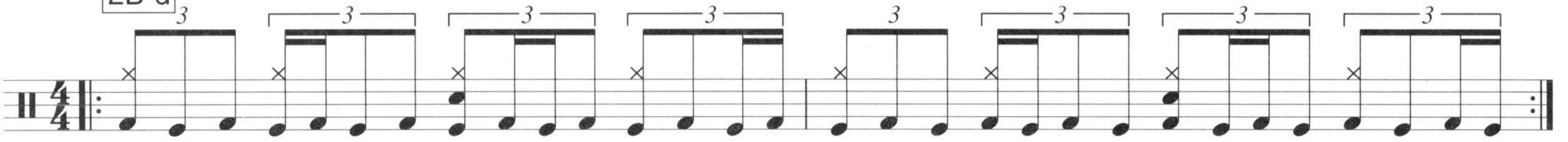

3A-a **Snare on 2 and 4**

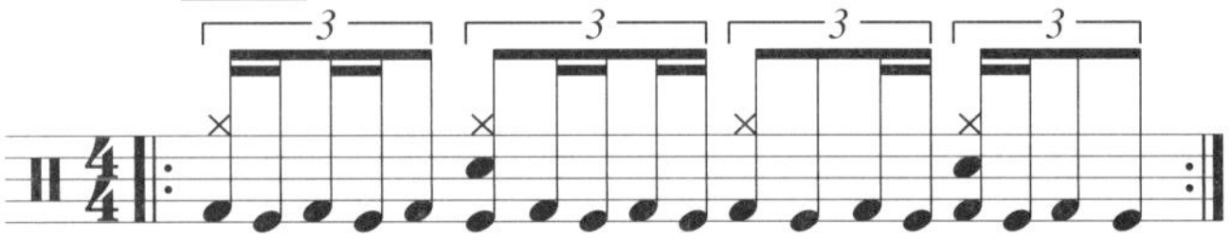

3A-b

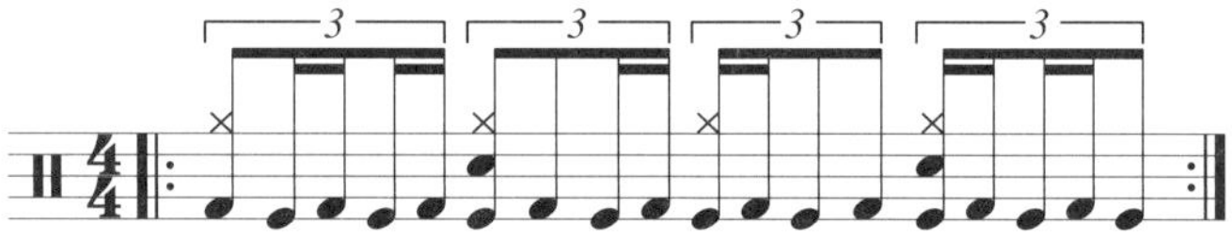

3A-c

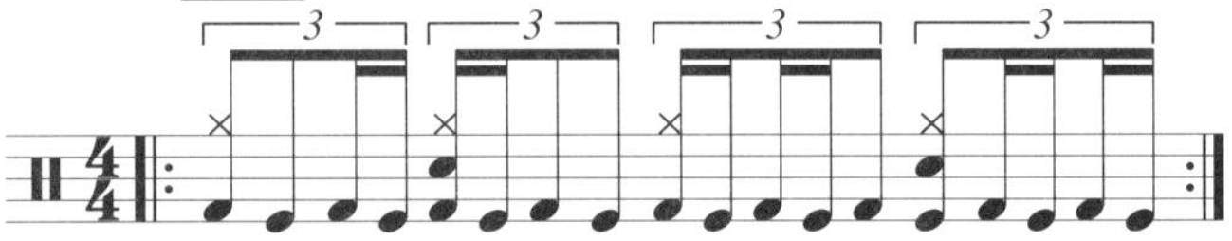

3A-d

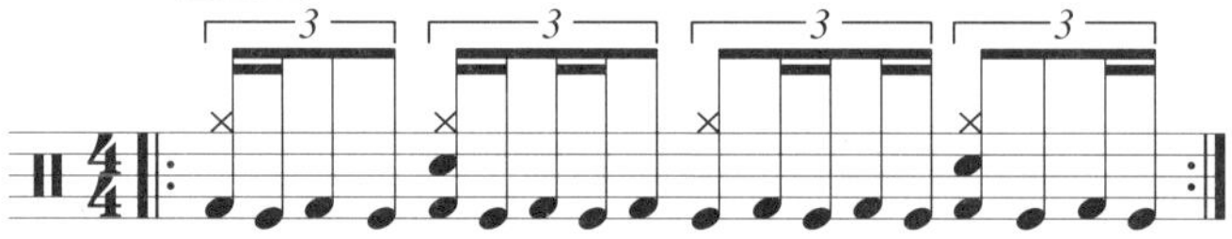

3B-a **Snare on 3**

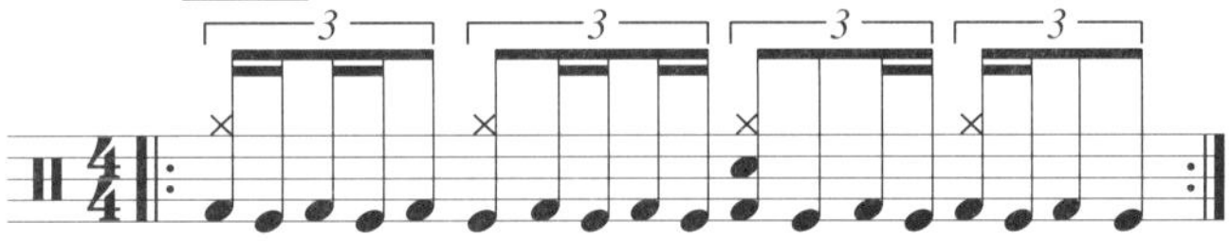

3B-b

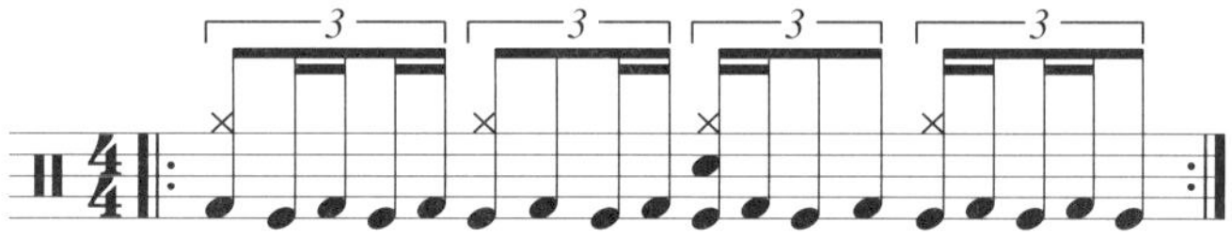

3B-c

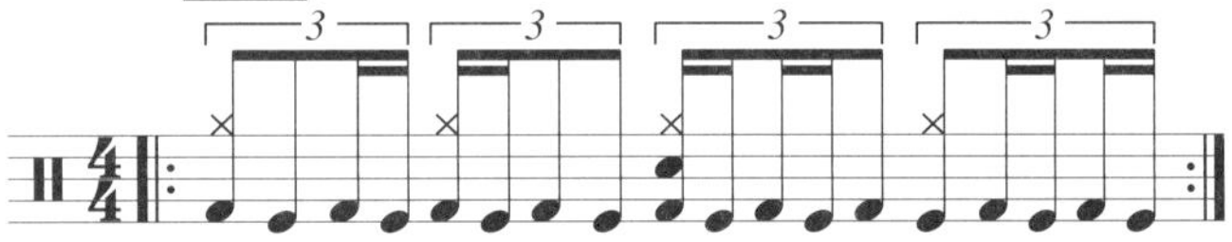

3B-d

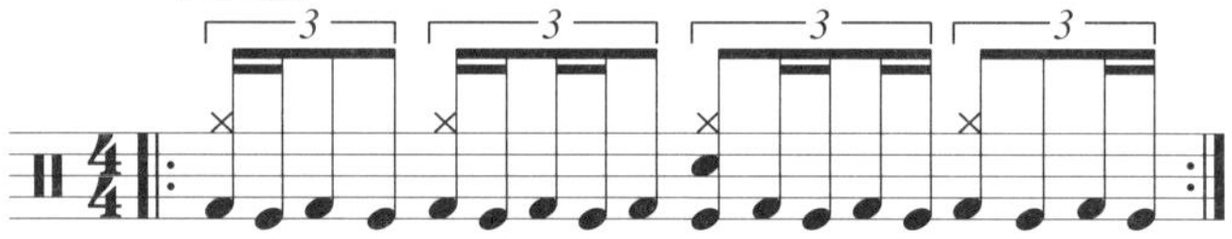

Five-Note Triplet Phrasing: Variation 1

Basic Phrase

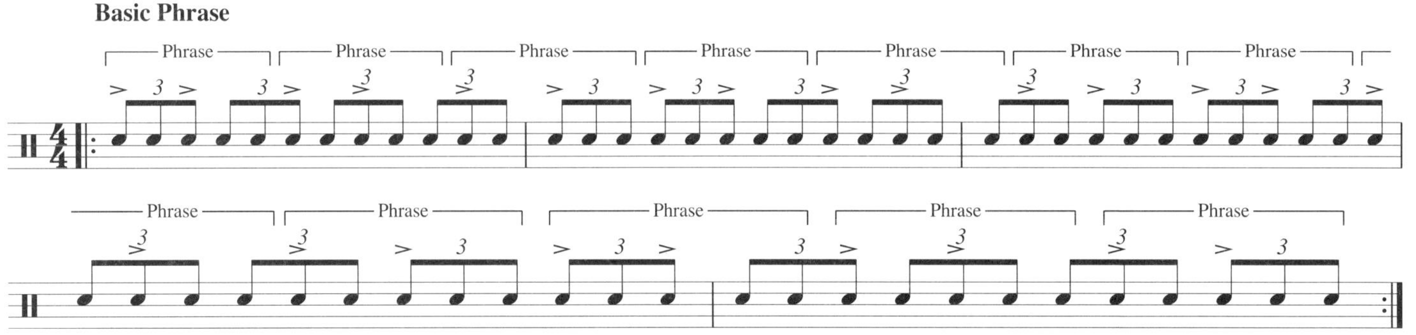

Accent Pattern
Layered Accent Pattern (snare accent only)
Ride Application
Track 111
Ride Application with Snare on 2 and 4
Implied Metric Modulation

Implied Metric Modulation: Four-Bar Application 1

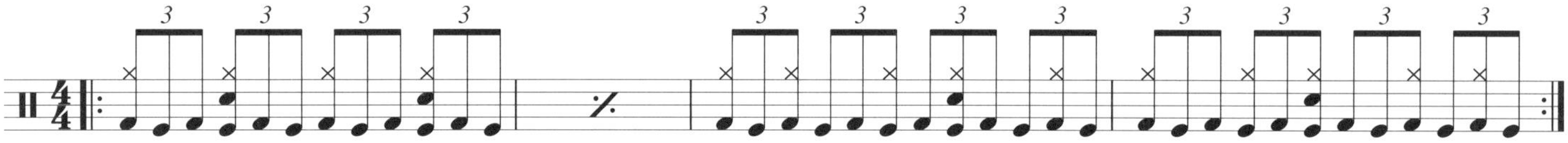

Implied Metric Modulation: Four-Bar Application 2

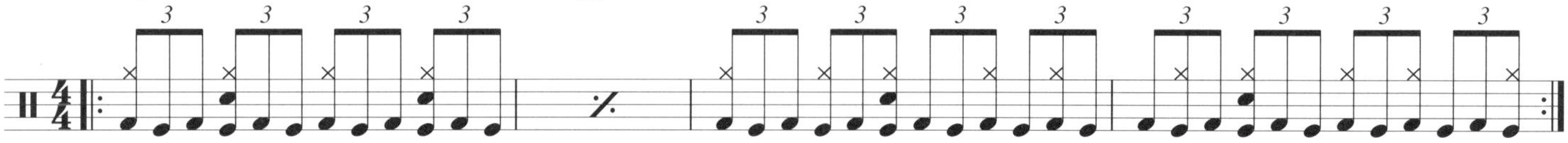

Implied Metric Modulation: Four-Bar Application 3

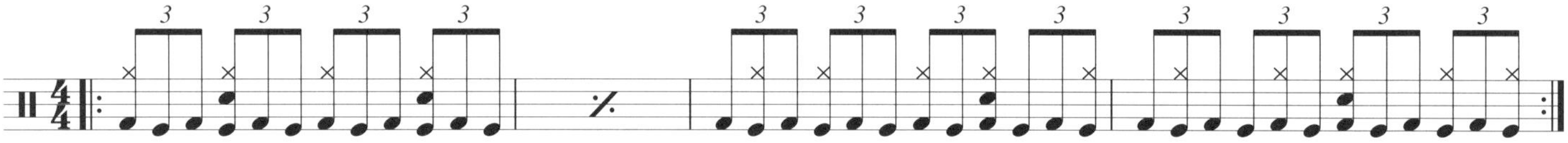

Implied Metric Modulation: Four-Bar Application 4

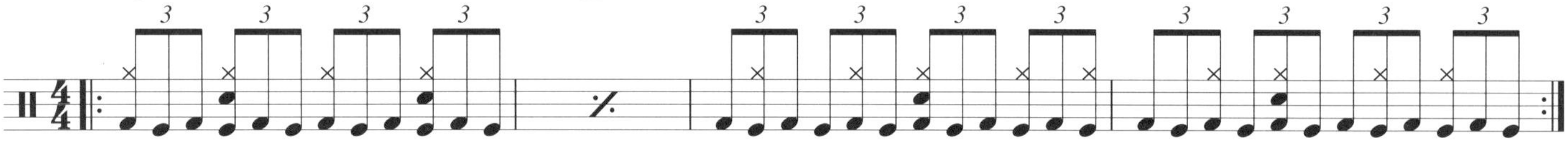

Track 112

Implied Metric Modulation: Four-Bar Application 5

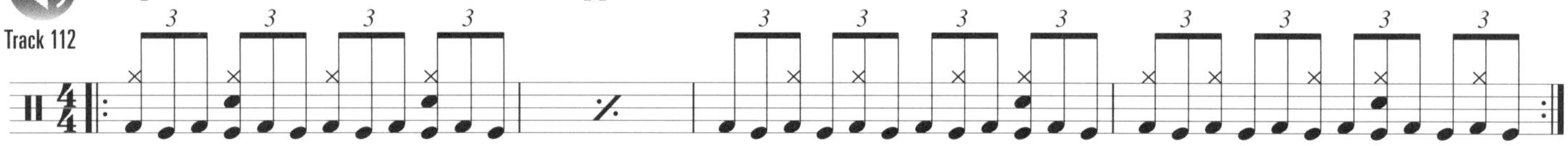

Five-Note-Triplet Phrasing Variation 2

Basic Phrase

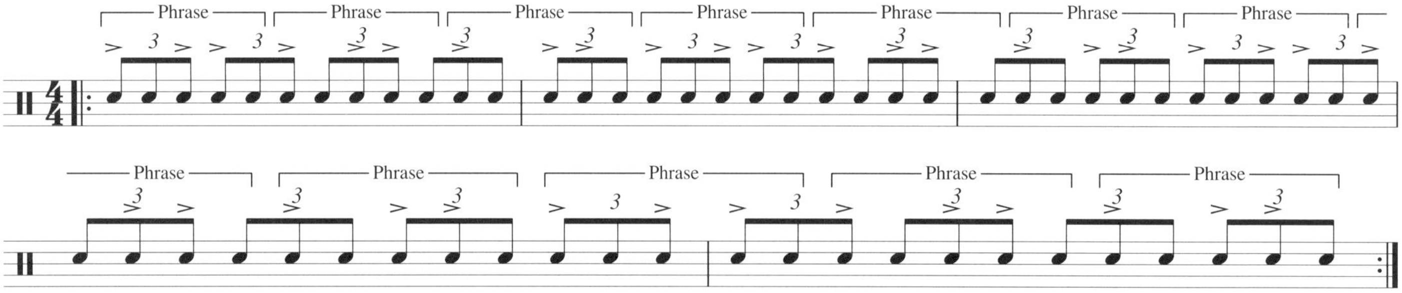

Accent Pattern

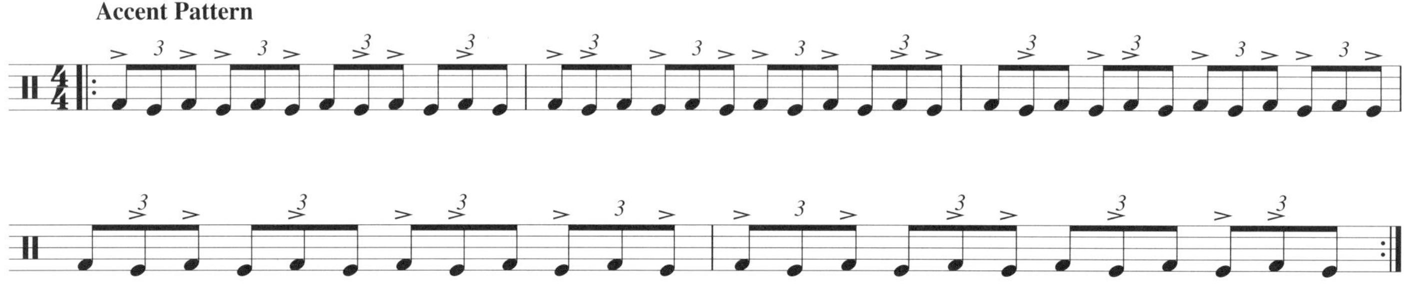

Layered Accent Pattern (snare accent only)
Ride Application
Ride Application with Snare on 2 and 4
Track 113
Implied Metric Modulation
Implied Metric Modulation: Four-Bar Application 1

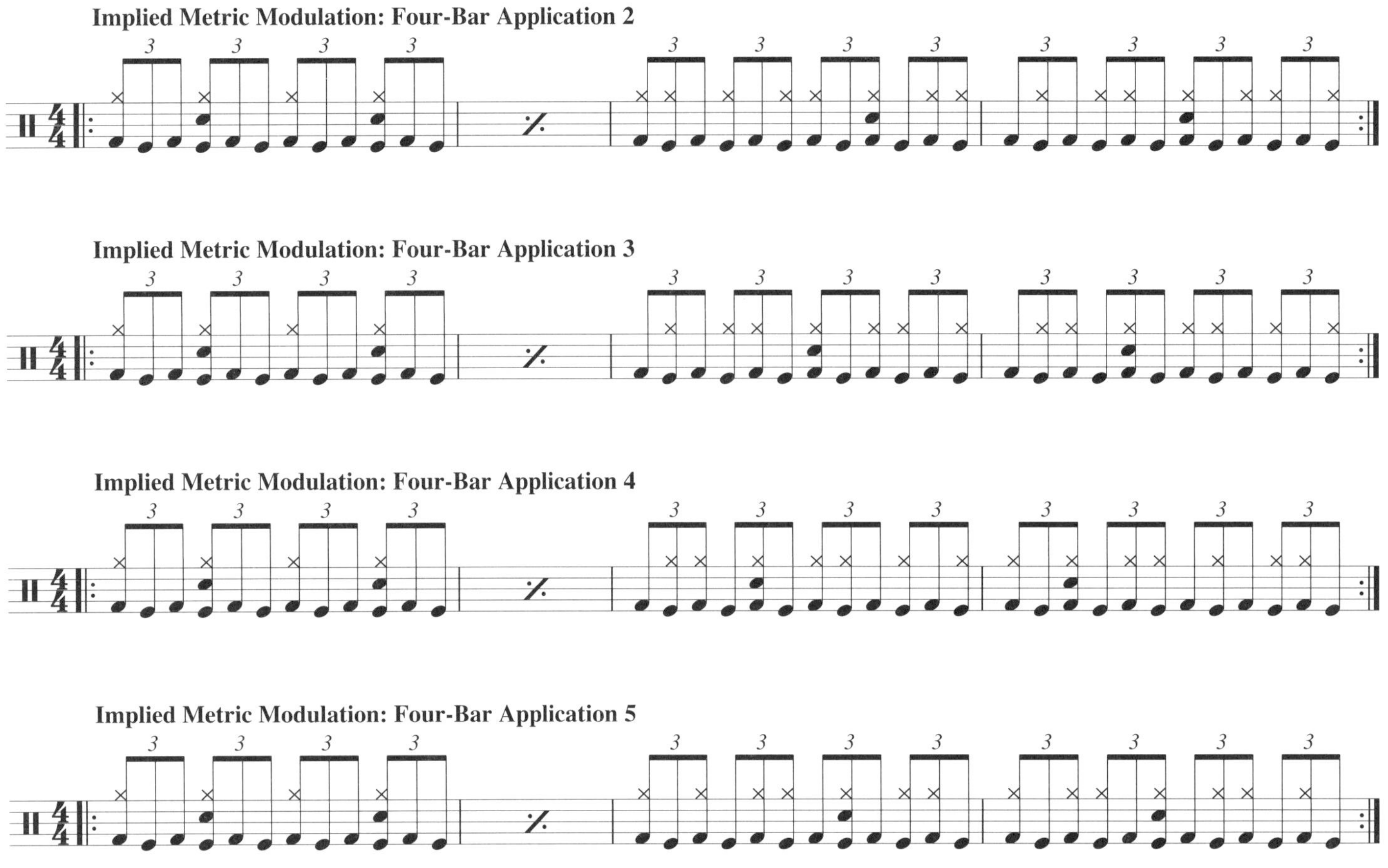

Five-Note-Triplet Phrasing Groove Applications

1C Snare on Fill in
2A Snare on 2 and 4
2B Snare on 3
2C Snare on Fill in
3A Snare on 2 and 4

Track 114
3B Snare on 3
3C Snare on Fill in
4A Snare on 2 and 4
4B Snare on 3
4C Snare on Fill in

Drumistic Discoveries

Use this page to log your original ideas based on the concepts from this chapter.

1

2

3

4

5

6

7

8

10 Phrasing Concepts—Fills

In this chapter we will explore the various fill applications which utilize the same phrasing concepts that where introduced in the previous chapter. Just as applying these techniques to grooves, your fill vocabulary will grow exponentially. My students and I have found a wealth of new fill ideas just by focusing on a couple phrases and exploring the endless orchestrations.

The same phrases that were studied in Chapter 9 will be explored in this chapter: 16th notes grouped as three and five-note phrases as well as 8th-note triplets grouped as four and five-note phrases. Even though some of the phrases contain 32nd notes or 16th-note triplets, the base phrase is built on the 16th-note or 8th-note triplet, respectively. Don't get confused with the smaller note values—the larger note values are the focus of the phrase.

In the following example, both fills are based on a phrase group of three 16th notes:

In the second measure, there are four notes within each bracket. This does not mean it's a four-note phrase. The main phrase is still three 16th notes, even though the third 16th note of each phrase is played as two 32nd notes.

Once again, take your time with these concepts. Intentionally dig into each one and fully absorb what they can offer. In time, you will start to see these ideas naturally surface within your playing, and then you'll know your abilities are growing to new levels! Practice with purpose. Stay focused. Work hard.

Practice Tips:

- Always know where beat 1 is of each bar by counting out loud.
- Never count the groupings. Always count the original note values.
- Use the Drumistic Discoveries to keep track or your original fills.
- Repeat. Rest. Recall.

"The greater danger for most of us lies not in setting our aim too high and falling short; but in setting our aim too low and achieving our mark."

—Michelangelo

Three-Note Phrasing

Basic 16th-Note Phrase

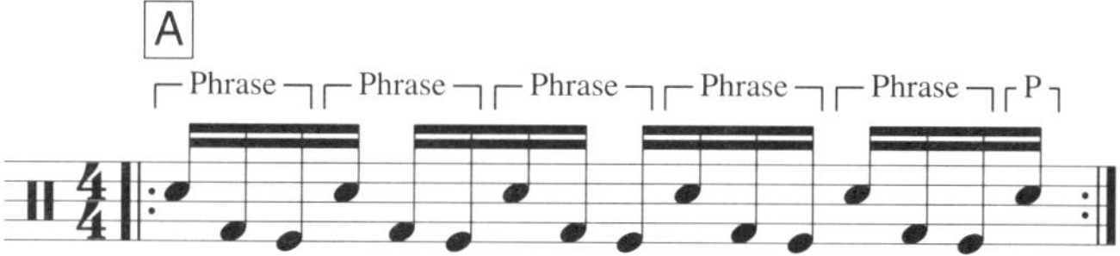

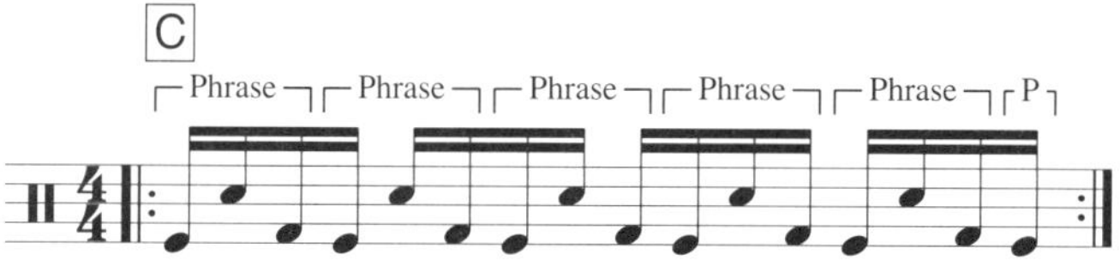

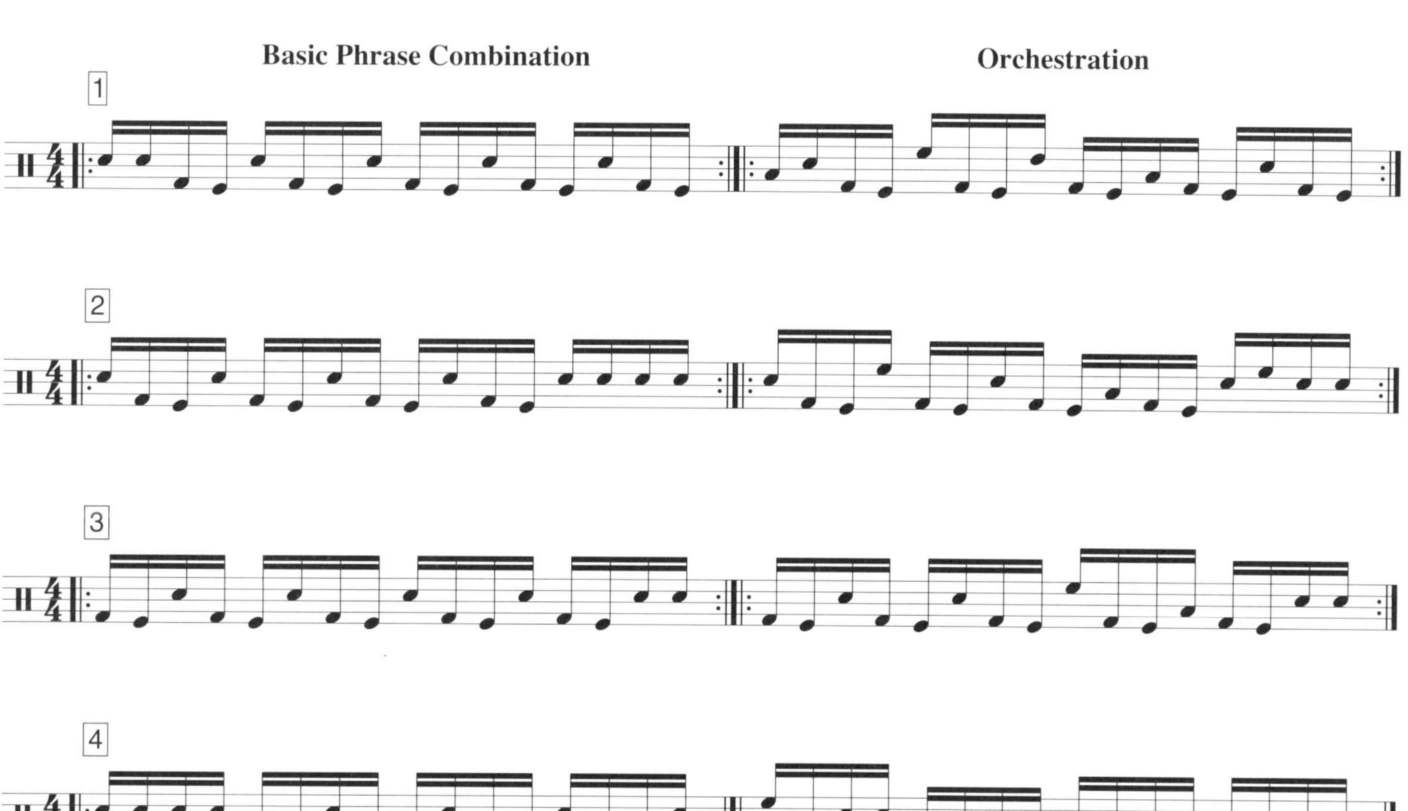

Basic 16th/32nd-Note Phrase: Variation 1

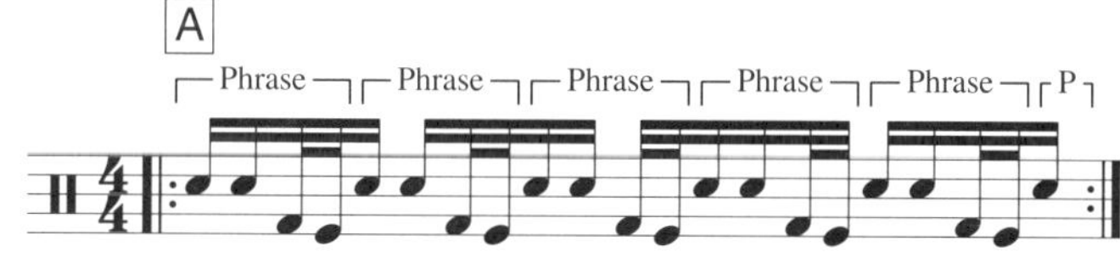

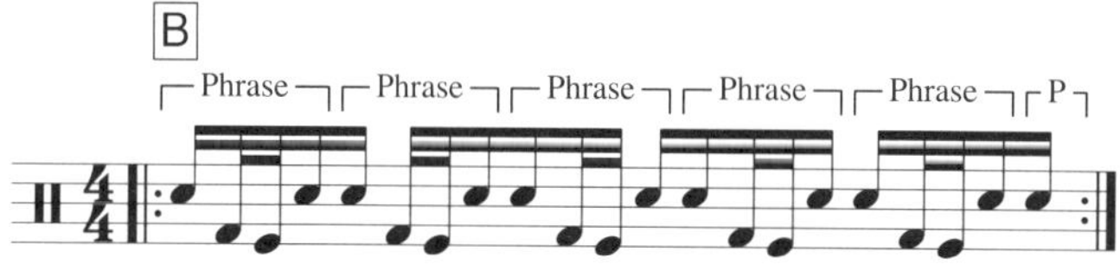

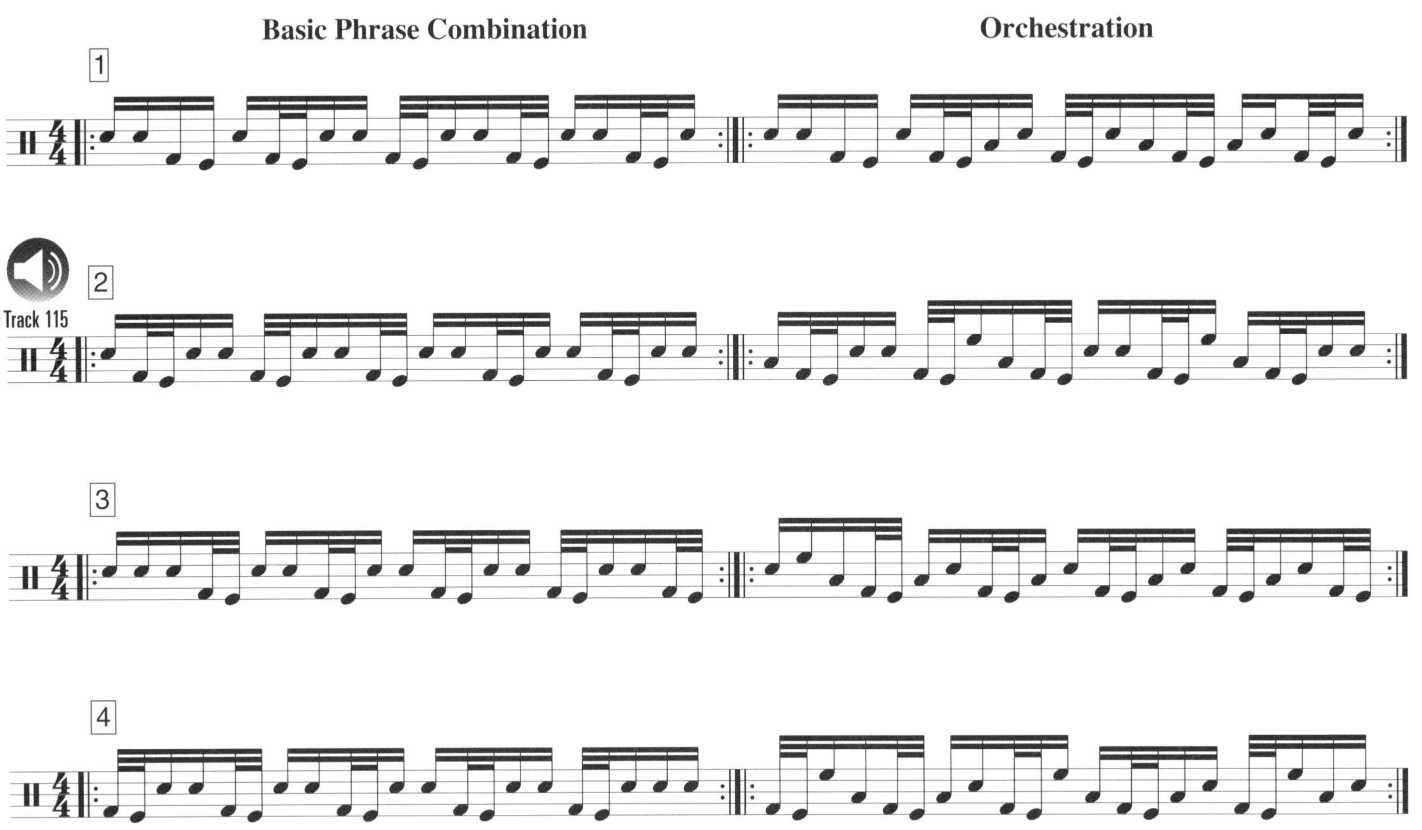

Basic 16th/32nd-Note Phrase: Variation 2

Basic 32nd-Note Phrase

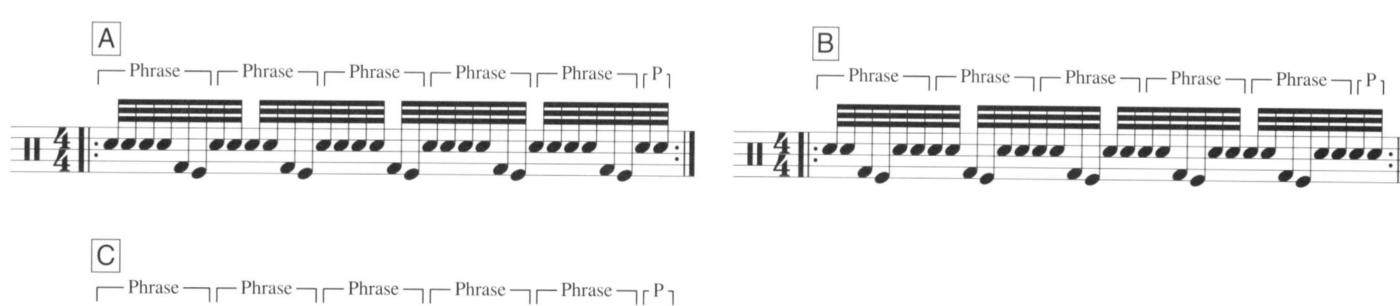

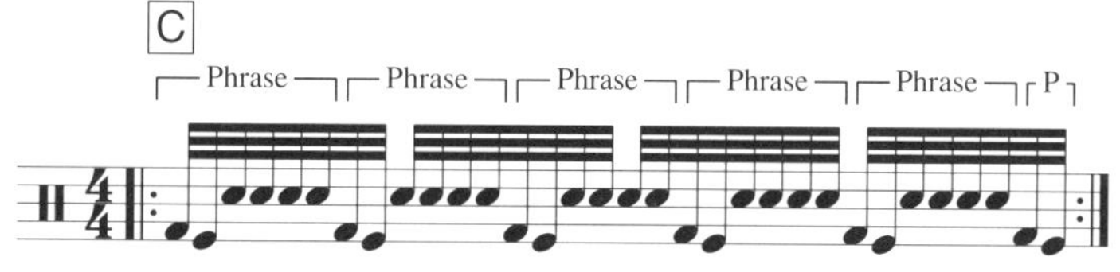

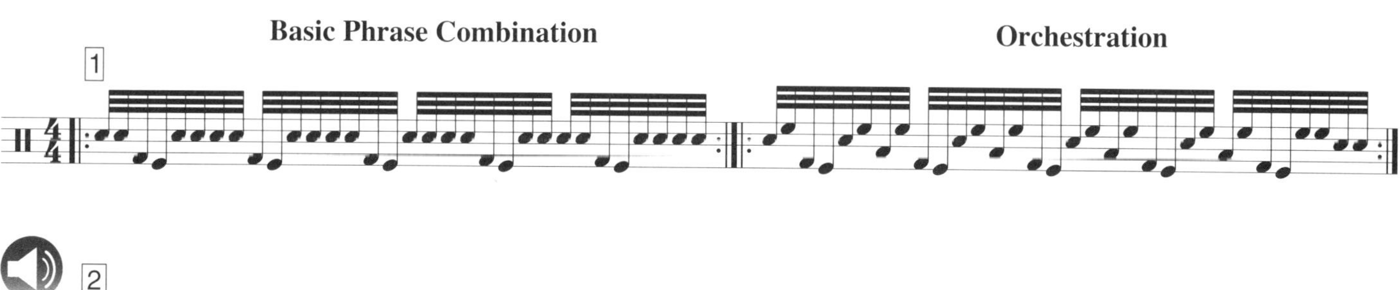

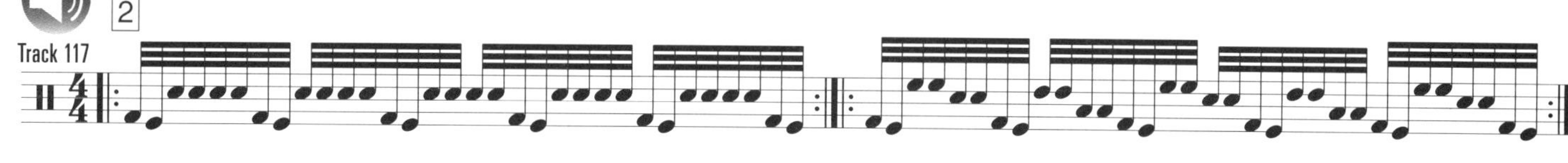

Basic 16th/32nd-Note Phrase with Cymbals

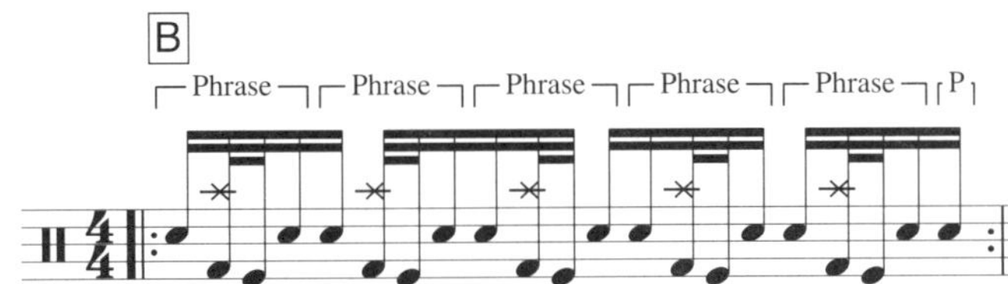

Basic 32nd-Note Phrase with Cymbals

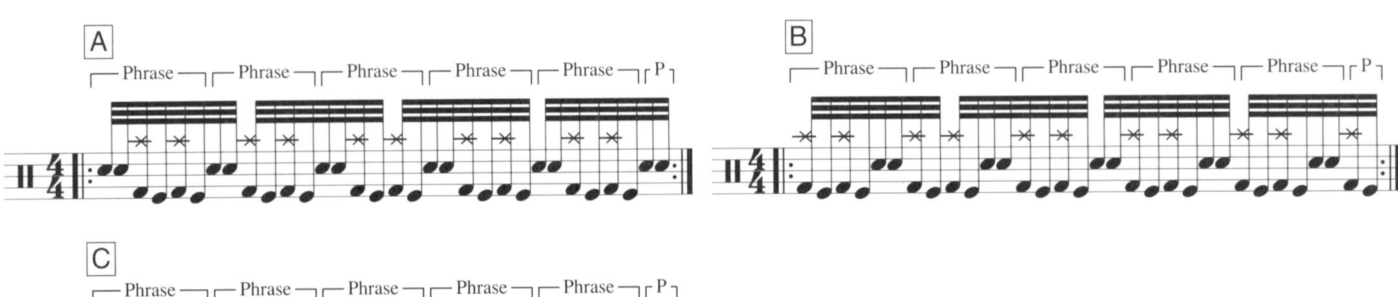

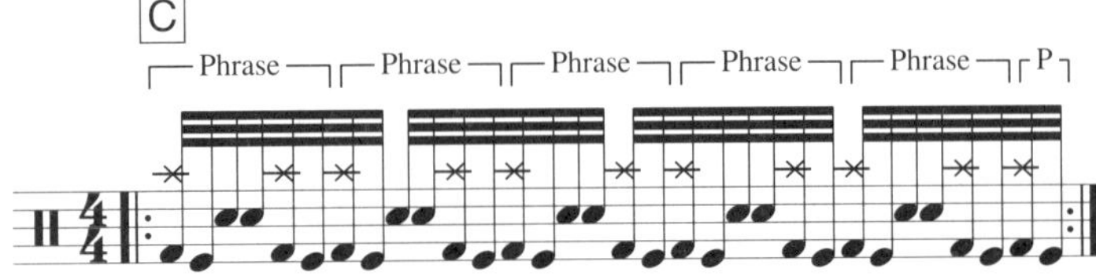

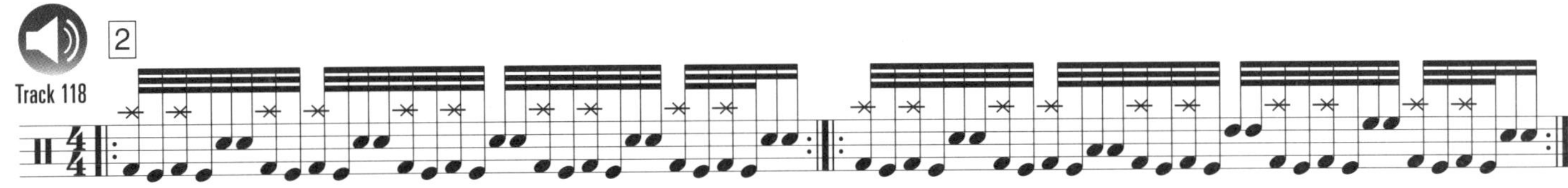

Five-Note Phrasing

Basic 16th-Note Phrase

A

B

C

D

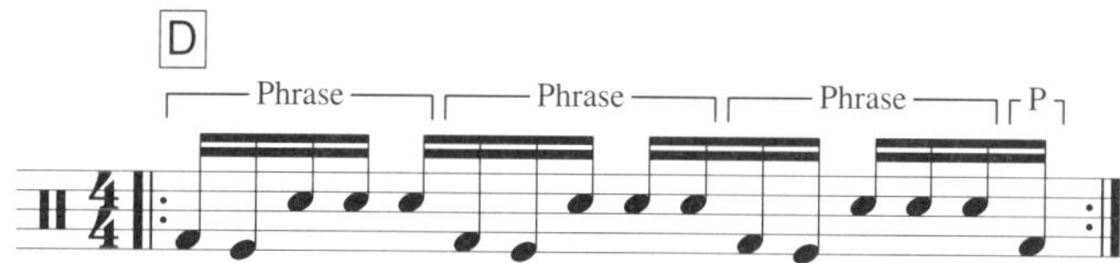

E

Basic Phrase Combination **Orchestration**

1

Track 119

2

3

4

Basic 16th/32nd-Note Phrase: Variation 1

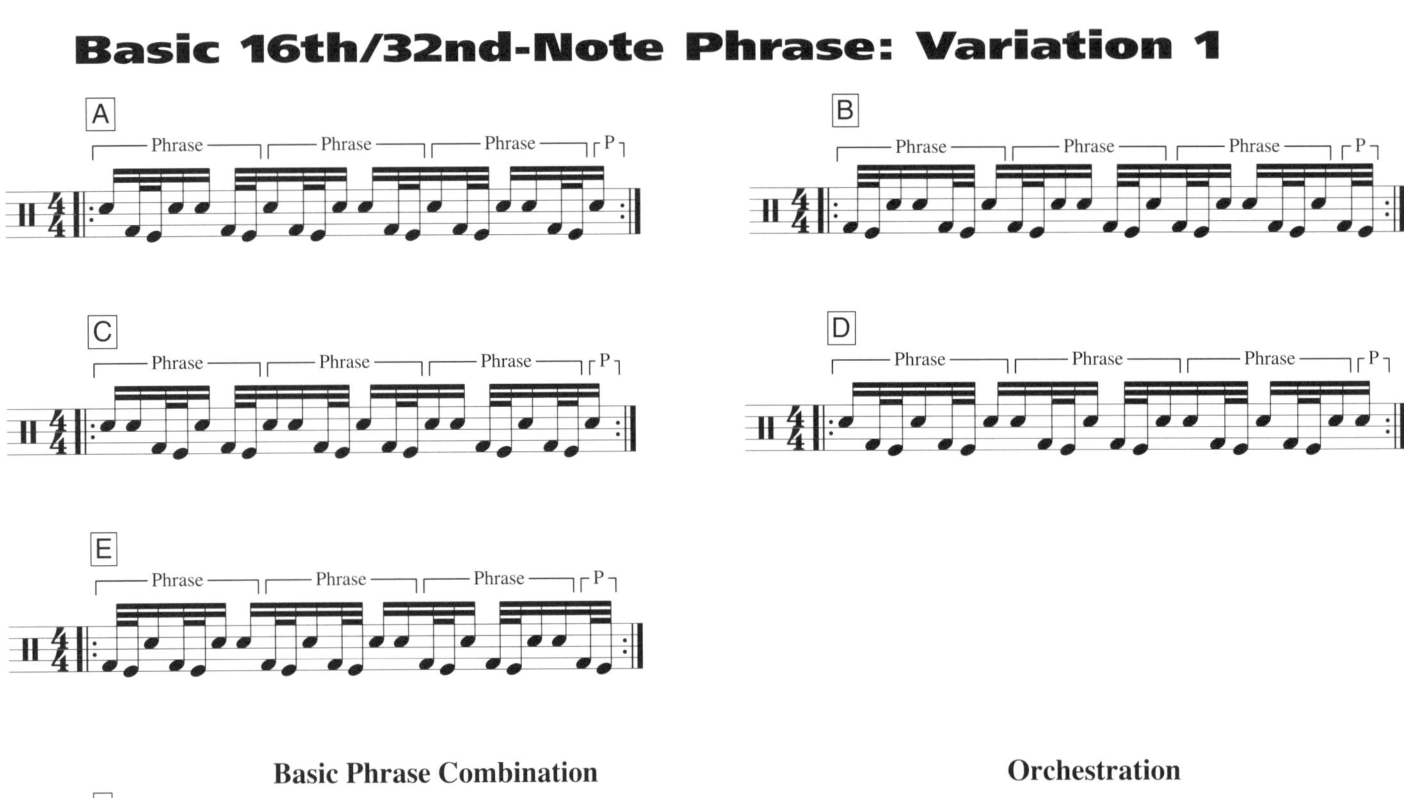

Basic 16th/32nd-Note Phrase: Variation 2

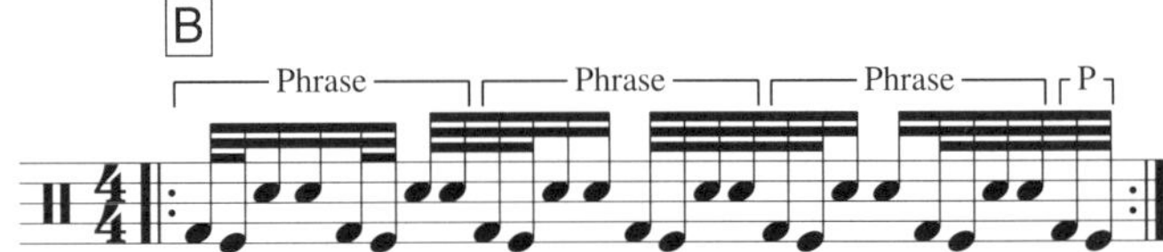

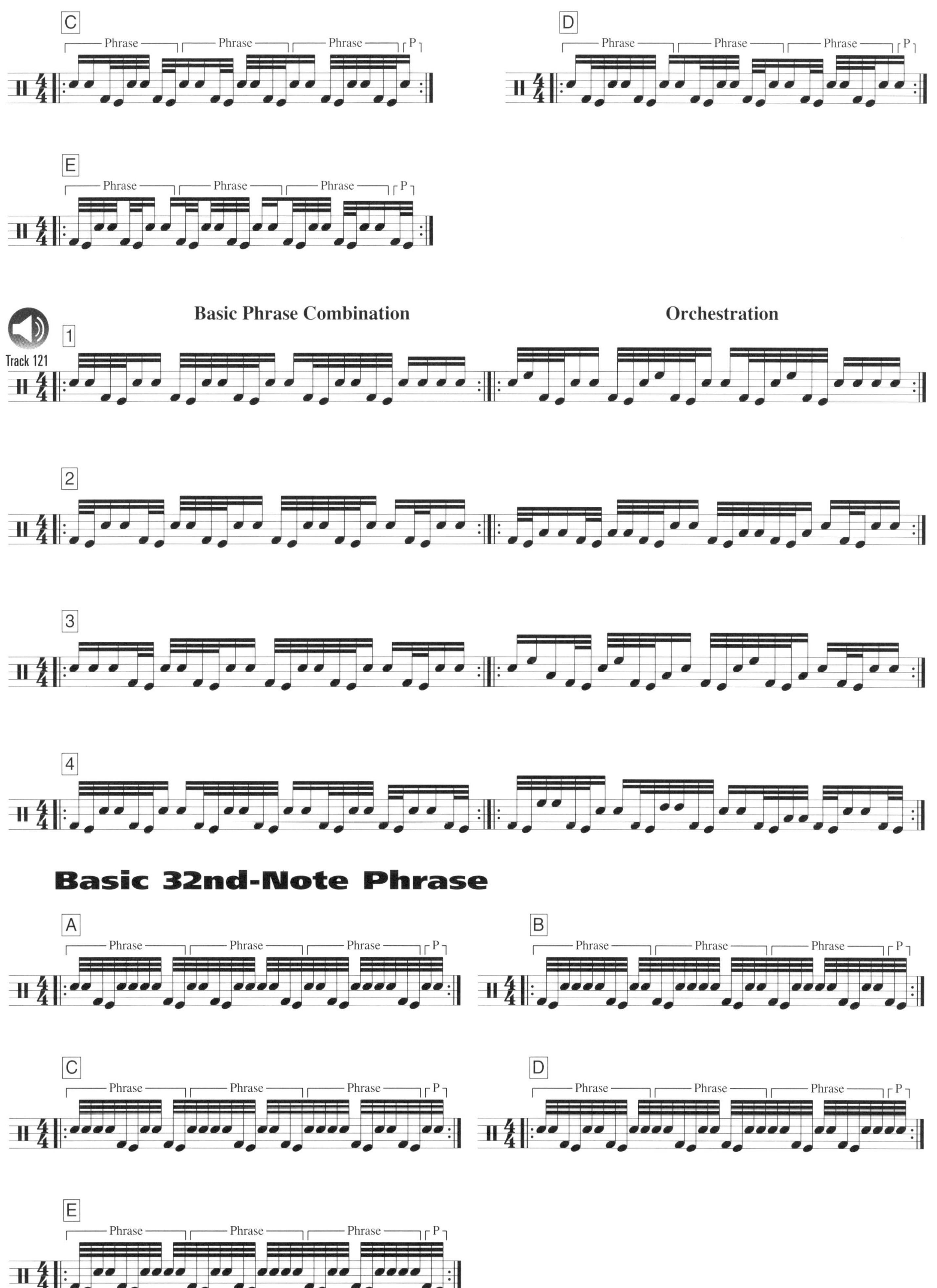
C
Phrase
Phrase
Phrase
P
D
Phrase
Phrase
Phrase
P
E
Phrase
Phrase
Phrase
P
Basic Phrase Combination
Orchestration
1
Track 121
2
3
4
Basic 32nd-Note Phrase
A
Phrase
Phrase
Phrase
P
B
Phrase
Phrase
Phrase
P
C
Phrase
Phrase
Phrase
P
D
Phrase
Phrase
Phrase
P
E
Phrase
Phrase
Phrase
P

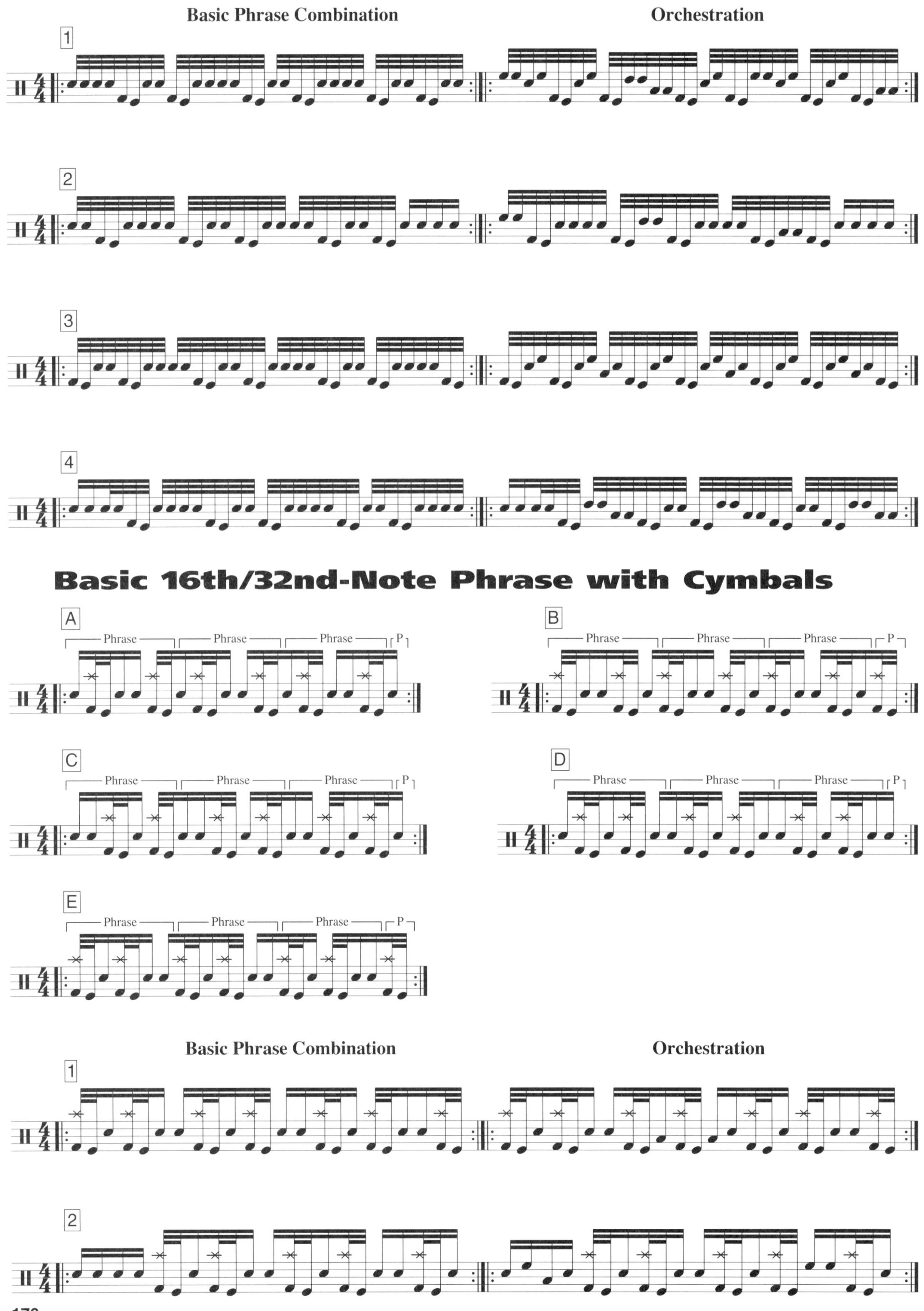

Basic Phrase Combination
Orchestration
1
2
3
4
Basic 16th/32nd-Note Phrase with Cymbals
A
Phrase
Phrase
Phrase
P
B
Phrase
Phrase
Phrase
P
C
Phrase
Phrase
Phrase
P
D
Phrase
Phrase
Phrase
P
E
Phrase
Phrase
Phrase
P
Basic Phrase Combination
Orchestration
1
2

Basic 32nd-Note Phrase with Cymbals

A

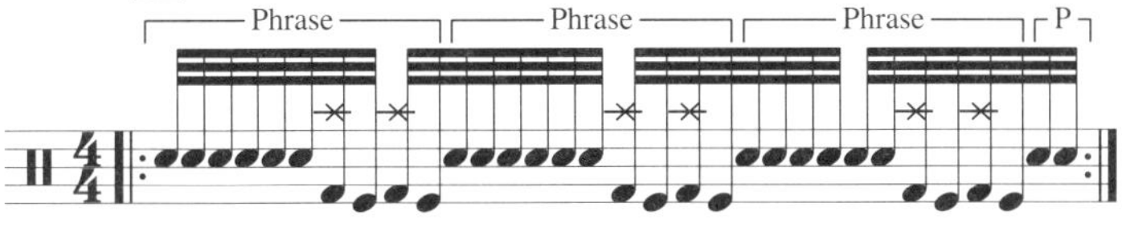

Phrase — Phrase — Phrase — P

B

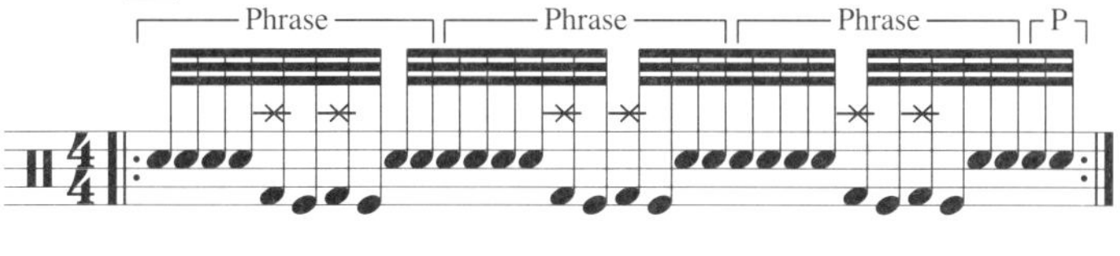

Phrase — Phrase — Phrase — P

C

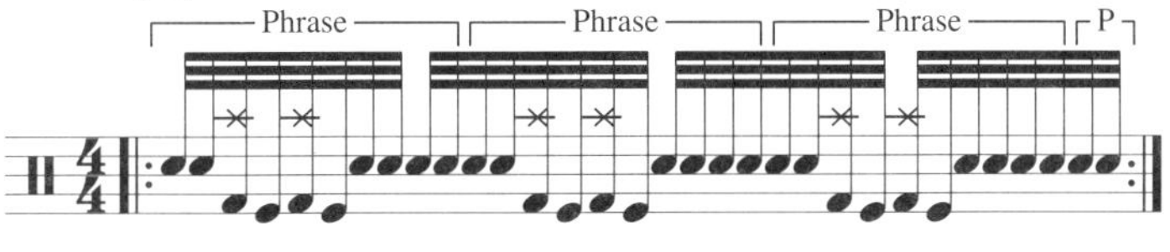

Phrase — Phrase — Phrase — P

D

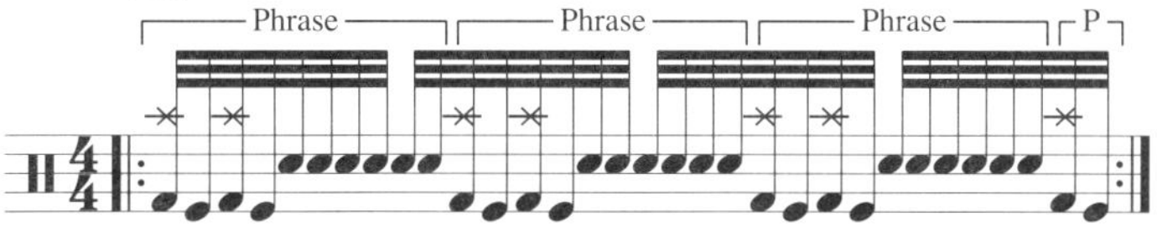

Phrase — Phrase — Phrase — P

E

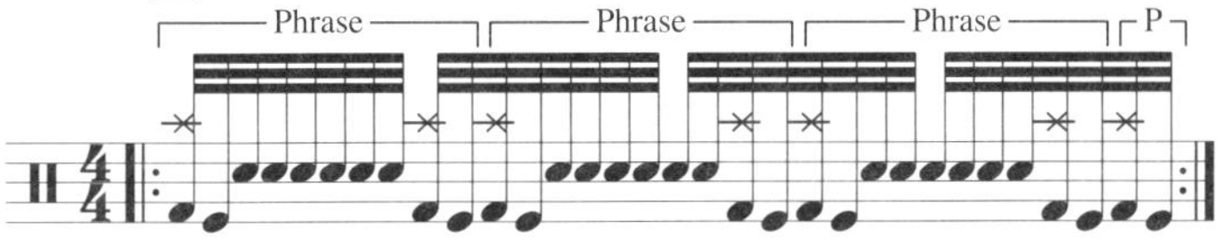

Phrase — Phrase — Phrase — P

Basic Phrase Combination **Orchestration**

Track 122

1

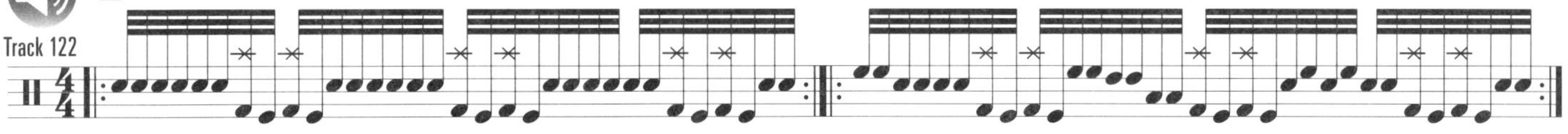

2

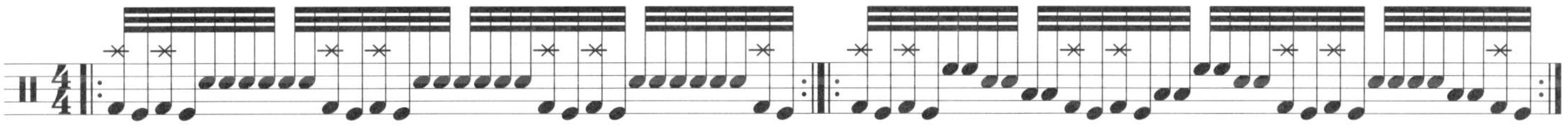

Three and Five-Note Phrasing Combinations

Basic 16th-Note Phrase

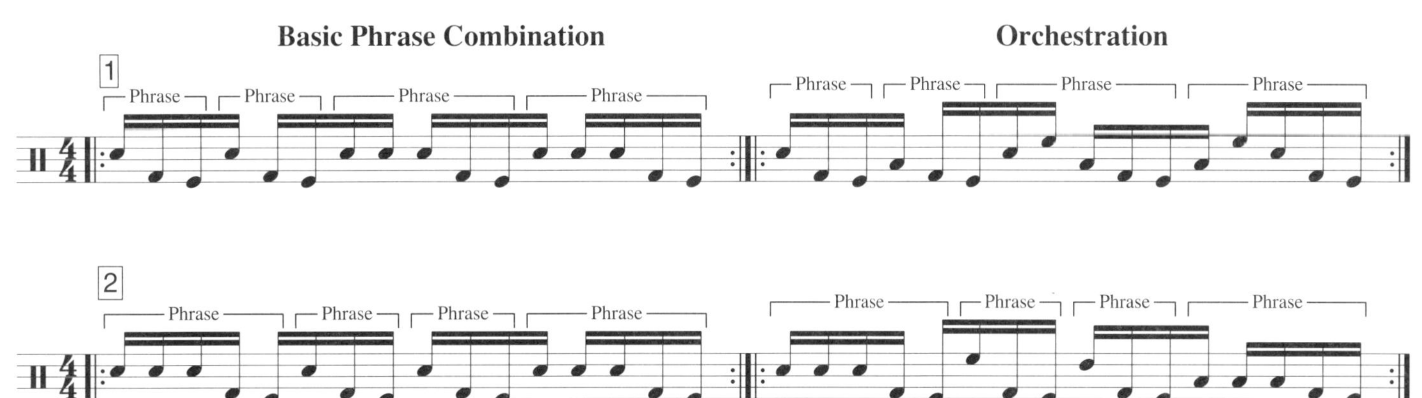

Basic 16th/32nd-Note Phrase: Variation 1

Basic Phrase Combination | Orchestration

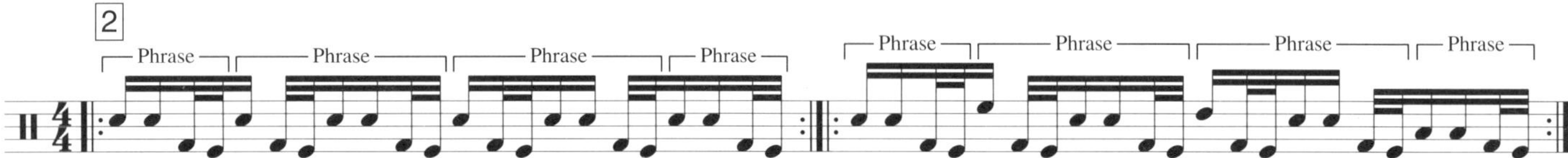

Basic 16th/32nd-Note Phrase: Variation 2

Basic Phrase Combination | Orchestration

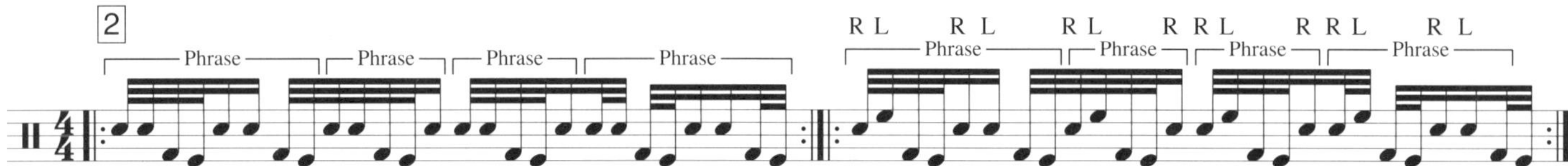

Basic 32nd-Note Phrase

Basic Phrase Combination | Orchestration

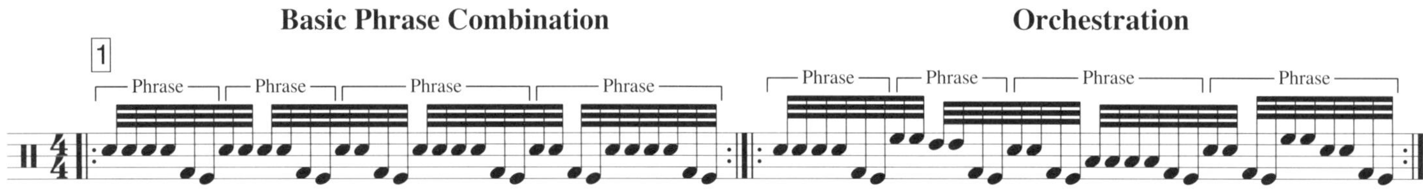

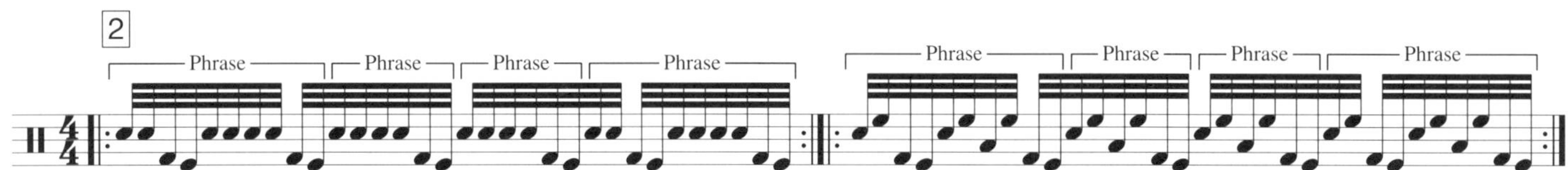

Basic 16th/32nd-Note Phrase with Cymbals

Basic Phrase Combination | Orchestration

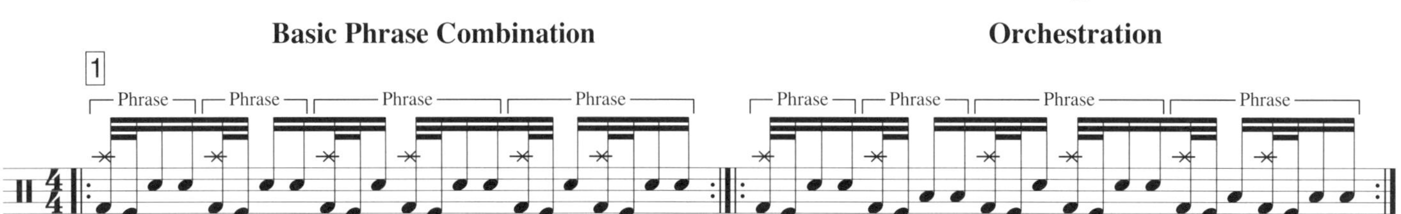

2

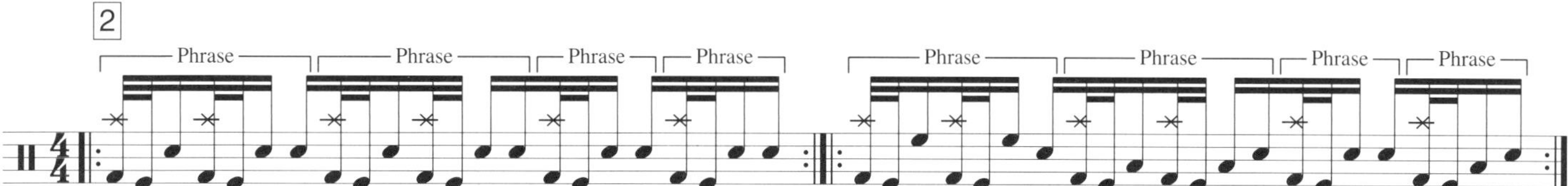

Basic 32nd-Note Phrase with Cymbals

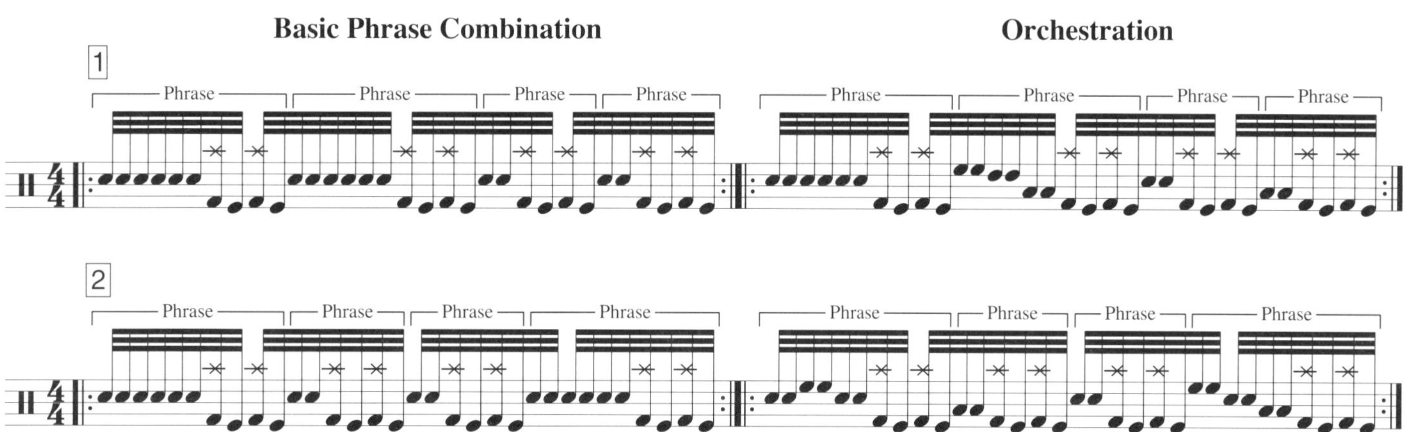

Four-Note Triplet Phrasing

Basic 8th-Note-Triplet Phrase

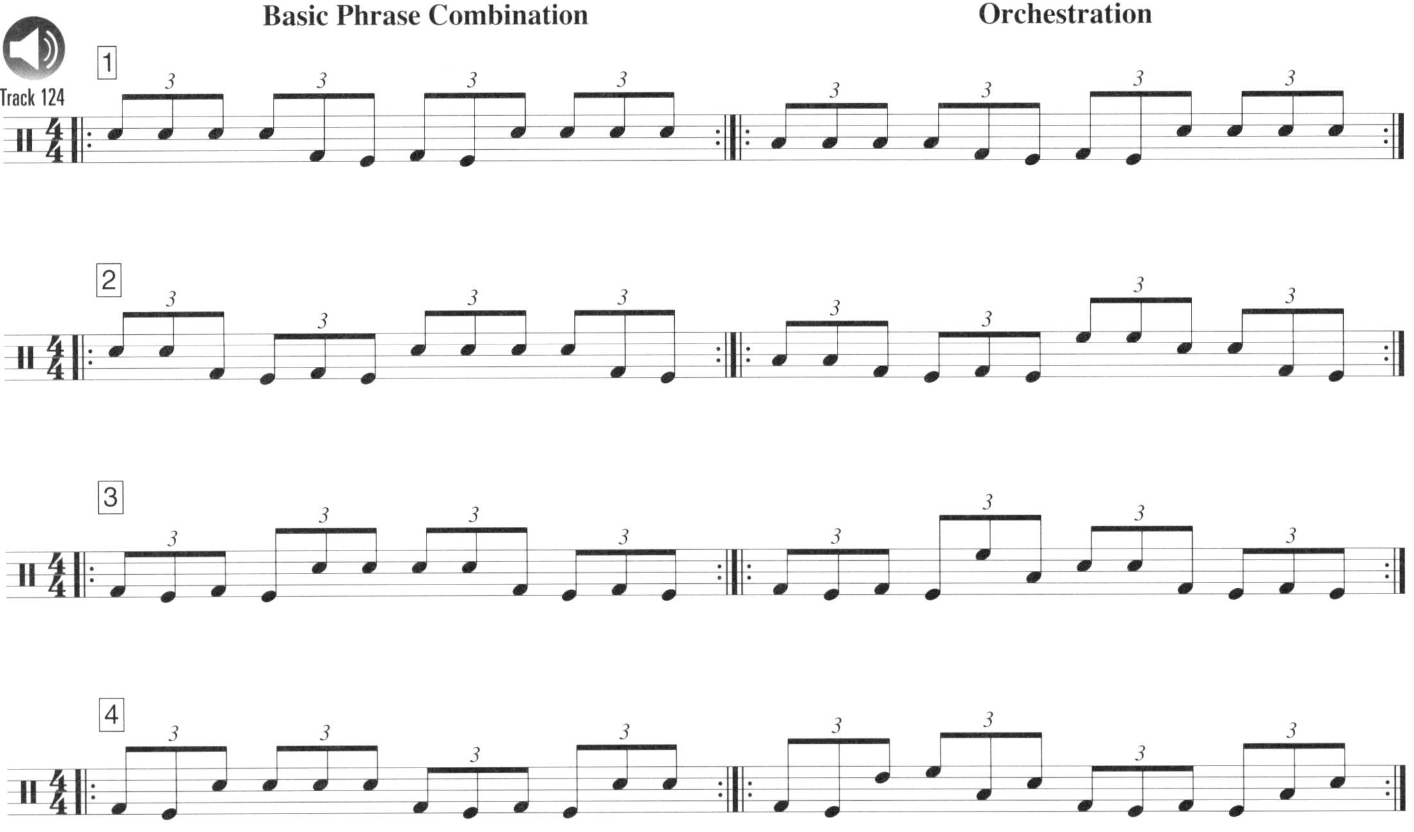

Basic 8th/16-Note-Triplet Phrase: Variation 1

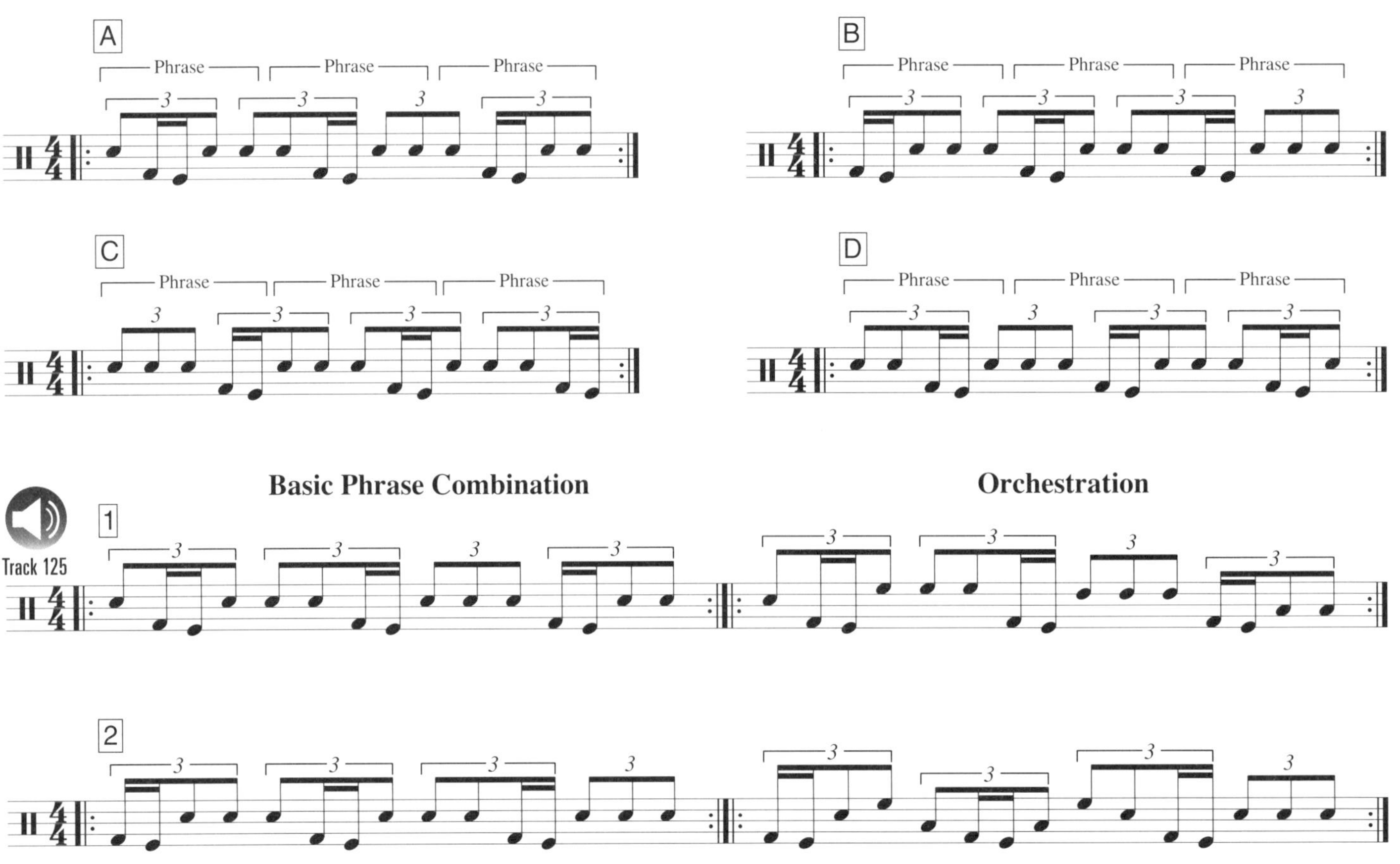

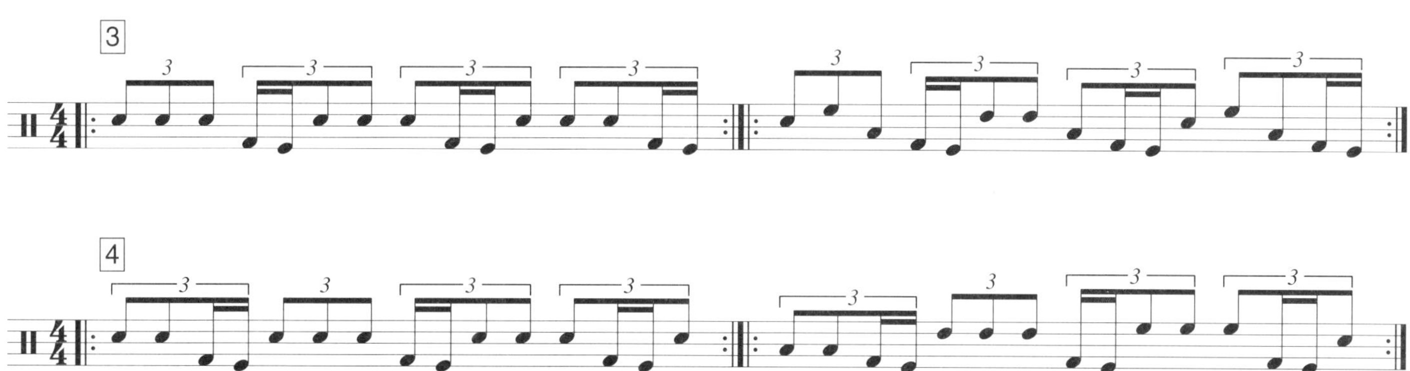

Basic 8th/16-Note-Triplet Phrase: Variation 2

A

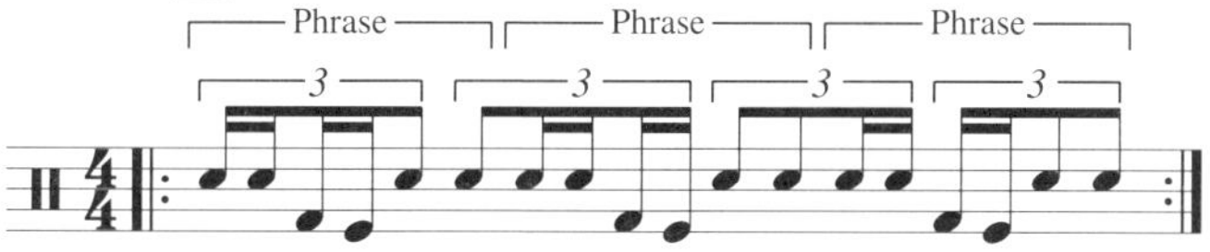

Phrase Phrase Phrase

B

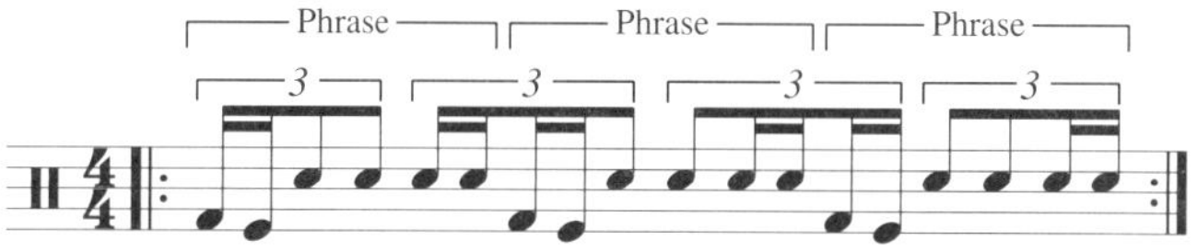

Phrase Phrase Phrase

C

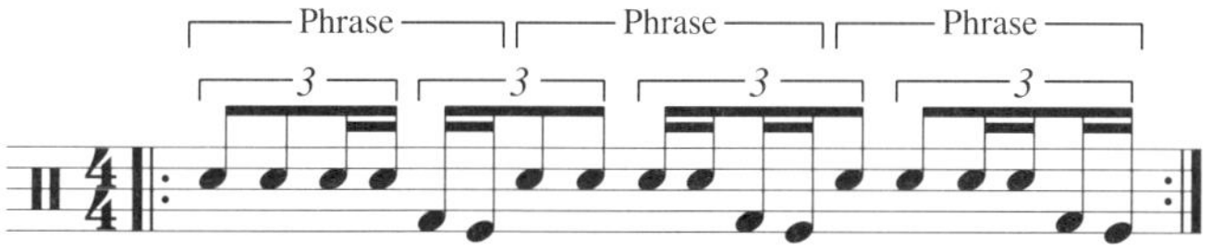

Phrase Phrase Phrase

D

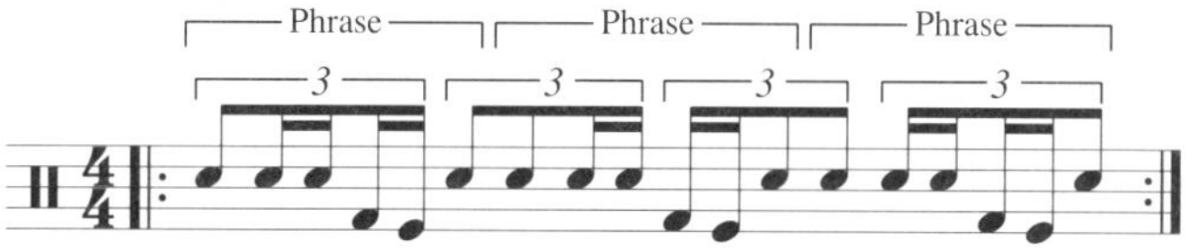

Phrase Phrase Phrase

Basic Phrase Combination **Orchestration**

1

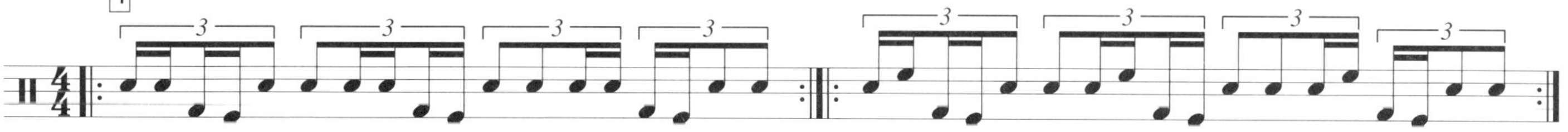

Track 126

2

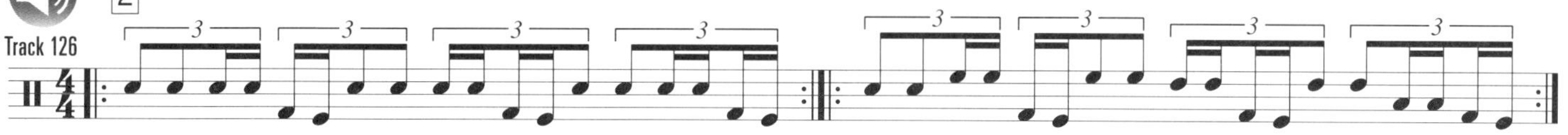

3

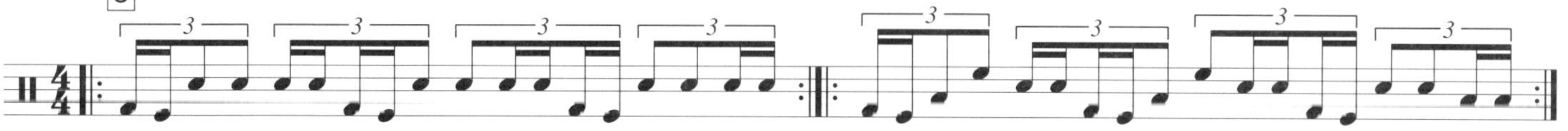

4

Basic Sextuplet Phrase

A

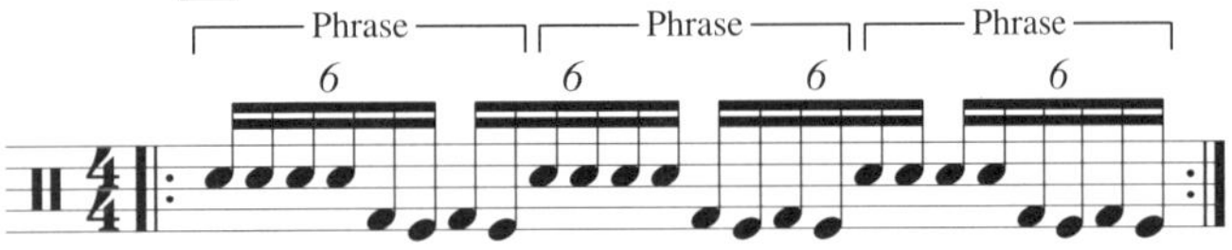

Phrase Phrase Phrase

B

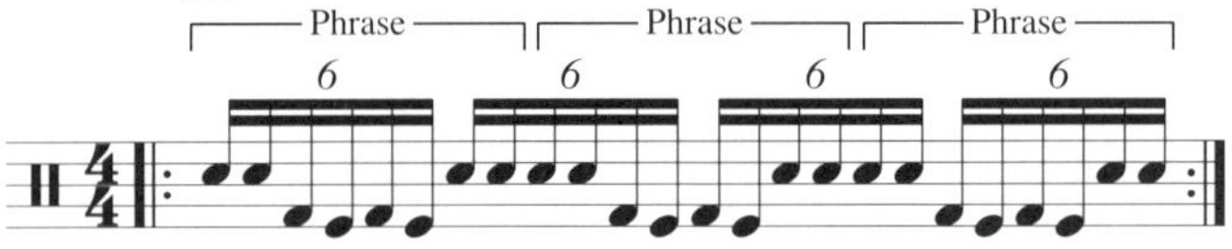

Phrase Phrase Phrase

C

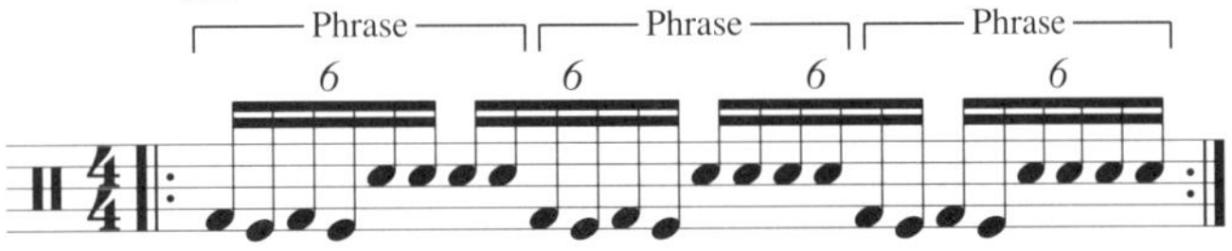

Phrase Phrase Phrase

D

Phrase Phrase Phrase

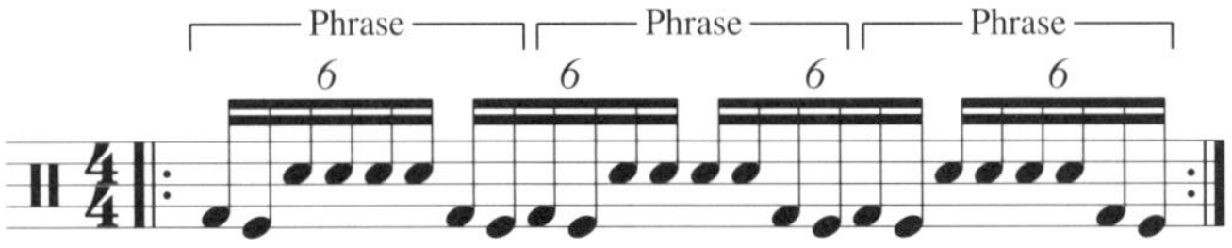

Basic Phrase Combination **Orchestration**

1

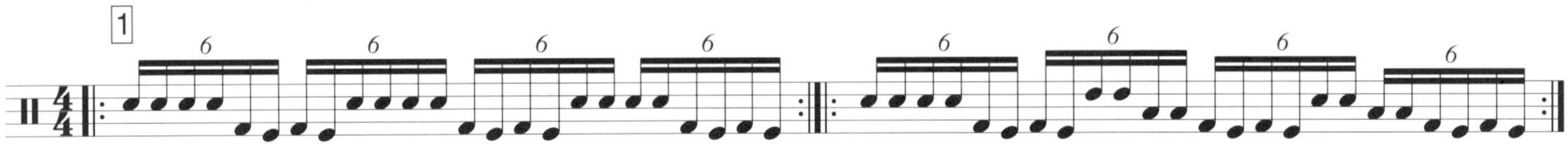

2

3

Track 127

4

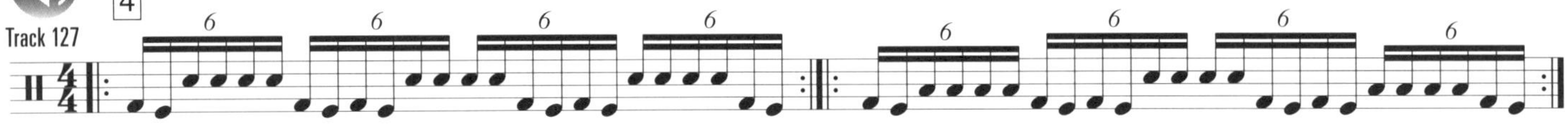

Basic 8th/16-Note-Triplet Phrase with Cymbals

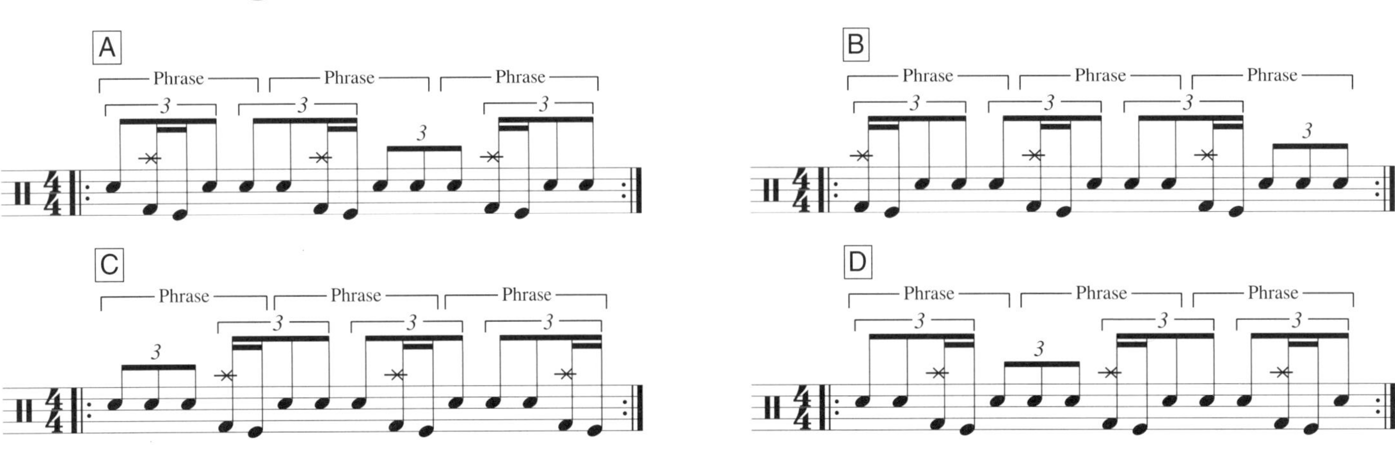

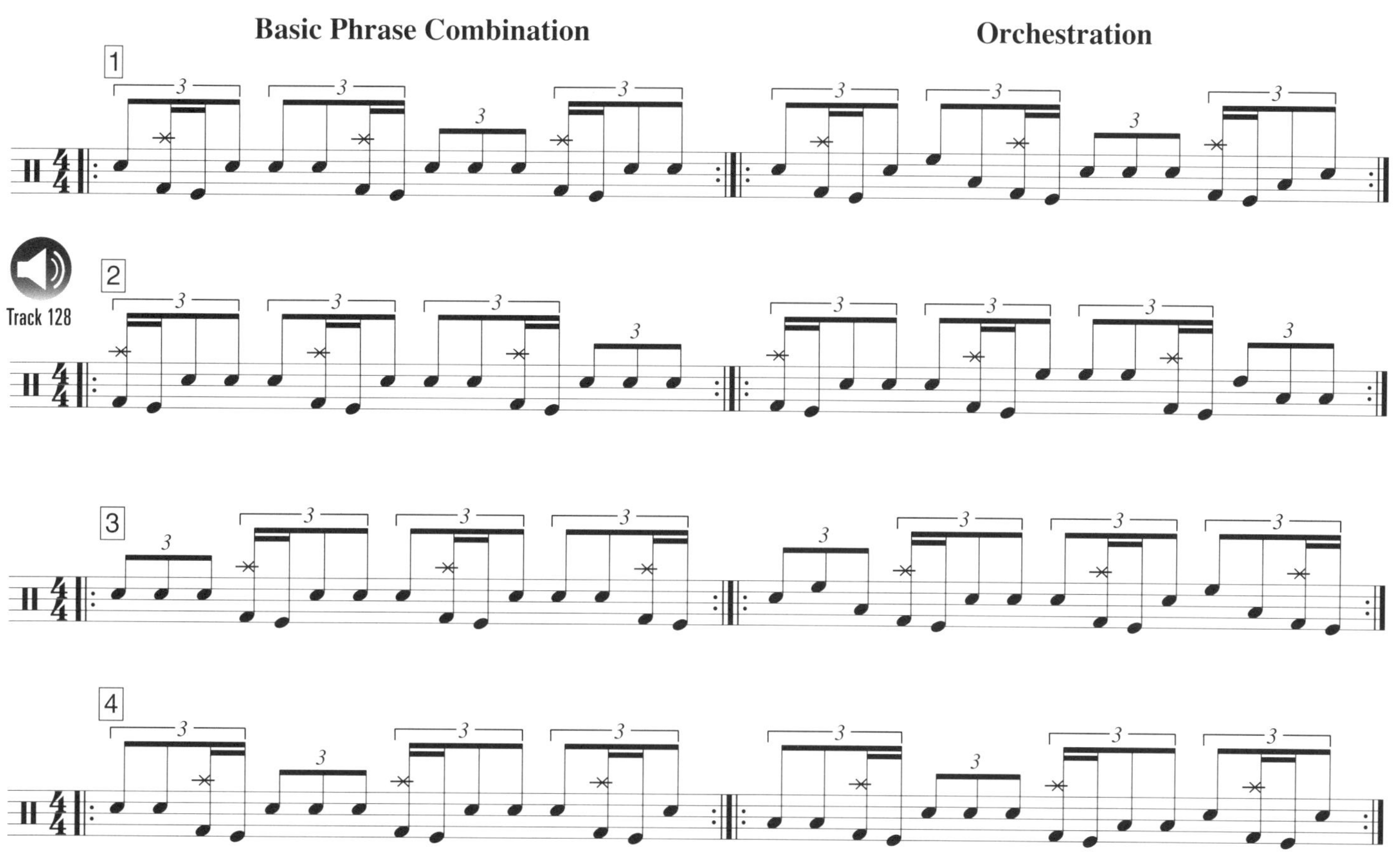

Five-Note Triplet Phrasing

Basic 8th-Note-Triplet Phrase

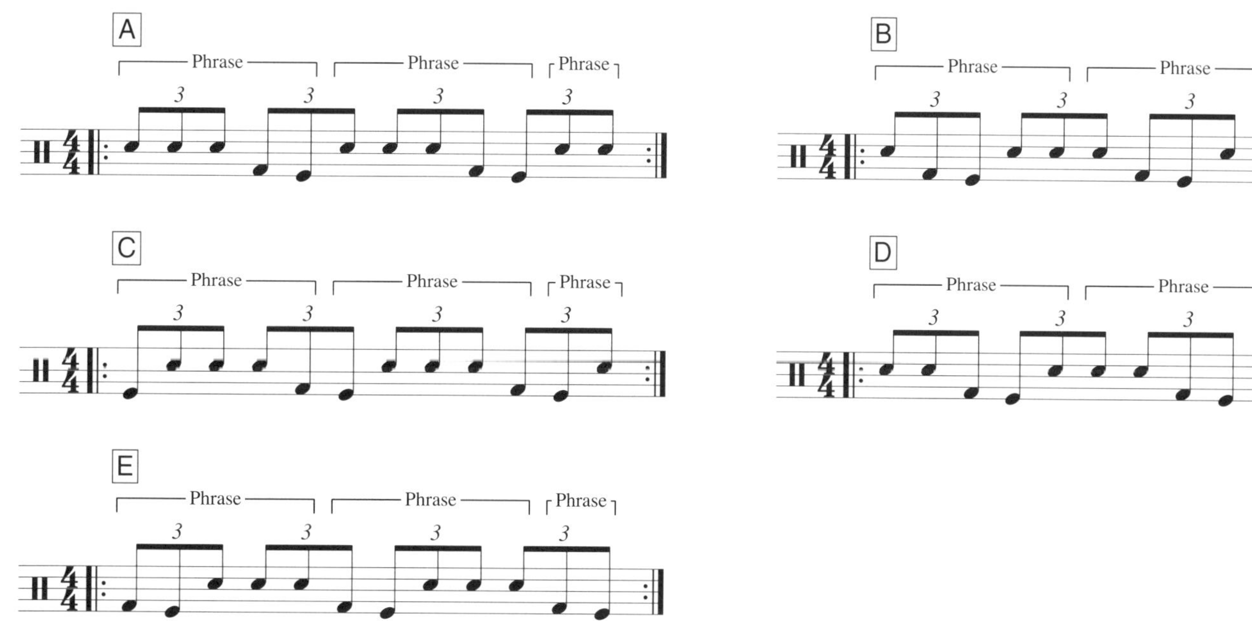

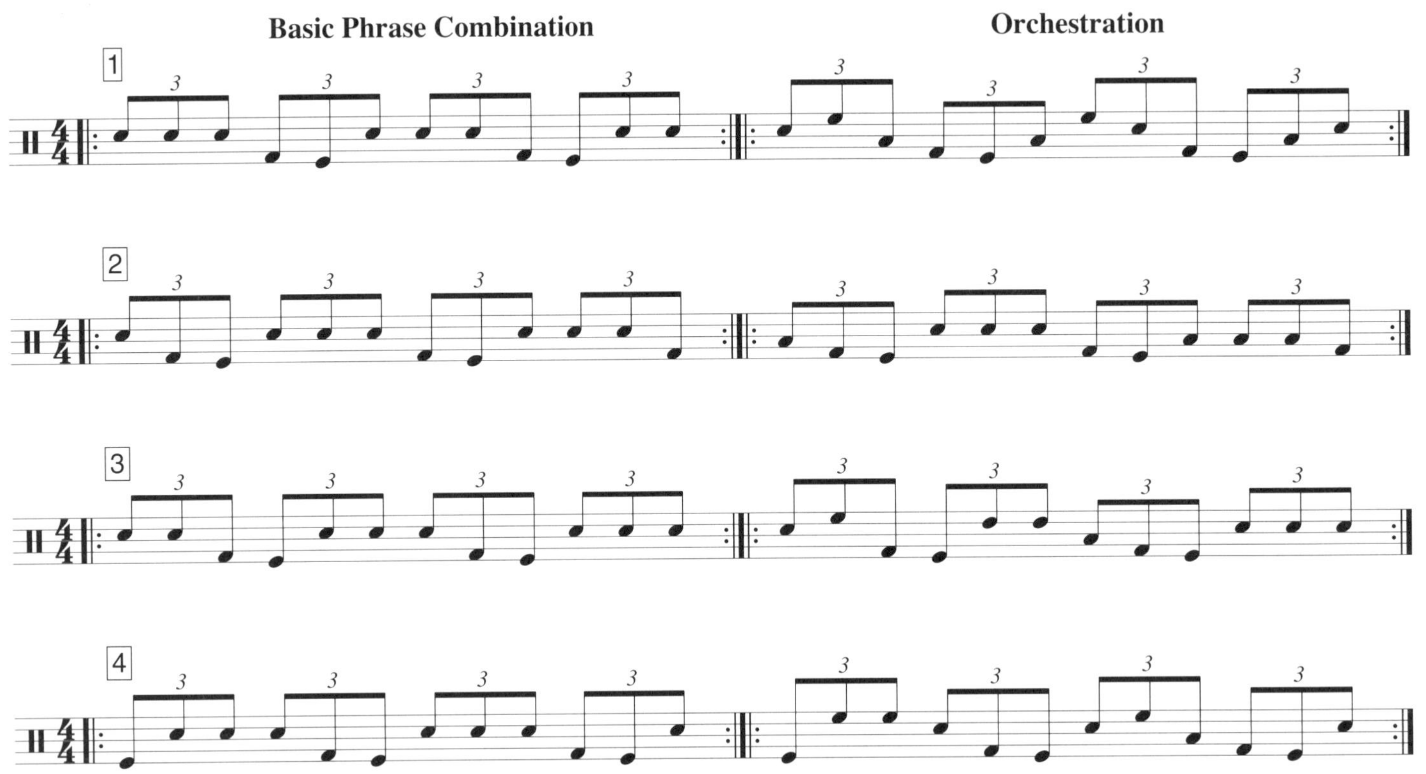

Basic 8th/16th-Note-Triplet Phrase

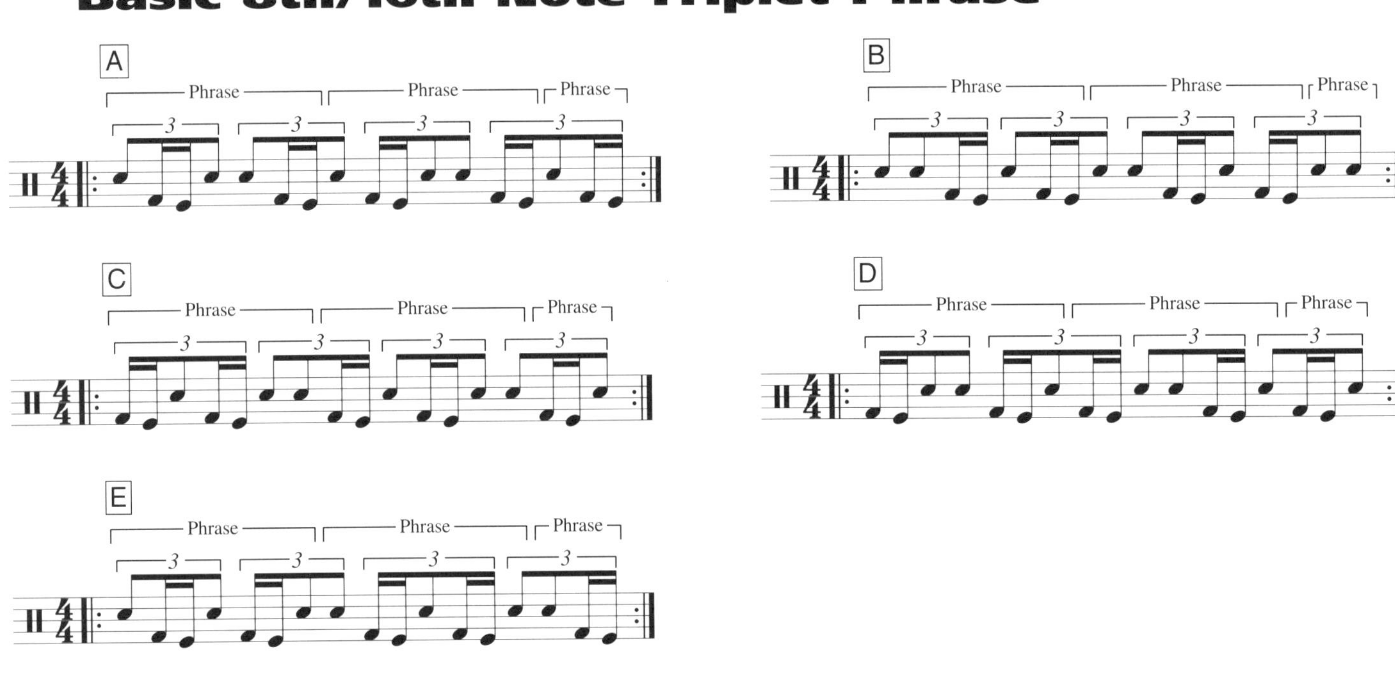

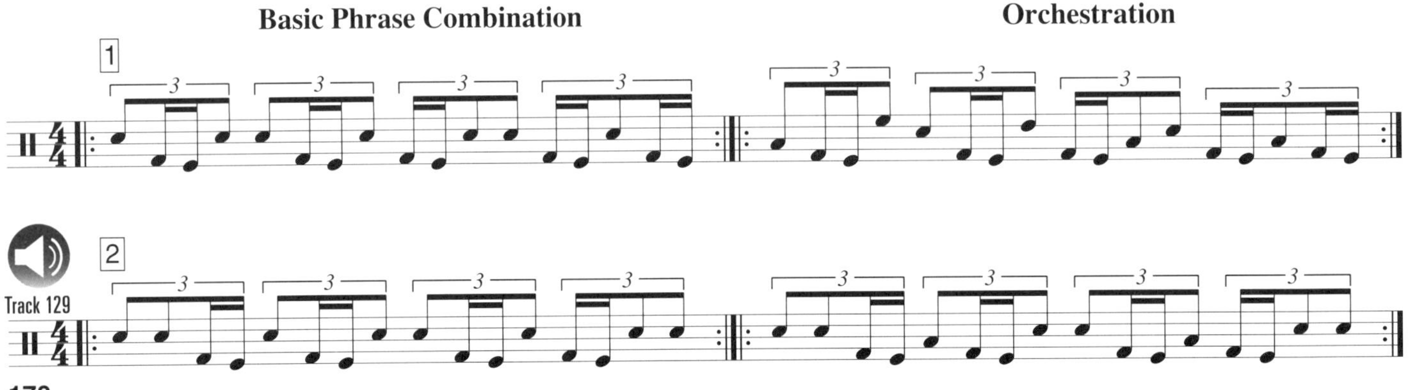

Basic 8th/16th-Note-Triplet and Sextuplet Phrase

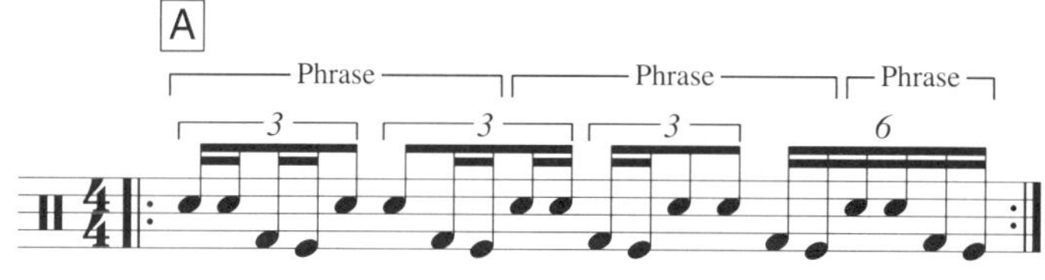

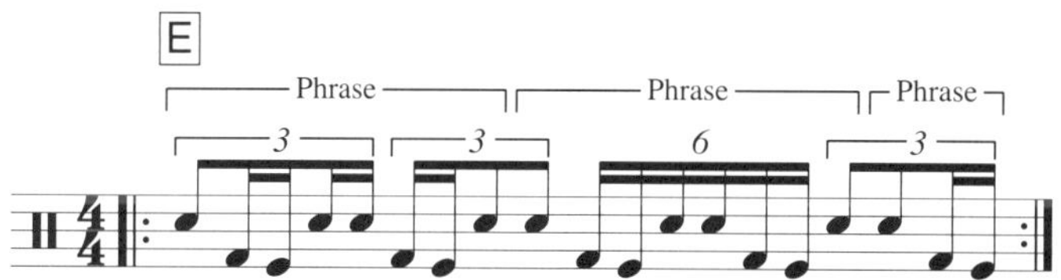

Basic Phrase Combination **Orchestration**

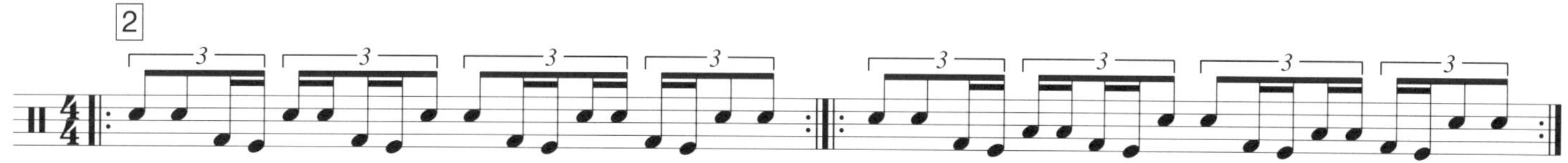

Basic Sextuplet Phrase

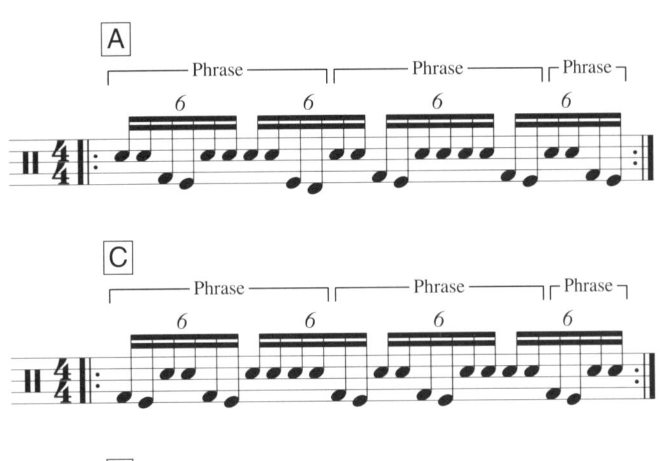

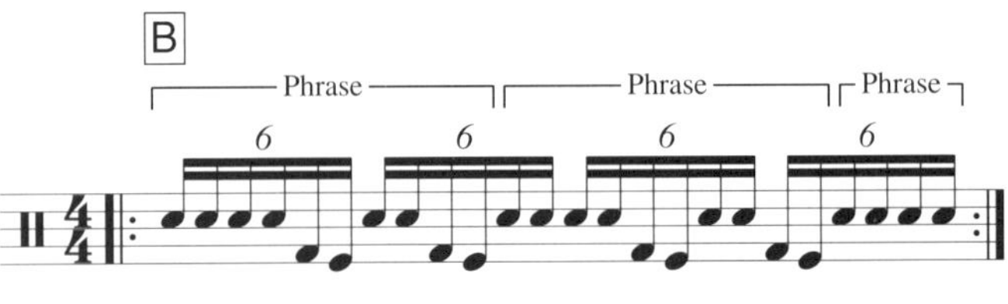

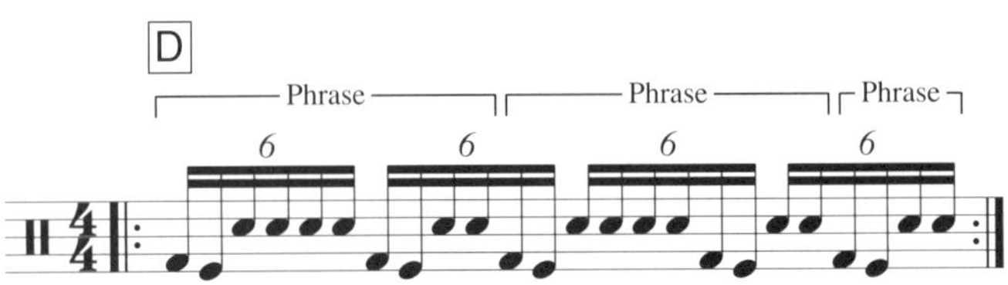

Basic Phrase Combination **Orchestration**

Basic 8th/16th-Note-Triplet Phrase with Cymbals

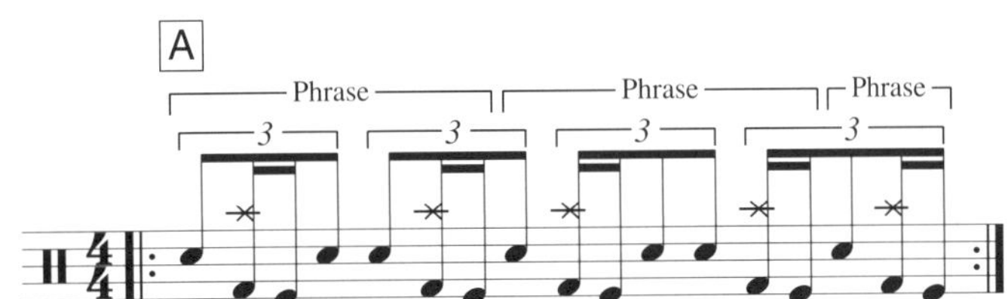

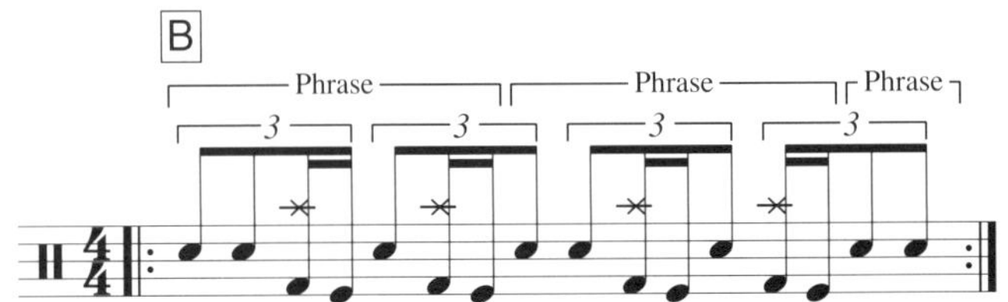

C
Phrase
Phrase
Phrase
D
Phrase
Phrase
Phrase
E
Phrase
Phrase
Phrase
Basic Phrase Combination
Orchestration
1
2
Basic Sextuplet Phrase with Cymbals
A
Phrase
Phrase
Phrase
B
Phrase
Phrase
Phrase
C
Phrase
Phrase
Phrase
D
Phrase
Phrase
Phrase
E
Phrase
Phrase
Phrase
Basic Phrase Combination
Orchestration
1
2

Drumistic Discoveries

Use this page to log your original ideas based on the concepts from this chapter.

1

2

3

4

5

6

7

8

Appendix

The following pages contain the exercises that are demonstrated in the accompanying video lessons.

Mirrored Warm-Ups and Coordination Exercises

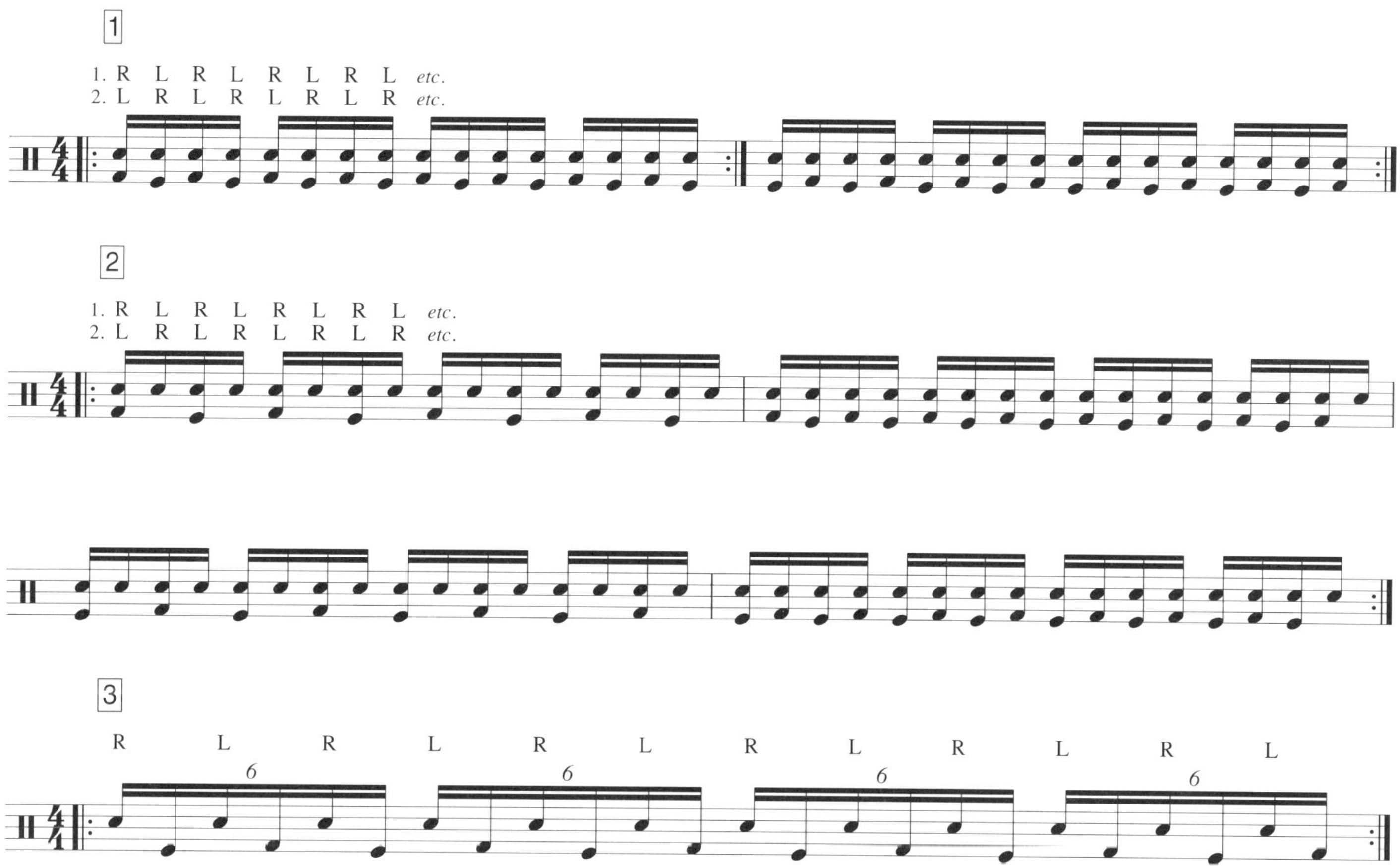

Dynamic Control Exercises

16th-Note Mirrored Grooves

Groove Warm-Ups

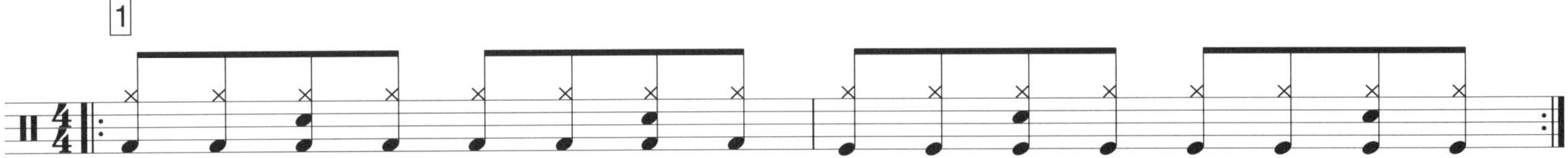

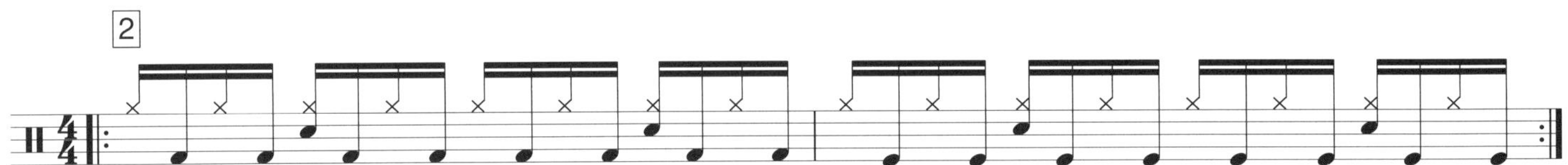

16th-Note Mirrored Grooves

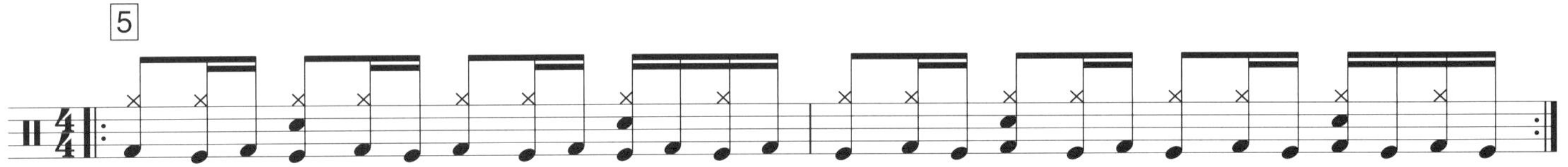

32nd-Note Ruff Warm-Ups

8

9

10

11

Ride Variations

A

B

C

D

E

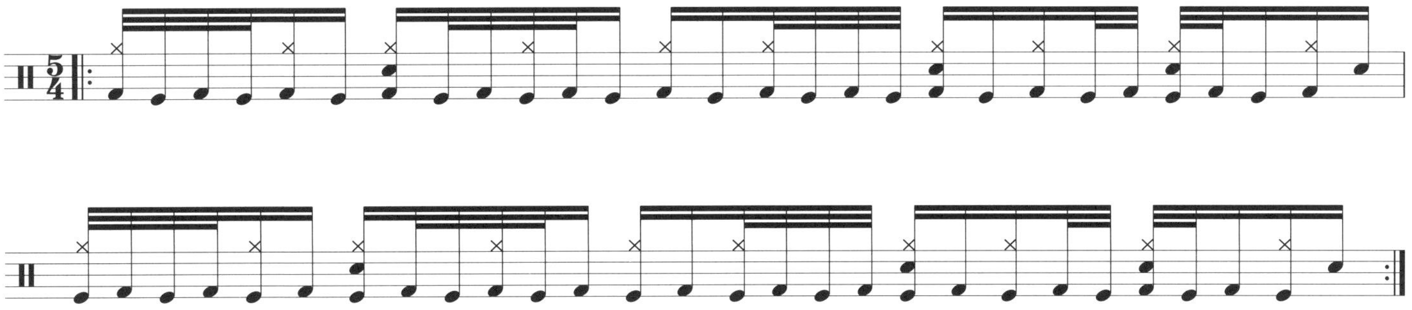

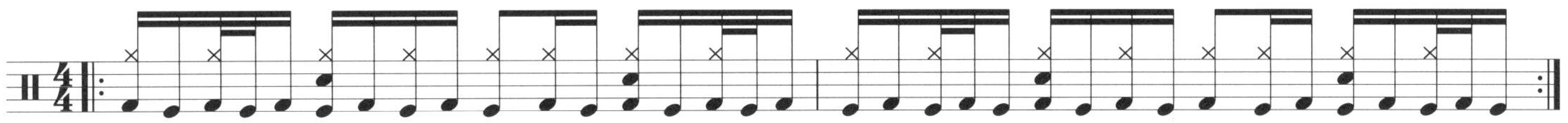

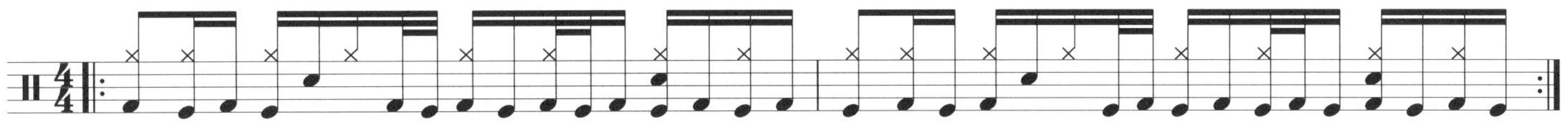

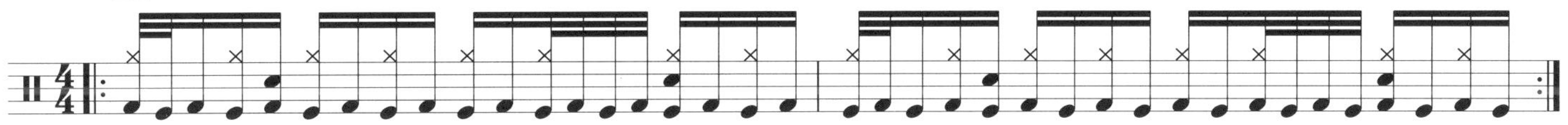

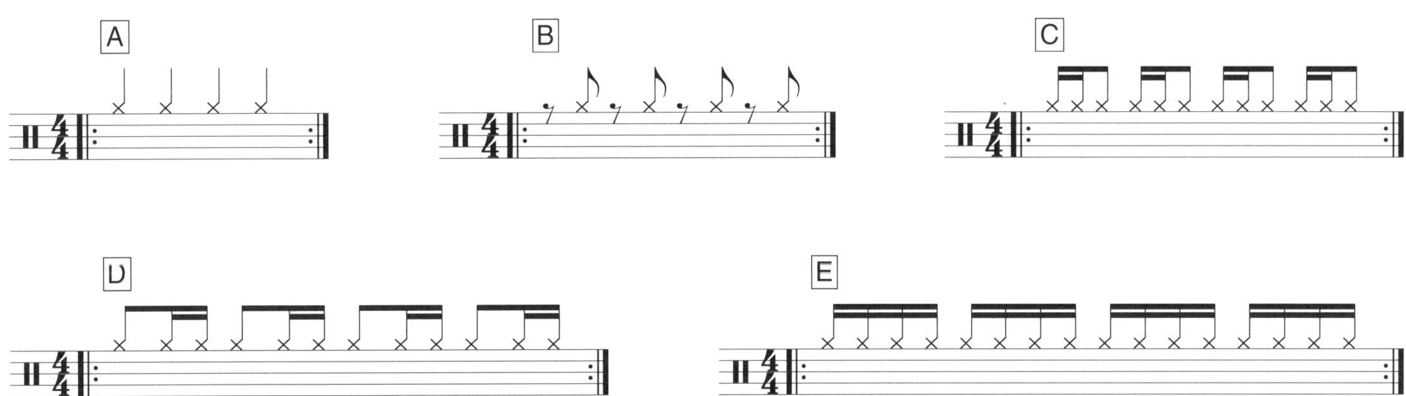

Triplet/Shuffled Mirrored Grooves

Groove Warm-Ups

Triplet Mirrored Grooves

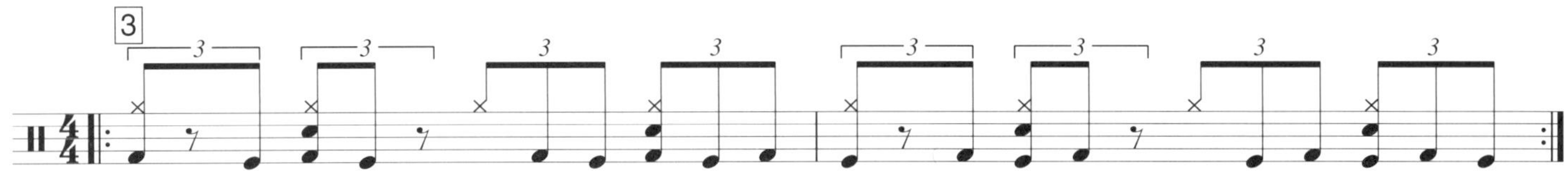

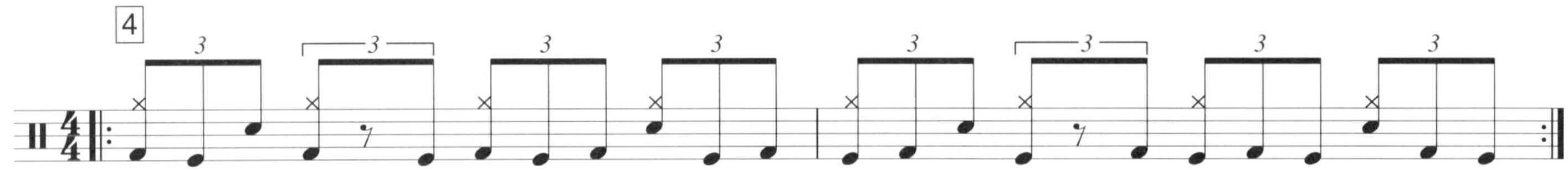

Double Bass Shuffle

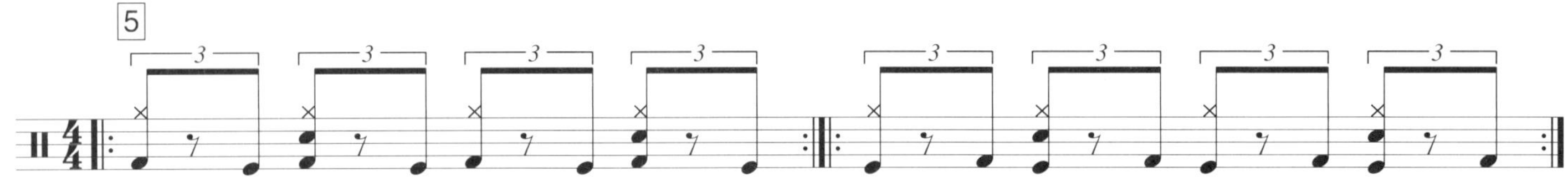

Double Bass Shuffle Variations with Fill-ins

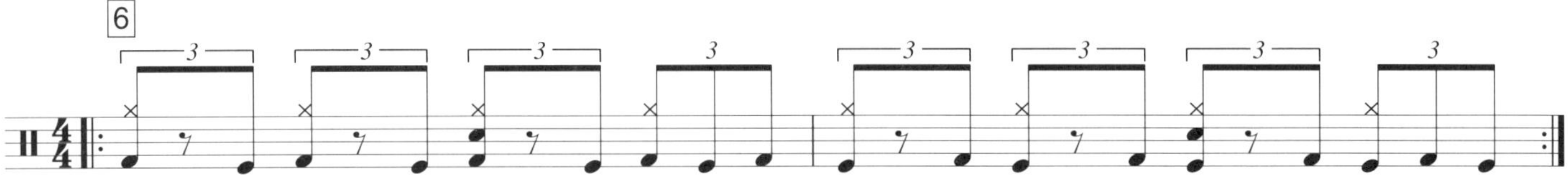

Ride Variations

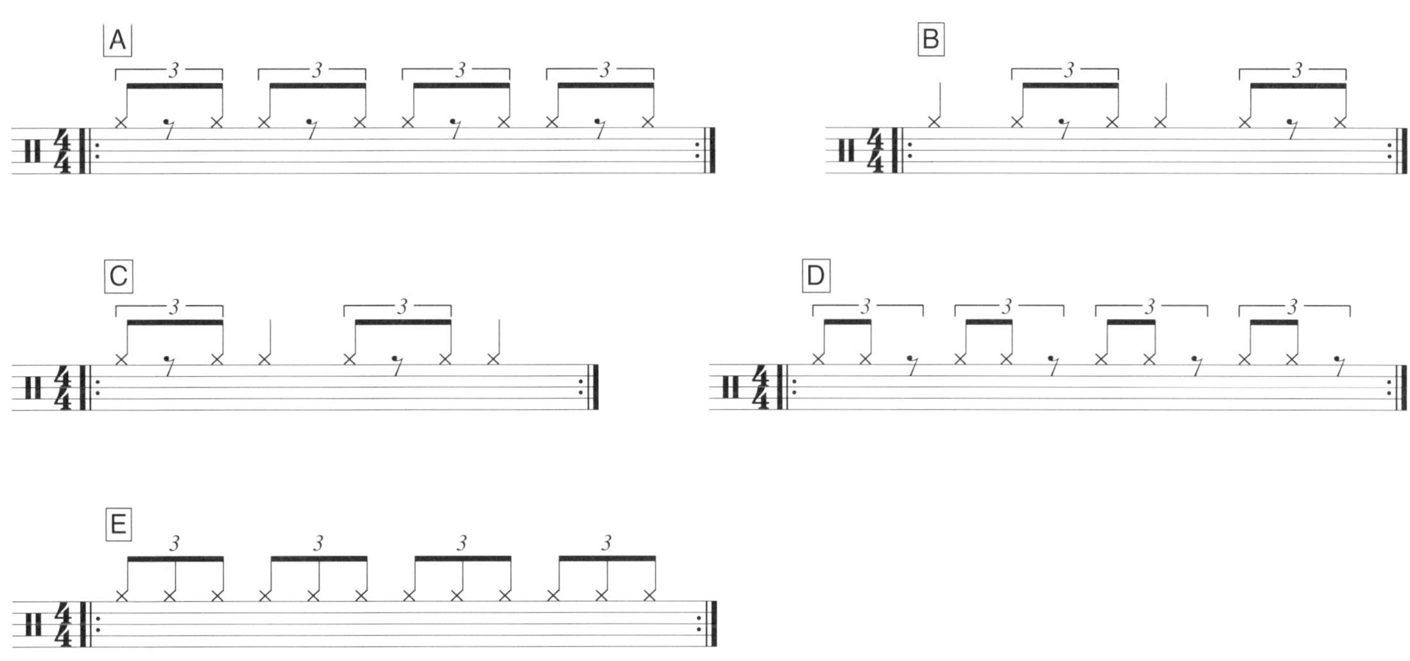

Endurance/Stamina Exercises

Ex. 1

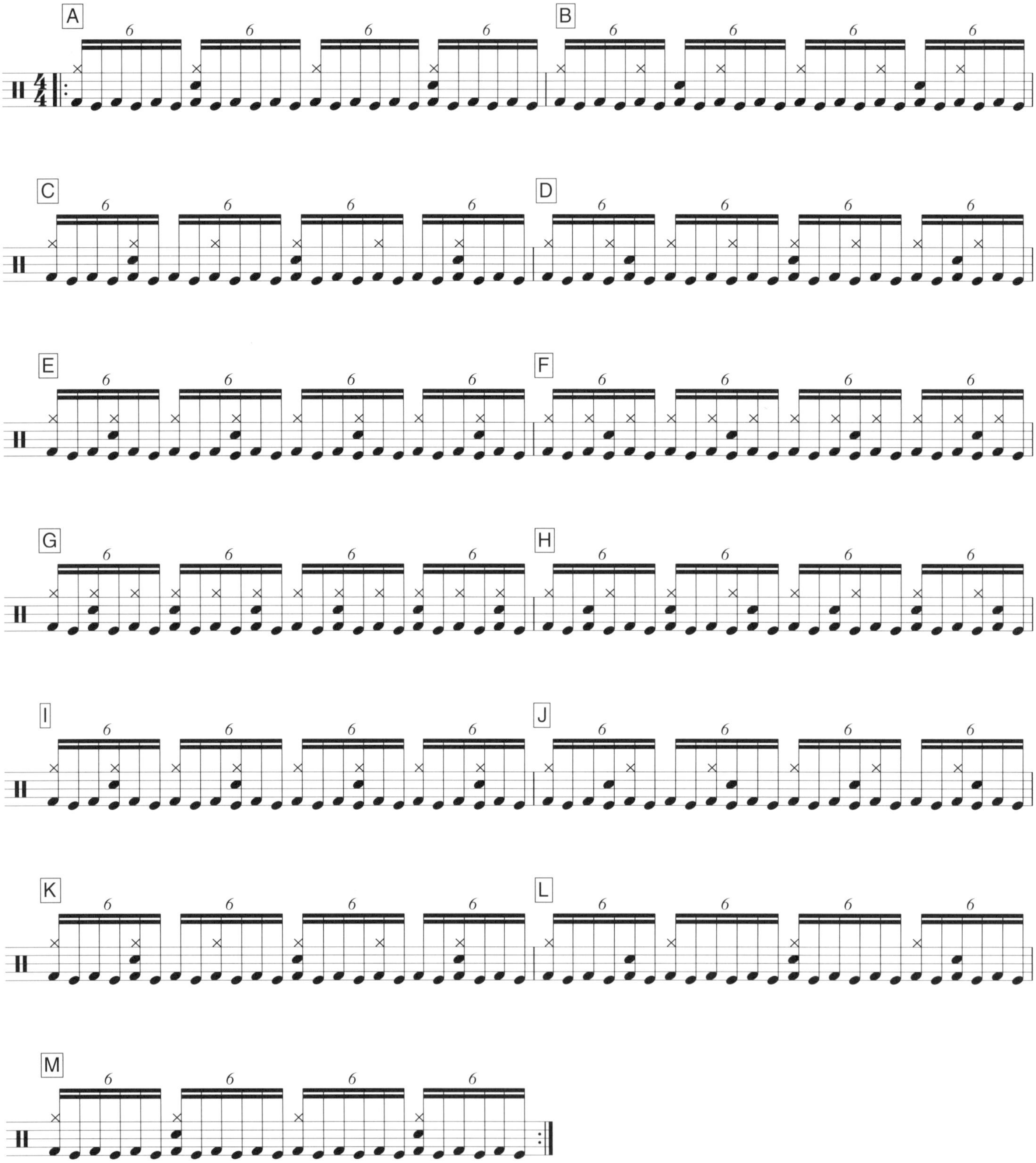

A B C D E F G H I J K L M

6 6 6 6 6 6 6 6

Alternate Bass Drum Pattern

Ex. 2 "5-Stroke Roll" 16th-Note Triplet

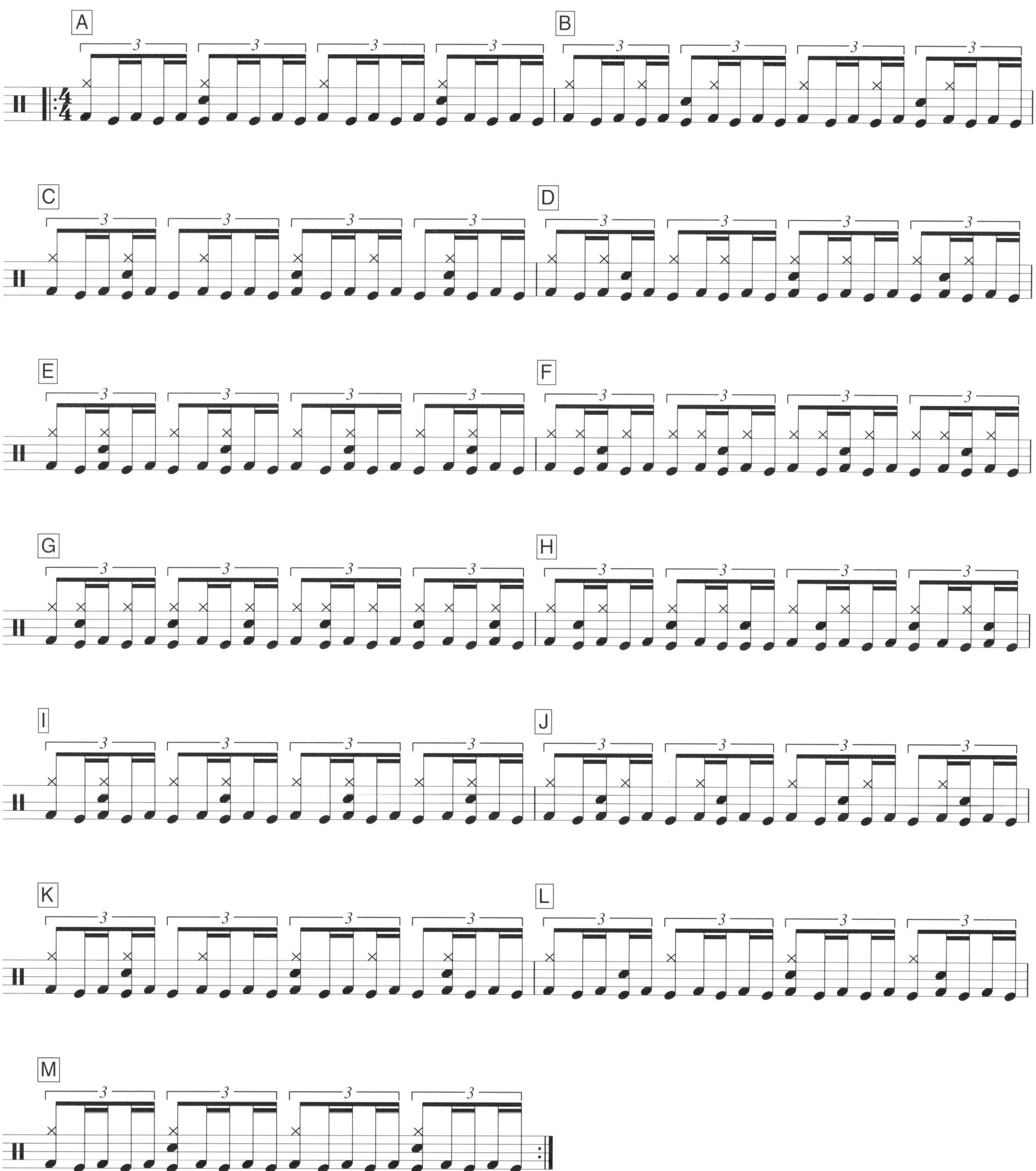

Double Bass Fills and Soloing Concepts

Standard 16th-Note Hand/Foot Combinations

Standard Sextuplet Hand/Foot Combinations

Hand/Foot Combinations with Cymbals

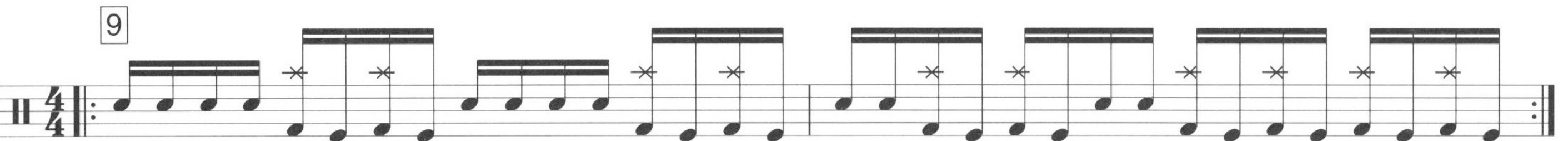

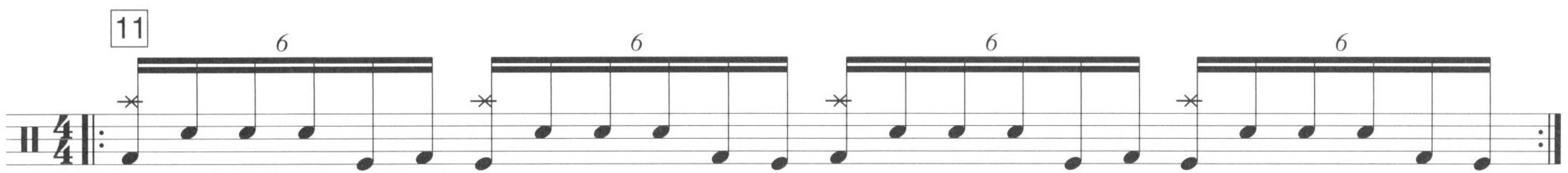

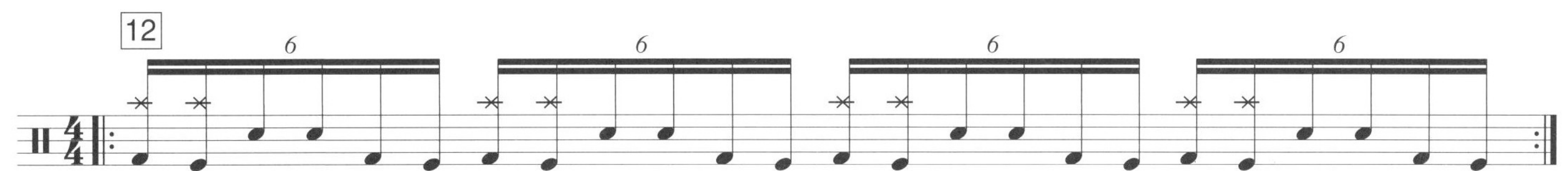

32nd-Note Ruff Fill-ins

32nd-Note Ruff Fill-ins with Flams

Live Performance Videos

"The Pound"

"Rock This"

"4 Pennies" (Drum Solo)

"Milkshake"